WHITEY'S STRUGGLE

ALSO BY T. J. ENGLISH

WHITEY'S PAYBACK

and Other True Stories

of Gangsterism, Murder, Corruption, and Revenge

T. J. ENGLISH

MYSTERIOUSPRESS.COM

OPEN ROAD
INTEGRATED MEDIA
NEW YORK

Copyright © 2013 by T. J. English

Cover design by Andrea C. Uva

ISBN 978-1-4804-1175-3

Published in 2013 by MysteriousPress.com/Open Road Integrated Media
345 Hudson Street
New York, NY 10014
www.mysteriouspress.com
www.openroadmedia.com

CONTENTS

CONTENTS

III. NARCO WARS, AT HOME AND ABROAD

IV. THE BULGER CHRONICLES

WHITEY'S PAYBACK

"Obviously crime pays, or there'd be no crime."

—G. GORDON LIDDY
WATERGATE BURGLAR

INTRODUCTION

J oseph "Mad Dog" Sullivan is a tough mammy jammy. Gangster, killer, fugitive from the law, prison inmate: Sullivan, seventy-three, has lived a life in the darkest corners of the known world. He is a hard man who has withstood the primordial dictates of crime and punishment, and he has done so without complaining. But by the fall of 2011—after a long career as a professional hit man for the Mob; after a lifetime highlighted by numerous escape attempts from penal institutions (some successful, some not so successful); after having been hunted down, shot at, captured and locked up—the clock is finally winding down for Mad Dog.

In year thirty-one of a life sentence, Sullivan's mortality loomed like the black raven that occasionally flew over the prison yard, sending a ripple of doom through the hearts of inmates. Recently, Sullivan had been treated for prostate cancer. During preliminary examinations, doctors determined that cancer had also developed in his right lung. Within weeks, he had half a lung removed. And still he wasn't out of the woods. Doctors suspected that the cancer had metastasized, that it was possibly in remission but could reemerge at any time to spread through his body like a raging wildfire.

Despite the dire prognostications, on this particular day Sullivan is in good spirits. He feels as though he's had a good run and mostly held up well against astounding odds. Never mind that fifty of his seventy-three years on the planet were spent in some form of incarceration. He feels lucky to be alive.

"It's kind of a miracle," Sullivan says in the visiting room at the Sullivan County Correctional Facility in upstate New York. "I should have been dead a long time ago."

I had been summoned to meet Mad Dog by the man himself. Through a mutual contact who had interviewed Sullivan and produced a cable television documentary about his life, I was told that he wanted to meet me. I had written two nonfiction books in which Sullivan's criminal exploits were prominently featured, and Joe was curious to know how I'd learned so much about him and the world he inhabited. Said the filmmaker: "He admires your work. He says you're one of the few people who got it right."

I was flattered and hesitant in equal measure. It has been estimated by law enforcement authorities that Sullivan, as a contract killer for the Mob, murdered somewhere between twenty and thirty people. What if Joe was not happy with me? Not only had I described some of his criminal exploits for the first time ever in a book, but, in my research for *Paddy Whacked: The Untold Story of the Irish American Gangster*, I'd even gotten hold of a manuscript of his unpublished memoir entitled *Tiers and Tears*. I quoted passages from the manuscript without ever asking Sullivan's permission—though I did cite the manuscript and made it clear it was Sullivan's writing. Even so, what I'd done was possibly an infringement of his rights; he had a good reason to be pissed off.

Knowing that he was safely locked away in prison, I could have ignored Sullivan's request for a meeting, but I felt that I owed him the courtesy. I had written about him and characterized his criminal career in print, and quoted from his writing without his consent. Plus, I was curious. Mad Dog Sullivan was a legend in New York crime circles, the last of a dying breed, an old-school, professional hit man for the Mob. I wrote Sullivan a letter to make sure he wasn't mad at me. When he answered that he was not, we made arrangements to meet at the prison.

For anyone with a professional interest in the criminal justice system—whether a cop, a lawyer, a parole officer, a judge, or a crime journalist—entering a penal institution is akin to descending into Dante's ninth ring of hell. Prison is, metaphorically speaking, the asshole of the universe. Many stories of the criminal life end up here, or in a cemetery, or in the witness protection program. Short of death, prison remains the great equalizer.

In the receiving room, you are stripped of all personal belongings, patted down, pockets emptied out. As you enter the facility, much like an inmate, you must be accompanied by a guard at all times. The automated bars slam shut behind you, and others open in front of you. You enter, and those gates also slam shut. As you descend deeper into the facility, you feel the free world slipping away like overcooked meat falling from the bone. You are passed from one armed guard to another, until you are ushered into the visiting room, which is also monitored by armed guards.

"I thought you might be upset with me," I said to Joe Sullivan, once we'd shook hands and sat down at a cafeteria-style table off in a corner of the room. "Having written about you," I continued, "quoted from your memoir, I thought you might want to wring my neck."

Sullivan smiled. "Hell no," he said. "What you wrote was accurate. In a way, I was proud, because you wrote about me like I was a historical figure." The aging gangster shrugged: "Who cares? All of that is the past. I can't change what happened. And there's no point in hiding it, because I'm never getting out of here anyway."

Sullivan and I had a lot to talk about. In his heyday in the criminal underworld, Mad Dog had been involved in some key events that I chronicled in my work, and I was fascinated to hear the details from his point of view. In the same regard, I had information and thoughts about certain events and people that Sullivan wanted to know about. Mad Dog regaled me with stories from his life of crime that were riveting and sometimes humorous. He told me how he escaped from Attica prison in 1971, the only man in history to ever do so. He told of meetings with Anthony "Fat Tony" Salerno; John Gotti; Jimmy "the Gent" Burke, of *Goodfellas* fame; and many other notorious mobsters. Joe had the Irish gift of storytelling. He was also a great conversationalist.

He listened to my thoughts and observations with great attention to detail. Though he was a man with little formal education, he possessed a sharp intelligence, and the hyperawareness and street smarts of a true hustler. He was friendly, respectful, convivial.

"Call me Sully," he said, after we'd been talking awhile. And that's when it hit me.

Nice guys make the best killers.

Joe Sullivan was a nice guy. He had the charm of a talkative cab driver, or a friendly bartender who has a talent for getting people to relax and unburden themselves. If you ran into him at a saloon or tavern, he was the kind of stranger who, over beers at the bar, would quickly and effortlessly draw you into a conversation, getting you started but then gladly letting you do most of the talking, asking interesting questions, making jokes and observations, loosening you up with the skill of a psychiatrist. Before long, you'd feel like Sully was an old friend. You'd be revealing things about yourself you didn't normally tell anybody, much less a complete stranger. Sully would also tell you stories, have you crying and laughing and listening in wonder. You'd want to match him yarn for yarn, to make him smile the way he made you smile. He'd say, "Sorry, I didn't catch that." So you'd lean in closer to tell him a particularly juicy detail or to deliver a punch line. And at that moment, without you seeing or noticing anything, Sully would whip out a gun, put it to the back of your head and blow your brains out.

I never set out to be a crime writer. In the mid-1980s, when I began my career as a journalist, I covered the waterfront, so to speak. As a freelance writer in New York City, driving a taxi at night to pay the bills, I was engaged in the classic American hustle. Back then, you could do it. You could live close to the bone and cover your bills while pursuing your craft, whether it was acting or filmmaking or painting or writing. To make any money at it, you had to maximize your talent and push the envelope. And so, as an aspiring journalist, I wrote about many subjects, including politics, sports, entertainment, and crime.

More and more, I came back to the subject of crime—not arbitrary crime, or so-called crimes of passion—organized crime, crimes set against a backdrop of sociology, ethnicity, culture, economics, and politics. Through the writing of many magazine articles and five non-fiction books, I have been covering this beat, off and on, for close to twenty-five years.

Given my chosen profession, I am sometimes asked, "What attracts you to the dark side?" I have a hard time identifying with this question. I do not write about serial killers, or psychological aberrations, or vampires, or zombies. Mostly, I write about crime as an extension of the American social and economic system. I write about the underbelly of capitalism, men and women attempting to manipulate the system to their advantage, and law enforcement's attempts to bring justice to this process. Sometimes, people in law enforcement are players in this underworld. They frame innocent people who they think deserve it, or attempt to manipulate a given situation to their advantage, driven by the desire for financial gain or career advancement or the esteem of their peers.

The world is a messy place. Ever since Adam and Eve were chased out of the Garden of Eden, we have known this to be true. It is the job of elected officials, civic leaders, and parents to promote the illusion that life is fair, people are good, and the world is an orderly place; our daily lives at home, school, or on the job are designed to lend credence and support to this illusion.

The journalist's job is to drag this fantasy out into the light of day, to pull back the curtain and make sense of what seems chaotic and difficult to explain.

I am not attracted to the dark side. I am attracted to the light, and what that light reveals about the true nature of the social universe.

The various articles in this collection were written over a twenty-two-year period. They reflect my interest in crime as a vast ecosystem, a parallel universe to the social and economic system we observe in the upperworld on a daily basis. The way I see it, one cannot exist without the other. In the United States, business, politics, and crime are frequently intertwined. What is happening below the surface shapes the world as we know it. What is presented to the public is occasionally wrapped in bullshit and lies.

For me, these collected articles are all basically about one thing: the pursuit of the American Dream. To the reader, the question is posed: How far would you go to achieve power and prosperity for you and your own? Some people, out of free will, dire circumstances, or temporary insanity, make choices that take them to the wrong side of the law. Chronicling the path of misguided souls and devious minds has become a big part of my calling as a writer.

It is worth noting that the pieces in this anthology were written for a variety of publications, and that I have never been under the employ of a particular magazine or newspaper. My status as a freelance writer, I like to believe, affords me a certain degree of independence. I am not peddling a specific ideology, nor do I represent the views of an established publication like, say, *Esquire* or the *New York Times*. Even though I have written for these periodicals, I have never been urged to adhere to a particular editorial point of view. I have never been pigeonholed in that way. My reporting is my own, and my point of view, when there is a need to assert it, is a consequence of my research and not an editorial dictate from above.

Creatively and spiritually, I am nurtured by the work. And the kind of reporting I enjoy most has to do with traveling to locales that serve as the setting and/or incubation chamber for the kinds of criminal activity I write about.

For a crime journalist, there are few undertakings more invigorating than traveling into a city—say, Kingston, Jamaica, or Hong Kong, or Ciudad Juárez, Mexico—in search of a good story. The trip must be planned with near-surgical precision. If you know what you're doing, some important interviews will have been set up ahead of time, so that you come into town and hit the ground running. You travel light, dress unobtrusively, carry little more than some research material, a notepad, a tape recorder, a laptop. You stay somewhere downtown in an anonymous hotel, a Holiday Inn or something similar. You circulate without calling attention to yourself, talking with people on all sides of the law, playing dumb, if necessary, to get what you need. You profess to have no ideological agenda, and hopefully you do not, for to tip your hand one way or the other can quickly rile passions and create untenable situations. You get what you need and then get the hell out of town as quickly as possible. Hopefully, the sources you have spoken with think little of your visit until after they see your article in print and react accordingly.

I do not whack people, but I can't help but think that what I do on these assignments is akin to being a hired assassin. You arrive from out of town as a mysterious stranger. Every move you make, every conversation you have, is geared toward a specific goal. The task at hand is to accomplish what you came for cleanly and professionally, and then—*poof*—disappear in a cloud of smoke.

Seated in the prison visiting room in upstate New York, Mad Dog Sullivan smiles at my analogy. He finds it cute. The idea that a writer's gathering information and putting words down on paper is in any way similar to the actions of a professional hit man is the kind of literary prestidigitation that brightens his day. Sullivan knows about high-intensity assignments that leave people scratching their heads, wondering what happened. But he also knows that the end result of his line of work is a dead body and shattered lives. "I belong in here," he says, "no doubt about that. If they were to give me the death penalty, I can't really argue with that, either, even though I don't want to die."

The immorality of Sullivan's actions is clear, but this does not stop the hit man from taking pride in his work. And this is where Sullivan and I sense a kinship, a mystical connection that can sometimes exist between a writer and his subject, no matter how contrary may be their backgrounds, lives, or daily existence. Sully and I come together out of a shared appreciation of craftsmanship.

Believe it or not, Mad Dog always operated within a personal code. For one thing, he has never been a rat. Many times since he began his most recent period of incarceration in 1981, he has been approached by federal agents and prosecutors offering him some kind of deal if he would testify against organized crime figures for whom he worked. Sullivan's response has always been the same: "Go fuck yourself."

The other part of Mad Dog's code has to do with being the best at what you do.

At one point in our conversation, I ask Sully to describe his cleanest and most professional hit. He described the planning and execution of a particularly perilous assignment with matter-of-fact satisfaction, how he stalked his victim—a notorious underworld figure—until he knew the man's daily routine. Sully described how he created a disguise and chose a particular caliber weapon best suited to the unique conditions of the shooting. One night, he penetrated the victim's inner sanctum—his favorite saloon. Joe got right up next to the guy, chatted with him at the bar for twenty minutes before shooting him once in the head, then walking—not running, walking—right out of the bar. His disguise was so seamless, and the act so sudden and unexpected, that witnesses gave three entirely different descriptions of the shooting, and a description of the shooter that guaranteed that Joe Sullivan, without the disguise, would never be identified as a suspect.

Sullivan's appreciation of a job well done extends to my own undertakings as a writer. Since he's been in prison so long, Sully has lots of time on his hands, and he's become a voracious reader. He is fascinated by the process of gathering information and getting it down on the page. He asks me if I use a tape recorder or take notes when I'm doing interviews. "How do you get people to talk to you?" he asks. He wants to know how I'm able to put so much into my writing and still keep everything organized. He's curious about how I'm able to remain mostly objective when writing about people that many would dismiss as "scumbags."

I answer Joe's questions, and he listens attentively to my answers.

I am fascinated by his life's work, and he is fascinated by mine.

Over a couple of visits to the prison visiting room, we continue our conversation. Often, Mad Dog and I become so engrossed that it's easy to forget where we are. The hours pass, the day drags on. We are merely two craftsmen—the assassin and the journalist—discussing the tricks of our respective trades.

The sixteen stories in this collection are republished here in their original form. With articles written fifteen and twenty years ago, it is tempting to go back and edit or rewrite from a revisionist perspective, to bend the information to a contemporary point of view. Fortunately, I am not the kind of writer who is obligated to make prognostications or provide "expert opinion" on the likely outcome of elections or sporting events. These articles represent the time in which they were written, snapshots from America's ongoing crime narrative.

The books I have written are sometimes from a historical perspective, but my journalism, as represented by these pieces, chronicles America's crime history in real time. To be judged fairly, they must be taken as investigations into an evolving phenomenon, though with the benefit of hindsight they can also—for better or for worse—be evaluated for their accuracy as harbingers of things to come.

The title of this collection—*Whitey's Payback*—is drawn from the most recent collection of articles dealing with the prosecution of Boston mobster James "Whitey" Bulger. The story of Bulger's capture and prosecution has many of the characteristics I most relish in a good story, namely, deeply rooted historical underpinnings that help explain a contemporary situation.

Having Mad Dog Sullivan and Whitey Bulger open and close this book has a certain symmetry: Taken together, they represent the last of a kind of old-school gangsterism that most people would rather deny ever played such a monumental role in American urban life.

Over the years, one fact has not changed: In the United States, the narrative remains open-ended. Being a crime journalist is the gift that keeps on giving. When gangsters, con artists, porn kingpins, and corrupt lawmen stop using the American Dream as their license to commit crime, I will stop writing about it. Short of that happening, I hope to see you again in another twenty-two years, with another collection of stories.

I.

BULLET IN THE ASS

*N*ot long after I published my first book, in late 1990, I received a call from an editor at Playboy. *The editor wanted me to write a feature article for the magazine. No major publication of this stature had ever before called me, out of the blue, with the offer of an assignment. It was a big step in my career as a journalist. The editor told me what they had in mind, though, frankly, I was hardly listening. I accepted the assignment immediately because it felt like an important opportunity. It was only later, after I'd hung up the phone, that it dawned on me what I was being asked to do: The story was to be an exposé on the Witness Protection Program.*

Can that even be done? *I asked myself.*

It was a good question, one I should have asked myself before I accepted the assignment.

The Witness Protection Program was, and remains, a highly covert federal program. It was designed to be secretive, a program that you could not trace or expose.

And so began a pattern for me of taking on certain reporting assignments with considerable fear and trepidation about whether or not that particular undertaking could be accomplished.

The article about the Witness Protection Program took six months of research and went down many blind and frustrating alleyways before appearing in the April 1991 issue of the magazine. The editors at Playboy *were pleased with the result and quickly came back to me with another assignment. They wanted me to write an article that charted the decline and fall of the Mafia in the United States.*

I had little interest in writing about the Mafia. In the early 1990s, I sensed there were many great stories to write about organized crime in America, but the story of the Mafia was old news. Even a story about the decline of the Mafia felt like old news. To me, magazine and newspaper editors were missing out on the most interesting crime phenomenon of our time: the emergence of newer ethnic crime groups that were using gangsterism and organized crime as a process of assimilation much like previous generations of Italians, Irish, and Jews had used crime as a way to carve out their own slice of the American Dream.

I told the editor at Playboy *that this was what I really wanted to write about. And so we came up with a compromise. I would do a series of three articles that would chronicle this transformation that was taking place in the American underworld. Two of the articles would be about the emergence of a new group, and the last article would be about the decline of the Mafia. The series was entitled "The New Mob" and it ran in the magazine over a nine-month period, from October 1991 to September 1992.*

Logistically and as a research assignment, the series was a challenge. It established a method for me that I have tried to continue throughout my career, which is to approach a subject with a wide lens and then zoom in on a particular storyline, to reveal the big picture and then focus on details within the big picture.

To write each of these articles required absorbing a tremendous amount of information, not just about the criminal activity of the subject I was writing about, but also the cultural and political factors that helped shape a particular criminal phenomenon or gang, both in the United States and the country of origin.

There was another proclivity that I established with this series that I have tried to replicate whenever possible, that of traveling, when it is called for, to complicated, challenging locales (in this case,

Kingston and Hong Kong) on high-intensity information-gathering assignments.

I am not a gratuitous thrill seeker. I do not bungee-jump or skydive on the weekends. And I do not, per se, take these assignments out of a Hemingwayesque sense of adventure. But I do relish the challenge of going into an environment that is new, a situation that requires street smarts and urban survival skills. I take pride in doing my homework and navigating these environments in a way that minimizes the opportunity for disaster. A successful research trip is one where you penetrate as deeply as possible, get the information you need—maybe even more than you hoped for—and then come home all in one piece, older and wiser and with experiences you remember for the rest of your life.

I have learned that these trips are often filled with fascinating moments that sometimes never make it into the article I am working on.

For instance, on my very first research trip for the Playboy *series, I found myself in central Kingston, a place I had never been before. If you are not from Kingston, and have never been exposed to extreme Third World poverty, the conditions in the shantytowns and tenement yards are shocking. In 1991, when I was first there, many of the neighborhoods were cordoned off by makeshift barricades. For fifteen years or so, the island had been in the throes of a wave of gang violence touched off primarily by the partisan wars between Jamaica's two main political parties. Each ghetto neighborhood was aligned with one of the two parties, and the gunplay and general violence, especially around election time, was horrifying.*

Over time, I established important contacts with a human rights organization based out of an office in downtown Kingston that was dealing primarily with the issue of police brutality in the city's poorest areas. They assigned me a guide, a kid who appeared to be about fifteen years old. One hot, tropical morning I set out with my guide on what would be an all-day journey around Denham Town, an especially rough shantytown right in the center of the action. The kid took me around and introduced me to wise neighborhood elders, shop owners, people at a bicycle repairman's shop, average denizens of this unremittingly poor but vibrant neighborhood. My guide introduced me as a journalist from the United States who wanted to know about life in Kingston during this time of strife and violence, and then I was more or less on my own. Some people did not want to talk to me; some did. All were startled to see something they rarely saw—an outsider from another country who was interested in hearing about the reality of their daily lives.

At one point in the afternoon, my guide led me into a sprawling tenement yard. He warned me that the physical terrain was ragged (no paved streets or sidewalks) and that sudden and explosive violence was always a possibility. The homes, such as they were, were wood shacks with roofs made of corrugated tin. We made our way around shacks and through the yards of what seemed like one huge collective living space. People gaped at me like I was a visitor from another planet, some smiled, some scowled. The entire environment was dominated by the sound of reggae music coming from distant radios or cassette players, and the pungent aroma of ganja.

Eventually, my guide led me into a yard where a group of four or five dreadlocked Rastas were sitting around a homemade grill roasting salt fish, listening to reggae and smoking from a huge chillum pipe. The look on their faces as I was brought into their lair on a leisurely afternoon was one of astonishment. They all looked at me, then looked at my guide, with an expression that said, "Junior, you better have a good reason for bringing this stranger into our yard in the middle of the afternoon while we be chillin' in our private space."

The kid explained, as best he could. The response was not enthusiastic. Two of the Rastas simply up and left. The other three stayed put mostly out of curiosity.

I attempted to explain what I was up to. The lead Rastaman—the one who controlled the chillum pipe—took it upon himself to scold me about exploitation and colonialism, explaining how absurd it was that they had to speak to me in a different language—American English—as opposed to their own Jamaican patois, so that I could understand them. Referring to our interview, he said, "Dis a colonial relationship." The others chimed in: "Ras clot."

I was sweating from the sweltering afternoon sun and the heat off the grill. The Rastaman had a valid point. I was there representing a big corporate American enterprise—Playboy—and I was asking them to share their experiences with me without them having any guarantee that what I might write would be accurate or informed. All I could do was try to assure them that my motives were sincere, that I was not ignorant of their plight, and that I was capable of seeing beyond a colonial or imperialist point of view.

As I spoke, they passed the pipe around.

"Let me ask you this," I said. "How many times have you had a journalist here in Denham Town, a white journalist from New York, here in your yard by himself asking to hear your perspective, your point of view, from your mouth? How many times?"

They were all quiet for a few seconds. The lead Rastaman said, "Nevah."

"Okay," I said, "Come on, then. At least you have to give me that."

One of the Rastas chuckled. The others hit the pipe, blew smoke in the air, and pondered what I had said. I sensed some of the tension drifting away with the ganja smoke. Now, as neighborhood people came and went, each of them looking at me as if I were a ghostly apparition, it was the lead Rastaman who took it upon himself to explain, "Him a journalist from Babylon, from New Yawk, him inna Kingston to get a bird's eye view of de politricks an' di violence."

I laughed when he said "bird's eye view." That was a fair description of what I was doing.

Eventually, the moment of reckoning arrived. The lead Rastaman handed me the chillum pipe. Everyone watched to see how I was going to react.

A number of equations ran through my head. First of all, my young guide had disappeared, so I was in the middle of a Kingston ghetto, sitting with a bunch of strangers, with no real idea of how to get back to where I came from. It was the kind of situation in which you would normally want to have your wits about you. Second, I knew from experience that Jamaican weed was about ten times stronger that what I was familiar with in the United States. All of this was weighed against the simple fact that if I expected to sit there in that environment, to come into those folks lives for an afternoon and ask questions, to not be judgmental, to show them that I could—to the extent possible in this transitory moment and on this transitory day—be one of them, I would need to take a hit off the pipe.

And so I did. With hardly a hesitation. And that changed every-thing. I was still an outsider in their midst, but we'd had a ceremonial exchange, a sharing of the pipe, and it meant a lot.

I recount this incident now because it has become, for me, a kind of metaphor—a parable—about having to make split-second decisions, trusting your instincts in a way that will determine whether you are able to absorb and understand the story you hope to write about. In a way, the lesson can be condensed into that hoary cliché, one of my favorites, that has become my guiding principle as a journalist.

If you can't stand the heat, stay out of the kitchen.

1.

THE WISEGUY NEXT DOOR

Playboy, April 1991

The Witness Protection Program has a remarkable purpose:
To hide hardened criminals among the general public.
What could possibly go wrong?

t was nearly twenty-one years ago that Michael Raymond, a beefy, Brooklyn-bred con man and stock swindler, got into a tight spot with the law. After a lengthy trial in Illinois state court, he received a four-year prison term for trying to use stolen Treasury notes to buy two small midwestern banks. A silver-tongued grifter with a robust appetite for the good life, Raymond had no intention of serving his sentence. Instead, he cut a deal with the feds.

What Raymond received, however, was far from your average, run-of-the-mill government deal. In exchange for testifying before a Senate subcommittee on stolen securities and the Mob, he was placed in what was then a new, top-secret federal program called WITSEC, short for Witness Security Program, now commonly referred to as the Witness Protection Program.

At the time, fewer than a hundred people had entered this experimental program, thought to be the government's most potent new tool against organized crime. Despite its controversial nature, the program had never actually been debated, or even proposed, on Capitol Hill. The U.S. Justice Department simply requested funds for "witness relocation" and the various appropriations committees gave it the rubber stamp. Over the next twenty-one years, the program would attract a vast following, not the least of which were more than 13,000 criminals and their family members coerced into its ranks. Back in 1970, though, WITSEC was a theory to be tested. And like any new theory, it had bugs to be worked out—bugs like Michael Raymond.

As part of this agreement with the overseers of WITSEC, Raymond was given a new identity and relocated to sunny Southern Florida. The government also immediately began paying him $1,500 a month, plus $50,000 for "job assistance." Over the next several years, Michael "Burnett," as Raymond officially became known, would learn to use WITSEC to underwrite one scam after another. During one deadly three-year period, three business associates of his disappeared under nefarious circumstances. One of them was a sixty-seven-year-old socialite and widow whom Raymond had been romancing. The woman was last seen getting into a car with him just hours after she cleared out her bank accounts. Raymond later became a prime suspect in her disappearance when an informant told local cops that he had bragged of killing her. "They're never going to find the stone she's under," he reportedly told the informant.

When Florida authorities began looking into the past of Michael Burnett, they were amazed to find that he had no personal history whatsoever. His life of crime as Michael Raymond had been effectively expunged, courtesy of WITSEC. Furthermore, the federal government helped Raymond disappear while the investigation was under way. He had intentionally violated his security, so the Justice Department—unaware that its prize witness was also a primary suspect—relocated him to another region of the country and covered his tracks after he left.

In the years that followed, Raymond often caught the attention of federal crime fighters. Although the U.S. Marshals Service—the branch of the Justice Department that administers the Witness Security Program—believed that his life was in danger, he moved around like a man without worries. He drove Cadillacs and wore mink coats, and his fingers sparkled with diamond rings. A gourmet chef with a taste for fine wines, he allowed his waist to grow in proportion to his criminal deeds, until he topped the scales near 300 pounds.

Now sixty-one years old, Raymond/Burnett is no longer in WIT-SEC. His long, notorious life of crime finally caught up with him when, after he resurfaced in Chicago a few years ago as an informant in an FBI sting operation, the feds caught on to his act. In 1987, he went off to prison on weapons possession; there were no deals left to be struck. For more than twenty years, Raymond had feasted on the federal government's naïveté and largess, turning the Witness Security Program into a criminal hideout.

The stupefying result of all this is that little has changed since the days when Raymond first made chumps out of the U.S. Justice Department. Although few inductees have abused WITSEC with the same panache as Michael Raymond, the twenty-one-year history of the program reveals a virtual catalog of failures, from recidivism through bureaucratic ineptitude to government callousness and neglect.

Throughout it all, WITSEC continues to grow, amassing a rogues' gallery of inductees. "Almost everything that could go wrong [with WITSEC] has, at one time or another," says Donald Bierman, a former Justice Department official who is now a criminal defense attorney in Miami. Bierman has had several clients enter WITSEC, often against his recommendation. "If you absorb enough scandal, eventually you become immune," he says. "Ironically, because of the program's long history of failure, it has now become virtually scandal-proof."

When forty-seven-year-old Max Mermelstein entered the Witness Security Program in 1986, it must have seemed like the last possible option. As the man who had run U.S. trafficking operations for a Colombian cocaine cartel for several years, he had a criminal career that had escalated to a point beyond his wildest dreams. From 1978 to the time of his arrest, Mermelstein is believed to have smuggled some fifty-six tons of cocaine into Florida. In a five-year period, he ran $300 million in laundered currency through Colombia and Panama.

Mermelstein never planned on a career in crime. After marrying a Colombian woman he met in Puerto Rico, he was introduced to Rafael "Rafa" Cardona Salazar, a major underboss for the Ochoa family, leaders of the Medellín cartel. On Christmas Day, 1978, Rafa inexplicably murdered one of his fellow drug runners after a long afternoon of free-basing cocaine. He and another smuggler then called on Mermelstein, whom he knew only casually at the time. They wanted Max to drive them around until they came down from their high. During the drive, Rafa, eyes ablaze, emptied five bullets into his roommate, who had been taunting him from the backseat of their rented van. "Just keep driving, Max. Don't say a fucking word," Mermelstein remembered Rafa saying.[1]

Having witnessed, but not reported, a brutal murder, Mermelstein was an accessory to the crime, which effectively put him under the thumb of the cartel. His criminal associations with Rafa, Pablo Escobar, and others flourished until June 1985, when he was jumped by a bevy of agents from the FBI, DEA, Customs, and assorted other branches of American law enforcement. After searching Mermelstein's home, the feds had enough on his drug operations to put him away for many lifetimes.

Faced with a life behind bars, Mermelstein remembered the words he'd heard many times from the murderous Rafa: "There are only two ways you get out of trafficking coke, in a box or in a cell." Mermelstein proved him wrong; he agreed to cooperate with the government and go into the Witness Security Program.

"The day I got arrested was the best day of my life," says Mermelstein, now living under an assumed name somewhere in the United States. "If it hadn't happened, I'd be dead right now."

To initiate Mermelstein into WITSEC required extraordinary measures. Sixteen members of his family, mostly relatives of his Colombian wife, had to be relocated into the United States. It presented the Marshals Service with a problem it has been forced to deal with more and more, as the so-called drug war escalates. According to the Justice Department's own statistics, nearly 80 percent of those now in the program are there because they or a family member testified in a drug-related case. More than one quarter of those are foreign nationals.

One might guess that with the Colombians, Mexicans, and Asians now entering the Witness Security Program, the Marshals Service would have devised a strategy for handling foreign refugees from our criminal-justice system.

Guess again.

Take the case of Arturo Jaramillo, Mermelstein's brother-in-law. Born and raised in Cali, Colombia, Jaramillo is described by his brother-in-law as "a quiet man who never wanted to be involved in drugs or violence." Still, he had been forced by Rafa to help dispose of his dead associate back in 1978, and he lived in fear of the Colombian drug merchants. When news of Mermelstein's "flip" reached him, he had no choice but to accept Uncle Sam's offer of a new identity in the United States. Although Jaramillo, his wife, and his young son spoke no English, they were inexplicably relocated to Memphis, Tennessee, a city not known for its racial tolerance.

The last time Mermelstein talked with his brother-in-law was November 13, 1986. "He was in a thoroughly morose mood," he says. "We tried to get an official assigned to his case to get him a Spanish-speaking psychiatrist—fast. What did the official do? He went on vacation."

One day later—on the day before his forty-ninth birthday—Arturo Jaramillo was found hanged in a closet of the small apartment WIT-SEC had provided for him and his family. He had looped a rope over the hanger rod, tied it around his neck, then pulled on the rope with both hands until he strangled himself.

"I'll always blame myself, in a way, for what happened," says Mermelstein. "But I blame the program, too. Nobody involved [with WIT-SEC] understands the Latin mentality or the Latin people. They take my brother-in-law, his wife and kid, and stick them in a place like Memphis. Aside from the fact that it is one of the most bigoted places in the United States, nobody there speaks Spanish. They couldn't get a driver's license, because the tests weren't given in Spanish. They were just dumped in an apartment and left to fend for themselves." Echoing the sentiments of many currently in the program, Mermelstein adds, "Nobody cared. Those asshole inspectors out there just didn't give a flying fuck."

Back in the early 1960s, when Attorney General Robert Kennedy first made the pursuit of organized crime figures a top government priority, a program for protecting high-profile informants and their families must have seemed like a dandy idea. As early as 1963, Kennedy hinted to the Senate subcommittee on organized crime that a program already existed on an informant level. Although official procedures had not been worked out, the means for protecting important witnesses were established that year when Mob hit man Joseph Valachi spoke before a Senate subcommittee on organized crime. His testimony was a revelation, and the fact that he dared give it at all was proof of the program's power.

Along with its potential as a crime-fighting tool, the concept of witness relocation contained a peculiarly American notion—a chance to correct past mistakes and literally become a new person. There was a kind of implied freedom in the program that suited the Great Society. The idea—that a lifelong criminal might somehow cleanse himself with the help of the federal government and emerge a chastened, productive member of society—was, of course, incredibly simplistic and naive. Yet so appealing was this concept that for years the public accepted the Justice Department's contention that the program was working, even as the horror stories mounted.

"In the beginning," says John Partington, a former U.S. marshal assigned to WITSEC, "we never had any manuals or textbooks to go by. Basically, we were making it up as we went along. Soon the demands became so great we just couldn't keep up. It became like the uninformed talking to the misinformed." The program was devised to handle fewer than thirty or forty elite witnesses a year. But during his fifteen years as a regional inspector, Partington would personally guard, relocate, and help falsify IDs for nearly 260 inductees.

"A big part of the problem," says Partington, now retired, "has always been that the program is run out of Washington. The bureaucrats don't seem to have any understanding of what's happening out there in the real world. They've never had to face up to their decisions."

For a long time, the Justice Department avoided making any written promises to witnesses. Only recently have inductees been required to sign a memorandum of understanding—known as an MOU. In the agreement, the Marshals Service makes it clear that while it will assist a witness in finding employment, it will not falsify credit or work histories. Thus, the witnesses are totally dependent on the government to find them work and are prone to looking for outside income. Says Partington, "You've got people in the program who are being asked to take on a lifestyle that they've never experienced before. We've got guys—lifelong gangsters—capable of making two and three hundred thousand dollars a year through crime, and here we are, asking them to work nine to five, five days a week, for maybe fifteen grand a year."

An even more insurmountable problem than the financial strains faced by those in the program is boredom. It doesn't take a criminal sociologist to figure that people accustomed to an exciting, high-wire lifestyle will have trouble adjusting to working-class sobriety. Such has been the case with thousands of inductees.

Henry Hill, the Mafia wannabe lionized in the book *Wiseguy* (the basis for last year's hit movie *Goodfellas*), is just one example. After a long career as a mid-level hustler affiliated with the Lucchese crime family in Brooklyn and Queens, Hill cut a sweetheart deal with the government in 1980 and testified against his former pals, Jimmy "the Gent" Burke and the late capo Paul Vario. Relocated to Redmond, a Seattle suburb, Hill found his new life to be interminably dull. As he put it at the end of the book and film, "Today everything is very different. No more action. I have to wait around like everyone else. I'm an average nobody. I get to live the rest of my life like a schnook."

The irony of course, is that Hill did not wait around. In May 1987, he was arrested on federal drug charges after an undercover agent bought cocaine from two underlings who fingered him. Like their boss before them, Hill's henchmen turned canary and agreed to testify against him in court. A jury took two hours to deliver a conviction.

Hill had a strong incentive to stay clean, yet his addiction to the excitement and danger of crime—and the notoriety it provided—took precedence, a fact amply illustrated at the time of his arrest. When confronted by Washington state troopers, Hill is said to have asked pleadingly, "Don't you know who I am? I'm Henry Hill—the wiseguy."

It's not hard to fathom the appeal the Witness Security Program might hold for a career criminal facing a long prison sentence. Although inductees are often warned that life in the program will not be easy, the difficulties seem remote relative to getting whacked with a baseball bat or stuffed into a car trunk.

The assumption, of course, is that the government will be able to deliver on most of what it promises. "What the government says it can do and what it has the ability to do are two different things," says Mermelstein, who has been relocated four times in the past four years. "I've known lifelong criminals with more sense of honor than some of the people who run this program."

The prime appeal of WITSEC has always been the manufacture of a viable false identity, supported by all the documents. Although the government continues to insist that it can process records at short notice, the history of the program suggests otherwise.

"Every week I was on the phone," says John Partington, "with some witness shouting in my ear, 'my kid wants to play little-league ball and he needs medical records.' 'My daughter wants to get married and where's the goddamn driver's license?' And what about a birth certificate? You need a birth certificate before you can do anything.

"Most times, these are street-smart people—hustlers. They're not Billy Grahams. They'd say to me, 'Just gimme a week. I'll get my own documentation.' And I'd have to say, 'But that's not legal. You do that and you're back to your old ways.' It was frustrating. Why should it take the government months to do what these people could do in days?"

Despite the obvious failings of the program, there has never been a shortage of criminals trying to get in. During WITSEC's most ambitious period, the mid-1970s, criminals were tripping over one another to cut a deal with the feds and get relocated. From 1971 to 1977, the annual number of inductees exploded from 92 to 450. The standards for admission broadened beyond organized crime to include people for whom the program was never intended—small-time dope dealers, innocent victims of crime, and white-collar stool pigeons. As those inductees worked their way through the system, new problems arose. Witnesses were told by the Marshals Service that they could no longer consider Atlanta, San Francisco, or San Diego for relocation, because those areas were full.

If providing full documentation and satisfying employment for lifelong gangsters with minimal job skills has presented the government with difficulties, finding adequate work for college-educated brokers and other white-collar types has proved an impossibility.

Consider the case of Marvin Naidborne, WITSEC's most notable white-collar failure. The bespectacled manager of a Brooklyn car-leasing agency, Naidborne had a character flaw: He was an inveterate gambler often in debt to loan sharks. Arrested in the late 1960s, he was given leniency and relocation and testified in a number of trials, where he fingered, among others, a bank president who had received kickbacks for extending loans to his buddies at the Italian-American Civil Rights League.

After relocation in the program, Naidborne, who had a degree in business administration, waited around for the government to come up with a job, as promised. One of the jobs was part-time work as a process server. "That's a great job," Naidborne later told a reporter. "I bump into someone who knows somebody in the Mob and I get killed."

In due time, Naidborne heard of an opening as general manager of a Volkswagen dealership that paid $42,000 per year. When he asked the Justice Department to vouch for him, his request was ignored.

Totally dependent on the government for subsistence, Naidborne spent the next few years working as a freelance rat fink. He would wander into the city, nose around and eventually present the government with a major crime case. He would collect informer's fees from the FBI or the DEA, witness fees from the Justice Department, and sometimes insurance rewards for recovered goods. In one newspaper article, federal officials confirmed Naidborne's claim that he had accounted for arrests across the country involving drugs, stolen and counterfeit securities, stolen airline tickets, and bookmaking rings. In a good year, he claimed he could make $30,000 as a Witness Security vampire. But it was a sorry, paranoiac life, said Naidborne, living on the run in bad motels. He blamed WITSEC: "They just don't care. They leave you there, out in the cold, like an animal. I don't want their money. . . . I just want a job, a chance to get my life straightened out."

Throughout WITSEC's troubled history, its flaws have frequently been fodder for investigative journalists. The Marvin Naidborne case led to a series of damning articles in Long Island's *Newsday*. In 1976, Fred Graham published a book called *The Alias Program*, a scathing view of WITSEC. The bad press resulted, in part, in hearings before the Permanent Subcommittee on Investigation, chaired by Georgia senator Sam Nunn. Federal lawmakers finally took a look at a program they had been routinely funding over the previous decade.

The result was an abundance of saber rattling—one senator called WITSEC "a body without a brain"—but little in the way of legislation. It wasn't until 1984 that Congress enacted the Witness Security Reform Act, a toothless capitulation to the powers that run the program. Since then, there have been no substantive Congressional reviews, and WITSEC's budget has steadily increased, from $2 million in 1972 to nearly $44 million in 1988.

The program's most obvious deficiency has always been the degree to which it provides a framework for criminals to prey on unsuspecting communities, as in the case of Michael Raymond. Although the Justice Department claims that the current rate of recidivism among WITSEC's inductees is less than half the national average for felony offenders, this has never been very comforting for local cops. When trying to get information on someone they suspect might be a relocated witness, more often than not they find themselves butting heads with an intractable Justice Department.

One case that nearly single-handedly sank WITSEC involved a bank robber and hardened lifer named Marion Albert Pruett. Pruett was released eleven months early from an eight-year prison term because he testified on behalf of the state of North Carolina in a murder case. After being relocated to New Mexico with his common-law wife, Pruett went on a violent rampage, murdering five people. One of those murdered was his wife, whom he bludgeoned with a hammer, strangled with a belt, then carried into the desert near Albuquerque, where he poured gasoline over her body and burned it beyond recognition.

When Pruett's case was brought before the U.S. General Accounting Office in 1982, it raised more than a few troubling questions. Local police in a number of jurisdictions had been trying to track him for years, but no one had been able to obtain information on his past. Even more pertinent was the degree to which informants like Pruett were supervised, and how closely there were monitored after their release from the program.

The Marshals Service may be correct in its claim that instances of people like Pruett's creating one-man crime waves are low, but there remain other troubling issues, such as the program policy toward innocent people who, for whatever reason, feel that they have been wronged as a result of WITSEC. In hundreds of cases, for instance, witnesses have used the program to dodge lawsuits and debt collectors. Some have even used it to keep divorced spouses from visiting their children. Once such case, involving a Buffalo construction worker named Tom Leonhard, went as far as the U.S. Supreme Court.

As a law-abiding patriot, Leonhard had been granted visitation rights to see his children each weekend by the courts of New York State. When they abruptly disappeared one afternoon with his ex-wife's new husband, Leonhard made the rounds of the local offices of the U.S. marshals, the FBI, and the U.S. attorney. For two years, the Justice Department refused to admit it had had anything to do with his children's disappearance.

It was discovered that the children had, in fact, been relocated, so Leonhard sued the government. Ultimately, a U.S. appeals judge ruled that since the officials of the Justice Department had "acted in good faith," the federal court would not second-guess the officials' "rational exercise of discretion." Leonhard and the New York courts were bound by the decisions of WITSEC.

This example and others like it illustrate yet another flaw in the program—one that the Marshals Service has never been able to reconcile. In promising to protect the new identities of its inductees, the Justice Department is torn between its obligation to the witness and its obligations to the public. The result is that it is often unable to fully protect the interests of either.

In contrast to the complex and abundant reasons WITSEC has never really worked as intended, the justification for its continued existence—according to those who support the program—is short and sweet: The Witness Security Program brings about convictions.

"You cannot make an organized-crime case in this country without it," says Richard Gregorie, a former assistant U.S. attorney in Miami who initiated hundreds of people—including Max Mermelstein—into the program during his seventeen-year government career. "Our system of law requires firsthand evidence. Hearsay won't make a case. Unless you have someone who can put the criminal there firsthand, a conviction isn't going to happen."

There is no question that the U.S. government has won a number of impressive victories in the past decade against what it likes to call "traditional organized crime." Together with the Racketeer Influenced and Corrupt Organizations (RICO) statutes, the Witness Security Program has played an important role in these convictions. Virtually every major Mob case in recent years has relied heavily on turncoat witnesses. Invariably, the promises of the program have laid the groundwork for informant cooperation.

The fact that it works as a crime-fighting tool evidently carries weight with legislators and the public. Both seem resigned to accept the concept of a flawed WITSEC, believing, perhaps, that by fabricating new names and identities for people, our government is proving its daring and omnipotence. The problem, of course, is that by allowing government this power, we are only encouraging arrogance and cynicism, a fact amply illustrated by those who run WITSEC.

The program is now headquartered in Arlington, Virginia, and is run by Gerald Shur. Described by one witness currently in the program as "a small man with a small mind and a God complex," Shur is often cited by inductees as one of WITSEC's biggest administrative problems. He is known as something of a monomaniac in the J. Edgar Hoover mold and his decision-making process has been called "dictatorial and capricious" by one former WITSEC employee.

Shur almost never talks to the press, and he turned down repeated interview requests for this article. Doug Tillit, a spokesperson for the U.S. marshals, responded by saying, "Our position is that there are some people who support the program and some who don't. There's nothing we can do or say about it." Shur has always preferred to let those who benefit most from the program—federal agents and government prosecutors—extol its virtues. As for its deficiencies, to say that WITSEC has engaged in a cover-up or two would be a quaint accusation. The program was designed to engage in deception.

It would be a mistake, however, to blame the failings of WITSEC entirely on Shur, or even on the inadequacies of the Marshals Service. The real question is not whether the program is badly administered, but whether or not it can ever be administered.

No single group has a more acute understanding of this than the witnesses themselves. Dozens have turned to the press or the courts seeking an outlet, usually out of frustration with the Justice Department's lack of accountability.

Most witnesses enter the program in such a state of paranoia and fear that they willingly follow the government's lead. For every Michael Raymond or Marion Albert Pruett—lifelong criminals who see WITSEC as just one more exploitable branch of the system—there are hundreds whose motives are more confused. Once persuaded by the government to become informants, they have little choice but to see WITSEC in the most helpful of terms, as a kind of redemption, a chance to cleanse their misbegotten souls.

Joe Labriola, a smalltime gangster from Connecticut, was looking for just such a cleansing in 1987 when he was busted for trafficking in cocaine. At the age of fifty-one, Labriola did not want to spend any more time in jail. Despite misgivings, he decided to become a government informant.

As with many criminals who do so, Labriola seemed to crave the approval of his masters. After each trial in which he testified against his former friends, he sought reassurance from the agents and prosecutors, who told him, "You did the right thing."

Had Labriola known that the suicide rate among inductees into WITSEC was many times higher than the national average, he might have asked himself an obvious question: Why? And he might have arrived at the obvious answer that those in the program were, after all, criminals, just like himself. To believe that the government would ever truly concern itself with his welfare required the kind of wishful thinking of which only truly desperate men are capable.

Throughout his cooperation, Labriola sought to endear himself to the only friends he had left—the lawmen. Often he would cook meals for the police and the prosecutors as they discussed his next day's testimony. Joe would regale them with stories from his Mob days, and they would all laugh and slap one another on the back. It was almost like old times when Labriola had told wiseguy stories with his buddies until the dim hours of the morning.

But there was a difference. These men were cops and he was not. At the end of each day, they went home to their wives and kids while he slinked around, feeling like a rat, hoping he wouldn't inadvertently blurt out some small fact that might betray his true identity. The contradictions in his life caused Labriola to suffer bouts of deep depression, which he sought to alleviate through the occasional use of cocaine and heroin.

In May 1990, Joe could take no more. Sitting on the bed in his tiny government-assigned apartment in Springfield, Massachusetts, he swallowed an entire bottle of medication he had been taking for high blood pressure, chasing that with illegal drugs. He left behind a suicide note in which he said he could no longer take the pressures of being a government witness. The last line, scrawled in what looked like a child's handwriting, read, "Don't be mad at me."

"You know," said a cop familiar with Labriola's case, "it's not all that shocking to me. Joe was in a lot of anguish. He never felt good about turning. It was an abrupt change in lifestyle. He was caught between two worlds and wasn't comfortable in either of them."

There were no federal agents at Labriola's funeral. He left the Witness Security Program the same way he entered it. Alone.

2.

RUDE BOYS

Playboy, October 1991

By beating the Italian Mob at its own game—drugs and violence—Jamaican outlaws have become a brutal, bloody force in gangland America.

The raid began as a faint wail, barely audible over the evening hubbub on the streets of Brooklyn. In Crown Heights, an impoverished community well acquainted with the ravages of the drug trade, the sound of approaching sirens was nothing new. But on this particular evening, the residents took special notice as the sirens got closer and louder. As of December 1990, most police activity in the neighborhood had been related to an expanding, violent group known as the Gullymen. Made up primarily of Jamaican nationals, they had become one of the city's most powerful gangs.

The "rude boys," as the gangsters liked to call themselves, had taken over Crown Heights' thriving cocaine and heroin trade and were living the life of newly crowned drug lords. When they weren't showing off the lavish accoutrements of their success in the clubs along the main thoroughfares, the Gullymen were ruthlessly reinforcing their criminal power. They took over a fifty-nine-unit apartment building at 1567 Sterling Place, and when the landlord threatened to call the police, he was gunned down in a third-floor hallway, his bullet riddled body tumbling over a railing and landing on the floor below.

"Dem rude boys think dey was God," said a woman who works in a barbershop near the gang's Crown Heights headquarters.

Once they were in control of the building, the Gullymen used it to sell dope and provide crash pads for recruits recently arrived from Jamaica. Gunfire echoed loudly throughout the building and out into the neighborhood. It became too blatant for the police to ignore, and on December 6, at approximately 8:00 p.m., a massive caravan of law-enforcement vehicles sped past the dilapidated tenements and shuttered storefronts. At the corner of Schenectady Avenue and Sterling Place, nearly 200 city and federal agents jumped from their vans and squad cars. Four SWAT teams of twenty-five men each began busting down doors and climbing through windows.

At the same time the agents were making arrests and confiscating cocaine, heroin, and illegal firearms in Brooklyn, raids were taking place on Long Island, in Albany, and in Dallas. The following day, front-page stories in the *New York Times* and the *Dallas Times Herald* and a report on NBC's *Nightly News* trumpeted the busts. A local newscast called it "one of the biggest raids in the city's history."

Federal agents familiar with the Jamaican gangs knew better than to gloat. Despite the massive show of force and the many arrests, the gang's leader, thirty-one-year-old Eric Vassell, was nowhere to be found. It was a sobering reminder of what the police already knew. The posses were here to stay.

With the establishment of crack cocaine as the single most lucrative underworld racket since bootleg liquor, the face of organized crime in America has changed dramatically. The once-legendary five families of Cosa Nostra have been destroyed in court; time has taken its toll. Into that void have stepped the posses, named for the westerns once so popular in Jamaica. Like their namesakes, today's cocaine cowboys adhere to the rules of the wide-open urban frontier. Old-World concepts of turf and protocol are rarely honored. Because the rude boys' ability to replenish their ranks seems limitless, even the concept of family is dispensable. Unlike the Mafia or the notorious Chinese Triads, the posses have little or no organizational structure and no apparent blood oaths or initiation rites. Each group has a leader, but there are no godfathers or capos or underbosses.

About the only thing the feds can say for certain is that the posses are more pervasive than anyone first imagined. From 1986 to 1989, there were posse raids in locales as disparate as Miami, suburban Maryland, Rochester, and Kansas City. In one massive raid in October 1988, more than 120 members of the Shower Posse, believed to be the largest in the United States, were rounded up in a sprawling twenty-state bust.

In 1989, the General Accounting Office, an investigative arm of Congress, published a report that identified twenty-one states in which posses had definitely established operations and ten states in which activity was suspected. "In the beginning, we looked at this group almost as a novelty," says a federal agent who had been investigating the posses for years. "Now it's become an epidemic."

In the early 1980s, when Vassell and his fellow Gullymen began selling cocaine on the streets of Brooklyn, the Mafia was still talked about as the only game in town. Most cops knew, of course, that Asian and South American sources controlled the major flow of narcotics, but it was the Italian-American mobsters who grabbed newspaper headlines and were portrayed in movies. The few Jamaicans involved in organized crime were thought to be little more that ganja-smoking Rastafarians who casually sold a little herb on the side.

Law-enforcement personnel knew little or nothing about the politics and economics of the West Indies. Sun, surf, and sand—that was Jamaica. As the 1980s wore on, they would have good reason to know more. On the streets of drug-infested immigrant neighborhoods such as Crown Heights, a new generation was arriving. Raised primarily in the decrepit shantytowns of Kingston, Jamaica's capital city, these newcomers were hardened gunmen from some of the meanest, most poverty-ridden streets in the Third World. They proved to be the perfect training ground for a group that had designs on the toughest turf in America. In part, the level of violence associated with the posses can be attributed to their perilous position in the drug trade. If the international narcotics business is a buzzing hive, the rude boys are the worker bees, pushing at the retail level whatever the Colombians, the Sicilians, and the Chinese are able to import. And out on the street, dealers and buyers don't carry American Express. When the deal goes sour, people die.

Even so, within the world of organized crime, where rolling up a high body count may normally be expected to earn you a seat at the head of the table, the rude boys are thought to be hopelessly volatile. More than 2,100 posse-related homicides since 1985 may have something to do with that opinion. Although it would be comforting to dismiss the posses' penchant for mayhem as the product of an inherently violent class of criminal, it would also be wrong. The roots of their behavior are buried deep in Jamaican society, where grinding poverty, violence, and fratricidal politics have been festering for years in the tenements and back alleys of the island's capital city.

McGregor Gully is a garbage-choked ghetto in East Kingston. Rubble and broken glass are everywhere. The residents live in crumbling concrete homes sheltered only by thin sheets of corrugated tin. In a nearby shantytown, the streets are teeming: Goats, dogs in heat, and raggedy children amble past graffiti-splattered walls and open-air fruit-and-vegetable stands. Mired in a world of poverty and neglect, the inhabitants of this and a dozen other ghettos just like it have been dubbed "the sufferers."

It was in McGregor Gully that Eric Vassell got his start. Like many a "Johnny-too-bad" growing up in Kingston's shantytowns, Vassell became involved in politics at a young age. With few jobs available, the sufferers turn to the political system for sustenance and self-esteem, trusting that the party they back will extend its patronage after the election. As one social activist in Kingston put it, only half jokingly, "Whether or not the party you support is in power determines whether or not you eat."

As a teenager in the late 1970s, Vassell joined a youth organization affiliated with Jamaica's ruling People's National Party (PNP). It was not exactly like joining the Young Republicans; it was more like joining a street gang. Guns were supplied, political contacts established, and the wide-eyed youths were indoctrinated into Jamaica's rambunctious political process.

Elections had been violent through much of the country's history, but it took a massive infusion of guns into Jamaican society in the 1970s to produce the current harrowing conditions. The many high-powered weapons that flooded into the country arrived at the same time the CIA, under its director George Bush, was widely reported to have taken an active interest in Jamaican affairs. The American rationale was unambiguous. Throughout the 1970s, the government had followed a leftist doctrine, courting Fidel Castro and the Sandinistas, among others. The opposition party was led by Edward Seaga, a friend of Ronald Reagan.

Destabilization of the Jamaican government paved the way for a Seaga victory. It also forced gunmen employed by the losing side to flee the island and face the victors' retribution. One favored destination for the losers, of course, was the United States, and this tide of well-armed Jamaican refugees produced America's initial wave of posse-related violence in the early and mid-1980s.

Along with grinding poverty and political violence, Jamaica's ghetto dwellers must deal with abuse from the island's security forces. The Council for Human Rights, located in tiny downtown offices near Kingston's once-thriving port, devotes the majority of its time to investigations of police beatings and shootings. "On a slow day," says the group's head, Florizelle O'Connor, "we might get four reports of brutality. When the police are really having a good time, we get anywhere from fifteen to twenty per day."

Outside O'Connor's office, in a cramped, sweltering third-floor hallway, residents gather to file official complaints against the police. In the first two and a half months of 1991, the *Daily Gleaner*, Jamaica's largest newspaper, reported 156 violent deaths, an average of two a day. Of those, nearly one quarter were killings by police.

A small, finely feature woman dressed in traditional African garb, O'Connor stands at the door of her office. "Here," she says, nodding toward a group of sufferers who have lost all faith in the law, "this is our future."

———

Through a maze of loosely connected one-room shanties, near the back of a bustling tenement yard, a twenty-eight-year-old bicycle repairman named Johnny extends his hand to a visitor. He wears his dreadlocks gathered in a ponytail that flows to the middle of his back. Johnny is not a rude boy, but he knows many young men who are. As a male in his late twenties who is not dead, in prison, or on the run, Johnny is viewed as something of a wise old man in Denham Town. He is at first hesitant to criticize life in Kingston in front of a stranger. Speaking in a heavy patois, he says of those who complain about their lot in life, "Dem people, dey get up inna mornin' an' see de sunshine an' dey curse de sun. Next day, dey see de rain fall, an' dey curse de rain."

As Johnny speaks, a scruffy teenage boy walks into his one-room shed. A gauze bandage soaked with blood is stuck to his forehead, and his neck bears a fresh five-inch knife wound. Shaking his head in dismay, Johnny sends the kid away, presumably to have his wound tended to by a neighborhood bush doctor.

As Johnny explains it, the young man was at a Denham Town "moulood," or yard party, the previous night. A gang of thugs associated with a rival political faction crashed the moulood, touching off a violent rumble. Surprisingly, no one was killed.

As he speaks, Johnny becomes more upset—and forthcoming—about living conditions in the ghetto. "De cost a livin' is killin' dese people," he laments. That day, the price of basic foods such as milk, flour, and butter had gone up once again. Along with everything else, malnutrition was a major concern, especially with the "lickle pickneys," or young children. "I'd like fe dem tings to change," he says pleadingly, "an' me know dem must change. Our youts is comin' up, an' we can't continue livin' like dis."

Despite the violence, Johnny refuses to bad-mouth the rude boys, or "badmen," as they are called in Kingston. If nothing else, the badmen are a force the establishment must reckon with, which gives them a certain stature in the ghetto. To some, they are seen as the inheritors of Afro-Jamaica's rebellious history, which began with the maroons, the seventeenth-century runaway slaves who refused to submit to their colonial masters, and continued through many violent uprisings in the centuries that followed.

It is no accident that reggae became the music of the rude boys. "Fe years, Rasta been persecuted by society," says Johnny. "Society chase de Rastamon, an' dem chase de badmon. So de badmon an' de Rastamon becomes friends. Just as Jesus Christ was walkin' an' him never choose a priest, an' him never choose a high man. Him choose some fishermon, a lowly mon."

The reverence with which Johnny and other ghetto dwellers view the island's gunmen is based on the realities of life in the ghetto. Brutalized by the police and ignored by their government, the sufferers are sustained by their own mythology. They see the outlaw as an avenging angel, a latter-day Robin Hood who steals from the rich and gives to the sufferers.

To illustrate this point, Johnny tells the story of Rhyging, the gangster/outlaw whose exploits have become ghetto folklore in Kingston. In 1948, Vincent "Ivanhoe" Martin, a twenty-four-year-old burglar and gunman from a West Kingston ghetto, escaped from prison. Nicknamed Rhyging, patois for wild, angry, or foolhardy, he eluded a massive police dragnet with the help of sympathetic ghetto dwellers. Johnny takes obvious pleasure in recounting the tale, made famous in the Jimmy Cliff movie *The Harder They Come*. "Rhyging de *baddest* badmon," he says, "but de people support him, fe him one a dem."

The visitor asks Johnny about another violent tale, one that took place in Brooklyn, where a family of four lived in a tiny apartment. One night, gunmen entered the apartment and brutally murdered the residents. One of the victims was a pregnant woman. The gunmen, believed to be posse members exacting revenge for a drug deal gone bad, deliberately shot the woman in the belly, killing her unborn child.

Johnny has heard this story before. A few weeks earlier, it made headlines in Jamaica. "Dem posses," he says, "Me hears dem de roughest, toughest. Killers!" He shakes his head, then adds in a firm voice, "But dem people carries wit' dem de sufferin' a de Jamaican people.

To the Gullymen's Vassell, organized gangsterism must have seemed like a natural career move. After spending many months shooting up rival campaign rallies and delivering votes with the barrel of a gun, he fled Jamaica after the 1980 elections. Upon his arrival in New York, all he had to do was adapt his skills to America's criminal marketplace, where prospects for advancement were vastly superior to anything back home.

At five feet eight inches tall, with a scrawny ghetto physique, Vassell was not physically intimidating. Soft-spoken, with short, neatly coiffed hair, he had a broad, toothy smile that made him look years younger than he was. Because of his diminutive stature, he knew the value of surrounding himself with physically impressive strong-arm men.

In Brooklyn, Vassell made contact with a group of Jamaican killers called the 98th Street Men, a resident gang near Crown Heights. With this group of trained hit men, Vassell targeted a section in the neighborhood then controlled by a small group of Panamanian nationals. "The Panamanians themselves were no slouches when it came to violence," says a New York detective formerly assigned to the Gullymen's turf. "But the Jamaicans just shot them right off the block."

Once he had established a base of operation, Vassell's drug business followed a pattern similar to that of other posses across the United States. Guns and henchmen flowed easily back and forth between Jamaica and the States. Violence was used not as a last resort but as a calling card. The Gullymen staked their claim through drive-by shootings—the gangland equivalent of a leveraged buyout.

· Despite his lack of formal education, "Brooklyn Barry," as Vassell became known on the street, possessed an undeniable business acumen. By the late 1980s, his operation included some forty Gullymen who were reaping combined profits of more than $60,000 a day. Business was so good that in 1988, Vassell sent Paul Moore, his brother-in-law, to Texas to explore the possibility of expanding their operation to include the sale of crack. Two murders and many assaults later, the Gullymen were the largest crack dealers in Dallas.

To a bunch of young ruffians weaned in a Kingston ghetto and only recently arrived in America, it must have seemed like a dream. They pulled up in a sleek, new BMW in front of their headquarters on Schenectady Avenue, the Crown Heights Soccer & Domino Association, dressed "spree-style," with gold jewelry on their fingers and around their necks.

One of the few Gullymen who refrained from indulging in opulent displays of wealth was Vassell himself, who preferred to explore other benefits of the trade. He would take his pick of the beautiful women gathered at the rude boys' favorite Brooklyn dance halls and have them taken to his apartment. Apparently, his reputation was hard to resist. As of last December, Vassell is said to have fathered nineteen children from thirteen women, or "baby mothers," as he prefers to call his ladies.

Having established himself as a prominent figure in criminal circles in America, Vassell found that his reputation was growing back home in Kingston. Like many posse leaders, during trips to Jamaica, he took money, clothes, and lavish trinkets to the sufferers, which he handed out in annual "treats," or street festivals. Brooklyn Barry was welcomed in McGregor Gully as a renegade hero who had returned to help redistribute the world's riches. Beauty pageants were held in which budding baby mothers were sponsored by Vassell and other members of his gang. For the adults, Vassell often took guns—"vote getters," as he sometimes called them—that he had purchased in Florida and Texas, packed inside television sets, and shipped via air freight.

The reigns of the Gullymen might have lasted indefinitely were it not for their tendency toward unpredictable acts of violence, which, as their business became more profitable and more unwieldy, inevitably turned inward.

Among Vassell's most visible lieutenants were Danny, Winston, and Fitzy Reid, three brothers from Kingston. Because the Reids had been with the government and the police department back in Jamaica, Vassell never completely trusted them, even though he valued their talent for mayhem. Fitzy was particularly brutal and had been used as the Gullymen's favored hit man on numerous occasions.

In late 1989, Fitzy was arrested on drug- and gun-possession charges. Vassell refused to post bail. When Fitzy had to sell his car to raise the money, it ignited a smoldering resentment that led to a series of murders and attempted murders within the gang. In May 1990, after a night of dancing at a popular reggae dance hall in Brooklyn, Fitzy was trailed by two gunmen as he walked to his new Mercedes. Someone yelled, "Hey, Fitzy!" as he got behind the wheel. He looked up just in time to catch the barrage of gunfire from an M-16 assault rifle. The shots wreaked so much devastation on Fitzy's body that initial reports of the murder stated that his head had been chopped off. Street talk held that Vassell had paid $25,000 for the hit.

In the wake of Fitzy's death, a distraught Danny Reid, already a cooperating witness, found new inspiration to tell everything he knew to FBI Agent Robert Chacon and Detective Tom Bruno, members of a task force that had been investigating the Gullymen for months. Reid's cooperation touched off a panic in Brooklyn posse circles, with dozens of rude boys tripping over one another to cut deals with the feds. "Generally, posse members are easy to turn," says one agent involved in the investigation. "I guess they're used to Jamaican law enforcement, where they might get shot at the drop of a hat. We give them a sandwich and Coke and talk to them in a nice voice and they act like puppies. They come right over and lick you."

In Brooklyn, the excitement of a major organized crime bust is soon consumed by the daily travails of life in New York. At 1367 Sterling Place, formerly one of the hottest coke and heroin locations in New York, only the bullet holes in the lobby walls are a reminder of the building's former status as a drug haven. "It's quieter, but I'm not saying it's any safer," says a woman who lives on the ground floor. When the sun goes down, gunshots and sirens are still a common sound. Five blocks to the east, a group of Jamaicans known as the Jungle Posse is said to be expanding its operation, hoping to capitalize on the demise of the Gullymen.

Vassell is still at large. Some say he's hiding in Kingston, while other reports suggest that he may be in Brixton, a densely populated Jamaican community in London. A profile on the television show *America's Most Wanted* reported that he might be in Long Island or Brooklyn.

Despite the increased success in capturing and prosecuting individual posses, federal agents are baffled by their continued growth. The problem, it seems, lies far beyond the traditional domain of American law enforcement. "We have a sayin'," explains Johnny, chewing on a piece of roasted fish in Denham Town. "If a fire, mek it burn. If a blood, mek it run." In other words, as long as Jamaica's sufferers see themselves as victims, a parade of aspiring rude boys can be expected to follow the Gullymen.

In Kingston, young boys continue to prowl ghetto neighborhoods with such names as Concrete Jungle, Lizard Town, Dunkirk, and Beirut. With their fathers dead, in prison, or off fighting for their little piece of the American dream, the youths' tough, streetwise exteriors mask a burning desire to find someone who cares for them, who has an eye out for their interests. With no families and few role models, they look to the rude boys.

Last spring, the talk of Jamaica was twenty-five-year-old Nathanial "Natty" Morgan, the latest gangster to follow the legendary Rhyging. Wanted for the murder of seven people, Morgan escaped from jail and had been eluding the police for the past five months. In the meantime, he continued his life of crime, robbing from the rich and allegedly giving money away to people in his home community of West Kingston.

The closest the police came to capturing Morgan was when they fired at him one night from a considerable distance. He ran, leaving behind a shotgun and a Bible marked OUTLAW NATTY MORGAN. Inside the Bible, he had written: I HAVE THE WILL TO LIVE AND NOT TO DIE, THOUGH I PREFER MY FREEDOM MORE THAN MY LIFE.

The *Daily Gleaner* chronicled Morgan's exploits with blazing headlines, and the youths of West Kingston dreamed of being just like him. "When he gave me his gun to hold," one youngster was reported to have said, "it made me feel like a general."

3.

HONG KONG OUTLAWS

Playboy, June 1992

From their base in Asia, the Chinese triads have taken over rackets around the world. Now they're coming to America.

Needle in hand, the junkie named Africa searches his arm for a vein. Any vein will do.

"Tie off, motherfucker," his friend Leon reminds him.

In his haste to satisfy his need, Africa has forgotten one of the most elementary junkie rituals: wrapping a strip of rubber cord around his bicep so that his veins bulge. That task accomplished, he pierces his right arm. His soft brown eyes lift toward the ceiling. He lies back on his mattress and lets out a long, mournful sigh.

In tiny, dormitory-size rooms in the Marion Hotel on Broadway in Upper Manhattan, Africa and Leon are free to indulge their self-destructive cravings. Both men have been diagnosed as HIV-positive; they are using the nine-story dwelling as a flophouse while they wait to die. Emaciated addicts, many of whom contracted the AIDS virus from using the dirty needles that litter the floors, wander squalid hallways, openly shooting up.

On the fourth floor, in Africa's room, forty-year-old Leon rhapsodizes about the increased purity of heroine now circulating in New York. A longtime addict, he gives his full endorsement to today's product: "The shit is slammer."

Leon's enthusiasm is understandable. In recent years, the quality and quantity of the dope has indeed been on the rise, as a result of the expanding efforts of a major new supplier: the Hong Kong mob. In Washington, D.C., Philadelphia, and other cities, evidence of its success is plain. Agents of the Drug Enforcement Administration (DEA) have reported unprecedented seizures of heroin coming into the United States. In Congress, hearings have been held to discuss smokable heroin, a choice for users who shun needles. In hospitals across the country, overdoses are on the rise.

To junkies like Africa and Leon, the identity of their ultimate supplier remains a mystery shrouded by myriad street sellers, mid-level suppliers, and international brokers. For people in law enforcement who follow the drug to its source, the facts are more discernible but far from comforting.

The heroin business is part of a sprawling international empire with its heart in Southeast Asia. Although the empire has existed for centuries, surprisingly little is known about how it works. Law-enforcement officials have struggled for years to understand how the heroin business interconnects with a staggering array of rackets from prostitution, gambling, and money laundering to the smuggling of illegal aliens. Impressed by the vastness of the empire, some have misleadingly dubbed it "the new Mafia." In law-enforcement circles, federal agents refer to it more pointedly as the Chinese connection.

In the 1980s, as the influence of Cosa Nostra waned, no criminal group in the world made more progress than that of the ethnic Chinese. Since the early 1950s, immigrants have been fleeing social and economic oppression throughout Asia, settling in South and Central America, Australia, the Caribbean, Canada, and the United States. The overwhelming majority of these immigrants have shown themselves to be among the most industrious citizens in the world. Although certainly smaller in size, the criminal element among them has proved to be equally industrious.

For decades, these Chinese criminal groups were content to operate within the confines of the world's Chinatowns, extorting small businessmen, extending usurious loans, and capitalizing on the Chinese community's insatiable affection for gambling. Today, the burgeoning heroin business has changed all that.

In 1984, Southeast Asian heroin constituted only 5 percent of the market in New York City, home to nearly half the heroin addicts in the United States. By 1989, that total had increased to 80 percent. The purity levels of China white, as the drug is commonly known, are so high that Mexican, Pakistani, and Turkish sources have been virtually eliminated.

Back in 1968, when "Popeye" Doyle shattered the French Connection and seized 246 pounds of heroin with a purity level far below that of China white, the supply dried up and prices soared. The most startling fact of recent years is that even with much larger seizures from coast to coast, junkies around the country hardly seemed to notice.

Says DEA Special Agent Richard LaMagno, who has been investigating the Chinese connection for years, "It's a whole new game. We're seeing volume and projected revenues that must make this the most profitable criminal business on the face of the earth."

The forces behind today's dope trade form a labyrinthine underworld that begins in the Golden Triangle—the poppy-growing region that encompasses northern Laos, Thailand, and Burma—and spreads to transshipment points in Bangkok, Taiwan, and Hong Kong. The controlling interests are diverse, yet for such a vast criminal network to exist, many international law-enforcement agencies suspect the triads, Chinese secret societies founded in the seventeenth century. Originally, an underground political movement formed to overthrow the corrupt Ming dynasty, triads evolved into a criminal brotherhood with similarities to the Sicilian Mafia.

Today, triad societies are spoken of with awe throughout the Far East. They are believed to control virtually all organized crime activity in Hong Kong. Their name derives from the equilateral triangle use as their symbol, representing heaven, earth, and man. Triad membership is for life. Traitors are executed, often with a single bullet to the skull.

The societies are currently facing the biggest challenge in their 300 years of existence. In 1997, the British government's ninety-nine-year lease on Hong Kong expires, and the territory comes under the control of the People's Republic of China. When the changeover comes, a considerably less tolerant regime will come with it. Enterprises that thrived under the laissez-faire capitalism could well perish in the grip of a totalitarian regime. Hong Kong's criminal element is understandably nervous. Already, law-enforcement groups around the world have been warning their governments of an impending triad incursion. In the next five years, triad members may outnumber the Mafia in this country three to one.

To understand why the triad members are running, it helps to pay a visit to Kowloon's Walled City, the territory's most notorious ghetto. Located in the shadow of noisy Kai Tak International Airport, the area—as is much of Hong Kong—is a tightly packed enclave of concrete dwellings, just 100 yards wide by 200 yards in length. Within the walls, a maze of dank four-foot-wide passageways leads underground. Overhead, exposed electrical wiring dangles precariously and pipes leak a rust-colored sludge. An occasional concrete stairwell leads into darkness.

In 1842, when China ceded Hong Kong to the British, it claimed jurisdiction over the Walled City. The British apparently felt the compound was more trouble than it was worth and refused to police or even govern its approximately 50,000 inhabitants. Predictably, the area became a triad breeding ground. Opium merchants, child-prostitution rings, and gangsters on the run found refuge here. Other strange activities proliferated, from the practice of unlicensed dentistry to the selling of poisonous snakes.

The Chinese government has made it clear that when it takes over in 1997, it would prefer that the Walled City not be there. In the spirit of cooperation, Crown forces have been slowly evacuating the area. Rodents and alley cats are now the primary inhabitants.

The Walled City is scheduled for demolition, a fate that some believe may await other triad sanctuaries come 1997. Although the homes may be destroyed, the residents and their enterprise will surely move elsewhere.

Tsim Sha Tsui, one of Hong Kong's many neon-lighted commercial centers, is a prosperous triad stronghold. The fruits of capitalism are amply displayed with glittering jewelry stores, huge shopping malls, and lavish nightclubs jam-packed within a few square blocks. The average citizen probably wouldn't know by looking at it, but the area is considered to be the domain of Sun Yee On, one of Hong Kong's largest triads. Many of the stores pay protection money; the nightclubs, bars, and restaurants are guarded by triad bouncers; and a portion of the profits from producing and marketing counterfeit brand-name merchandise goes to Hong Kong gangsters.

Beyond Tsim Sha Tsui, in a small coffee shop on the outskirts of Kowloon, a young Sun Yee On member has agreed to talk. Knowing that the betrayal of his oath is punishable by death, the man—we'll call him Louie Leung—will answer questions only if his real name is not used and the location of the interview is not described in much detail. "I must warn you," he tells the interviewer, "if anyone learns of this conversation, both me and you will be in a lot of trouble."

The motive for Louie's willingness to talk stems from his dissatisfaction with triad life. Five years earlier, far away in Brooklyn, two fellow Sun Yee On members were executed on the street in the middle of the day. New York police suspect that the murder of Billy Wong Ming-fung and Wong Chi-ming, both twenty-five, arose from a power struggle for control of an illegal casino in Chinatown. The case was never solved, but Leung claims he knows who ordered the killings. "Sun Yee On offices in New York hired professional assassins to murder their own members," he says.

He goes on to say that he was disgusted that triad officers would order the killing of fellow members. "I was always told that when there are disputes between members, no matter what, we should sit down and work it out. As far as I am concerned, Sun Yee On violated its own oath." Since the murders, he says, he has tried to avoid triad activities and live a "clean, law-abiding life."

But Leung's growing disenchantment with his triad affiliation was a long time coming. Eighteen years earlier, when he was first inducted into Hong Kong's secret criminal fraternity, he couldn't have been more proud. Like many youths that have come from poor and working-class families, he was recruited while hanging out in video arcades and playing soccer in his neighborhood.

When Leung was barely a teenager, he was roughed up by a group of gang members and told that if he didn't want it to happen again, he would have to join their organization. He acquiesced. For one year, he waited to be initiated, a period known in the triad lexicon as "hanging the blue lantern."

One evening, Leung and a group of twenty or so other youths were rounded up by their *dai lo*, or "big brother," who had sponsored their memberships. The inductees were scared to death. "There was a small shrine in the room, with a statue of an ancient Chinese warlord. We were each given a stick or two of incense, which was lit. Then we recited the thirty-six oaths, extinguishing one incense after each oath. We all stood in a circle and they pricked our middle fingers with a needle. A drop of blood from each of us was mixed with water in a bowl. The bowl was passed around and we all had to take a drink."

An egg with a face drawn on it was placed before the group. Each inductee was told to slice the egg with a knife. The egg represented the face of an informer. By cutting the egg with a knife, the triad members pledged to seek vengeance against any member who cooperated with the police.

"From that day forward," Leung says, "I am a triad soldier, what we call a Forty-Nine. If I talk with anyone outside the group about triad business, my whole family will die. I will be killed by a tiger in the forest. If I go swimming, the fish will eat me."

Having become part of one of the oldest and most revered criminal organizations in the world, he began practicing the ways of the brotherhood, triad style. "Me and the other Forty-Nines, we meet maybe a few times a month. We discuss new groups operating in our territory. Should we beat them up, take them out? We go to the market for extortion. We take maybe five dollars each from all the small businessmen. When we walk into a restaurant and eat, we don't pay for the food. We just sign the Sun Yee On symbol on the bill and walk out."

After eight years of dedicated involvement, Leung was promoted to the prestigious rank 426, or Red Pole fighter. Only the triad leader, or Dragon Head, can authorize such a promotion. In ancient times, the Red Pole was the triad's most respected warrior, a proletarian symbol of righteousness and liberation. Today, his primary role is to punish triad rule breakers and terrorize shopkeepers who are slow to pay extortion.

"If some brother make a mistake," he explains, "we slap him in the face and give him a verbal warning. If he don't listen, we beat him up. Then we cut him. Also, we protect businesses in our territory. One time there was a shooting in some Sun Yee On mah-jongg club. We tell the parties involved, 'Listen, go make your living somewhere else.' They didn't listen, so we went after them."

Leung is quick to add that, given the triads' reputation, violence is not often required. Any Hong Kong businessman knows the routine. In fact, many so-called legitimate businessmen are themselves members of a triad, having joined to enhance their chances of succeeding in a highly competitive environment. This relationship between business and criminal elements has been termed the "Chinese waltz," and it is a dance familiar to any Chinese gangster—from low-level racketeers like Leung to the most powerful international heroin traffickers.

When asked whether or not it would be possible for a professional criminal to exist in Hong Kong without being a triad member, Leung laughs. "Yes, of course. If this person had a death wish."

The omnipotence of triads is a shared preoccupation in Hong Kong. At least once a week, the *South China Morning News*—the territory's largest English-language newspaper—contains a triad-related article. Estimates by the Royal Hong Kong Police place membership somewhere around 160,000, or three percent of the population. There are close to fifty triad groups, with turf established along territorial lines.

Typically, rank-and-file membership is composed of working-class kids roped in at a young age, enamored with the triad's ritualistic trappings and the sense of importance provided by the secret societies. Yet the attractions have proved to be far-reaching, with solicitors, policemen, an occasional legislator, and white-collar types having opted for the triad life.

Despite a long-standing ordinance that prohibits Hong Kong residents from joining secret societies, attending triad meetings, or possessing paraphernalia that in any way relates to their activities, the societies' broad sphere of influence has consistently bedeviled law enforcement. "We try," says David Tong, an assistant commissioner with Hong Kong's Customs and Excise Department, "but so many citizens are fearful and uncooperative."

Tong's office on the ninth floor of the Harbor Building overlooks Hong Kong's port, which hosts a colorful panorama of ferries, junks, sampans, and other seagoing vessels. Gulls sweep the shoreline looking for morsels amid a constant swirl along the docks. The harbor is the world's second busiest, after Rotterdam, with as many as 5,000 craft passing through each day. For Tong and other lawmen, it is a continuing nightmare.

Shipments of China white are smuggled through Hong Kong's port every day. Fishing trawlers chug up the coast from Thailand and offload the dope in the South China Sea. Small junks bring the contraband to Hong Kong's container terminals, where triad members see that it is unloaded. This pattern was first established a century ago, when the British government systematically foisted tons of opium on an unsuspecting Chinese populace, creating millions of addicts. "Today," says Tong, "the heroin trade is carryout."

It would be inaccurate to say that triads control the heroin business. An individual Chinese entrepreneur in the United States can initiate a major deal, whether he is member of a triad or not. It is unlikely, however, that the deal will proceed as smoothly as he would like without some help from the triads. A well-known code phrase or secret handshake associated with the Sun Yee On, 14K, or Wo Hop To triads can consummate a deal. Triad connections move the dope from Hong Kong to Europe and the United States.

The loosely structured manner in which triad affiliations enhance large-scale dope transactions has perplexed some Westerners. Trained on a generation of *caporegime, consigliere,* and *capo di tutti capi,*

American law enforcement has had a hard time grasping the opaque ways triads operate internationally.

At the street level, of course, the triads function much like criminal mobs everywhere: Gangsters enforce their will through fear and intimidation, and group loyalty is brutally upheld. Unlike the American Mafia, though, which has a rigid corporate structure, upper-echelon triad members are free to initiate criminal projects on their own and use their affiliations as they see fit. "It's more in the nature of a brotherhood like the Freemasons than a Mafia family," says a senior officer with the Hong Kong police.

Over the years, triads have firmly established their role as an integral part of free-market capitalism, but they can play the other side of the fence as well. In the face of competition from American and European expatriates, for instance, some Chinese businessmen have exploited the triad mystique while espousing the belief that it represents a sacred historical tradition.

But that game is just about over. Now that they face the prospect of a hostile government at the century's end, triad members are eager to make one final big killing under the old regime. To do so, they are pushing their drug trade with extraordinary vigor. It is, quite literally, their passport to the world.

In New York City's Chinatown, the prospect of Hong Kong's impending change in status has already begun to reshape the community's traditional boundaries. Elaborate triad-run smuggling networks, in which illegal aliens pay huge fees to be shuttled through Canada and Central America, are flourishing as never before. Adjacent neighborhoods like Little Italy, once a Mafia stronghold, have been pressured by immigrants from Hong Kong, Mainland China, and other Asian ports of call.

For many years, Chinatown's ruling structure has remained the same. Tongs (business associations) dole out jobs and housing to loyal members. Violent street gangs, allegedly controlled by the tongs, uphold territorial boundaries. Whether or not an infusion of triad gangsters will unsettle this balance of power is a source of much debate.

According to Leung in Hong Kong, one triad has already begun to stake its claim. On frequent visits to New York, he says, he has met many fellow Sun Yee On members. "One guy," he contends, "a Red Pole fighter, was sent to Chinatown for one reason: to oversee the migration of Sun Yee On into the United States. The vessel they hope to use, he says, is the Tsung Tsin Association, one of Chinatown's wealthiest tongs. Situated in the heart of Chinatown, the association's seemingly placid, nondescript redbrick facade is the perfect cover for one of Chinatown's liveliest gambling dens.

In 1988, infighting over a Tsung Tsin Association election led to a number of shootings. One longtime member filed a lawsuit alleging that fraud and bribery tainted the election of the association president, Tony Ng. The lawsuit claimed that Ng had been placed in office by Paul Lai, a former president and current association "adviser for life." According to Leung, both Ng and Lai are Sun Yee On members, having been initiated into the society in a secret Hong Kong ceremony.

The fraud and bribery charges against Lai were never proved, but in a 1988 judicial hearing, even more serious allegations were raised. A lawyer for the complainant accused Lai of hiring a gang of thugs, whom he housed in an apartment on the fourth floor of the association. When asked about his triad affiliation, Lai denied even knowing what the word meant.

The possibility that one of Hong Kong's largest triads has already penetrated Chinatown presents a daunting challenge for American law enforcement. In the past, the Chinese community was always allowed to monitor itself. Only when gang violence spilled out into the street did police intervene, and even then charges were haphazardly pursued. To many, Chinatown's peculiar isolation stemmed from a tacit agreement between cops and the tongs, well known for their ability to grease a palm when necessary.

Leung says, "Sun Yee On wants to follow the Hong Kong style. You have to understand, Chinatown is not Hong Kong. They know they must move slow and make all the right contacts so they can place their people in power."

With few Asian cops or agents, American law enforcement is ill equipped to deal with criminal developments in Chinatown. In their attempts to understand triad groups, many of which speak different dialects, police have to deal with a closed and distrustful Chinese community, the product of years of neglect.

Any Chinese citizen who is pondering whether or not to cooperate with *low fan*, as Caucasian police are sometimes disdainfully known, might want to consider the case of Steven Wong. Born in Hong Kong and raised in Chinatown, Wong infiltrated the United Bamboo, a powerful Taiwan-based triad, in 1985. Neither a cop nor a criminal in a bind, Wong was simply a citizen fed up with the stranglehold criminal groups had on legitimate businesspeople in Chinatown when he agreed to help in a police investigation.

"Every day I would read the Chinese newspapers," says Wong. "I see the problem. Kids dropping out of high school, being gunned down. We have ninety-nine percent of our population living in fear of the one percent who are bad."

Posing as a Chinese gangster with Mafia connections, Wong worked his way into the inner sanctum of the United Bamboo, a group with deep-rooted political connections in the Taiwanese government. Wearing a recording device strapped to the small of his back, he even recorded his initiation into the triad, the first time any such event had ever been taped by cops in the United States.

With a lean, muscular physique and steely glare, Wong approached his undercover duties like a method actor preparing for the role of a lifetime. Since he was a teenager, he had wanted to be a cop. Throughout the investigation, says Wong, agents and prosecutors constantly reassured him there would be a job for him in law enforcement when the case was over. "They tell me, 'Steven, you're a hero. We can use you.' "

By the time FBI agents made their arrests of eleven United Bamboo members, Wong had risked his life making heroin deals and even contracting to commit a murder. The case was tried in federal court using the RICO statutes. Wong was grilled on the witness stand by eleven defense attorneys, who accused him of being, among other things, a Communist agent and a lifelong gangster.

The trial resulted in the only conviction of a major triad group in U.S. history. Afterward, Wong inquired about his job. "They told me,

'Mr. Wong, you are not eligible for a police job because you were a member of a criminal organization.' " Wong was dumbfounded. He had joined the United Bamboo solely as part of the investigation.

Having testified against his fellow Chinese, Wong was ostracized in the community. The FBI told him there was a contract out on his life. He was offered relocation through the Witness Protection Program, which he refused, asking, "Why should I have to live my life in hiding, like a criminal?"

Today, Wong works in a restaurant outside New York. He rarely shows his face in the city before midnight; his memories of the United Bamboo case haunt him. "They never did let me be a part of the team," he says of the cops, agents, and prosecutors he worked with. "They never trusted me because I was not one of them. To me, Chinatown was at stake. But they didn't care about anything except improving their careers."

If Chinese organized crime were still only a Chinatown problem, American lawmen would not be sounding alarm bells. The fact that second- and third-generation Chinese-American criminals have branched out, however, is impossible to ignore. There was a time when Chinese heroin dealers made distribution arrangements only with Italians. Now, police sources say, the Chinese are willing to deal directly with Dominican and African-American groups, the primary street-level distributors of China white. The Mafia, no longer the feared presence it once was, has been relegated to a lesser role.

Far away from New York, in hill regions of the Golden Triangle, fields of poppies are in bloom. The plant's slender four-foot stems are topped with brilliant, multicolored petals and a core bulging with opium. DEA intelligence reports say that the last three years have produced record crops of raw opium sap, which is extracted and used as the base ingredient for heroin.

In many ways, the drug trade is just an example of the way the Hong Kong Mob has always done business, and it is the base for the triad's international expansion. By exploiting their connections throughout the world, heroin brokers reap huge profits, which they in turn launder through Hong Kong banks or use to finance multimillion-dollar real-estate deals. "Some traffickers are quite well regarded," explains a Hong Kong investigator with triad expertise. "To them, heroin is just a commodity like sugar. You could put it on the stock exchange. These people don't have to look at users on the street in Washington, D.C., or New York. They aren't concerned with some poor black kid in Harlem. It's just a business, plain and simple."

Junkies all across America have reason to rejoice. Soon, the latest shipments of China white will be blanketing their neighborhoods. A new generation of heroin addicts is about to be born.

In the Marion Hotel, Africa cooks up a righteous batch. This time, he remembers to tie off. The needle is poised; a vein is bared. Down the hall, a junkie moans, his voice reverberating through an open window and out into the street.

Africa is asked if he ever wonders about the origins of his dope.

"Who gives a fuck?" he replies. The needle enters his vein with a pop.

4.

COSA NOSTRA TAKES THE BIG HIT

Playboy, September 1992

The Mafia's official bird—the stool pigeon—is singing a treacherous song.

By the time Mafia capo Peter Chiodo looked up from under the hood of his Cadillac, he had already been shot once in the ass. Weighing in at 547 pounds, Chiodo was an easy target. On a clear afternoon in May 1991, after he had stopped at Pellicano's gas station on Staten Island to check his engine, a car screeched into the station and two men jumped out, guns ablaze.

Despite being hit, Chiodo pulled a weapon from inside his jacket and managed to return fire. An auto mechanic standing nearby dove under the Cadillac for cover as the gunmen chased Chiodo around the gas station shooting indiscriminately, riddling the blubbery Mafioso with twelve bullets. Chiodo finally fell flat on his back. As blood oozed from his wounds, somebody stole his gun. Then a neighborhood onlooker ran up and exclaimed, "Geez! What a shoot-out!"

The shooting of Peter Chiodo may not have been the sloppiest Mob hit in history, but it ranks right up there. Even with Chiodo's girth and lack of mobility, the hit men failed to get the job done. Four months later, Chiodo was wheeled into a New York courthouse. Understandably perturbed by the attempted hit, he turned stool pigeon, testifying about a huge racketeering scheme that allowed four of New York's five Mafia families to seize control of the New York Housing Authority's profitable window-replacement businesses. He also described his own lucrative career as the Mob's man in control of the International Brotherhood of Painters and Allied Trades, a job that frequently involved intimidation and murder.

Chiodo's rise and fall eloquently symbolizes the pathetic state of Cosa Nostra, circa 1992. He was a powerful capo grown fat on his own success; he was the intended victim in yet another inept Mob hit resulting in yet another high-level informer; and he was a murderous criminal who was allegedly reformed through his act of contrition and became a card-carrying member of the federal Witness Protection Program. Today, for the first time in history, there may be more "made men" in the criminal justice system than there are on the street.

"Yeah, you could say the Mob is all fucked up," says Joe Pistone, a former FBI agent who went undercover as a Mafioso for six years. "There was a time when a guy was supposed to get whacked, he got whacked. Now they even have trouble getting that right."

Henry Hill, the wiseguy whose years in the Mob were immortalized in the movie *Goodfellas*, says, "It's a horseshit life, the Mob. Always was. I guess more and more guys are starting to see the way they get treated."

The Mob is currently being chased out of many of its traditional territories. In New England, the powerful Racketeer Influenced and Corrupt Organizations Act has been used to gut the Patriarca family, once a sprawling criminal organization with members in Rhode Island, Massachusetts, and Connecticut. In Pennsylvania, the Bufalino family and the murderous Scarfo Mob have been decimated. Nicodemo Scarfo, whose organization controlled that rackets in Atlantic City, is in federal prison with a life sentence. These high-level convictions follow earlier law enforcement successes in former Mafia strongholds such as New Orleans, Chicago, and Cleveland.

In New York, recent prosecutions have overwhelmed the city's infamous five families. Beginning in 1986 with the Commission case, which resulted in three of the most powerful Mafia leaders in America being put away, the legal onslaught has been staggering. In the past four years, leaders from all five families have been busted on RICO charges, culminating in the highly touted conviction of Gambino family boss John Gotti, the alleged *capo di tutti capi*.

In contrast to their American brothers, Mafiosi in Italy still know how to handle a prosecutor. Last May, they took out a top Italian Mob buster (Giovanni Falcone) by detonating a bomb as his motorcycle drove past. In America, the man might have been peppered with movie offers.

Beginning with the testimony of Joseph Valachi in the early 1960s, the Justice Department—aided considerably by the Mafia's own lack of quality control—systematically eroded the once-vaunted oath of *omertà*, which historically ensured that those who talked died. Today, with the prospects of long sentences and the existence of the Witness Protection Program as a viable career alternative, stool pigeons such as Chiodo and Salvatore "Sammy the Bull" Gravano (the man who brought down John Gotti) willingly come forward.

"The rules have changed," says Ronald Goldstock, director of the New York State Organized Crime Task Force. "It used to be that a low-level Mob member might come forward, and he would be seen as a traitor to the organization. Now we've seen mobsters at the highest levels—Bonanno, Fratianno—talk. They not only testify but wear wires, write books, and have agents. Their attitude is, 'This is not the same organization it once was. There is no honor left.' Now everyone feels free to break the code."

Along Mulberry Street, in the heart of New York's Little Italy, the changes have been apparent for some time. A few of the old restaurants remain, including Grotta Azzurra and Umberto's Clam House, where "Crazy" Joe Gallo got whacked while having a late-night snack. Neon signs still advertise cappuccino, espresso, and Italian pastries, sold mostly to tourists in the neighborhood. Scenes from all three *Godfather* movies were filmed in Little Italy, and the Italian residents who remain seem determined to keep up appearances. Italian flags flutter from lampposts and the sounds of Sinatra emanate from corner smoke shops.

In reality, the neighborhood is a dwindling ethnic enclave overrun by more recent immigrants, mostly from Southeast Asia. Mott Street is still lined with seafood and produce stands, as it has been for generations, but the merchants are Chinese and Vietnamese rather than Italian and Jewish.

John Gotti hung out regularly in Little Italy right up until his most recent arrest and resulting conviction. To admirers, Gotti's insistence on maintaining links to the old neighborhood reflected well on his sense of tradition. It was here, in a hallway in the back of the Ravenite Social Club, that Gotti was recorded wishfully telling an underling, "This is gonna be a Cosa Nostra till I die. Be it an hour from now, or be it tonight, or a hundred years from now when I'm in jail. It's gonna be the way I say it's gonna be—a Cosa Nostra."

At one time, such confidence would have been justified. Long before Gotti sipped his first cup of cappuccino on Mulberry Street, the concept of a criminal underworld had taken root. At the turn of the century, the Black Hand ruled the tenements and small businesses in Little Italy in New York and elsewhere. Tireless extortionists, members of the Black Hand sought to establish themselves as men of virtue, as mediators in a bustling, fresh-faced immigrant community.

As the newcomers assimilated, things changed. Leaving the antiquated ideas of the Sicilian Mafia behind, the new generation of mobsters embraced free-market capitalism. During Prohibition, they were handed a product that everyone wanted and a marketplace without competitors. Naturally, their business thrived and they were able to expand and diversify.

Over the decades, the Mafia derived much of its strength from links with the so-called legitimate establishment. In dozens of cities across the United States, the Mob became deeply entrenched in the fabric of American society through political connections and influence with organized labor. Although the Mafia never really had the national hierarchy some journalists and historians suggest, virtually every major industrial city had an organized crime structure loosely based on Charles "Lucky" Luciano's model, whether it was called the Commission, the Syndicate, the Outfit, or Cosa Nostra.

The reason behind the success of the Mob was clear. *Omertà* was caught up with the Italian image of honor and manliness. It is not manly to snitch. The very foundation of the Mob was based on the idea that if a member spoke to the police, the press, or even to other associates about his criminal dealings, he would sleep with the fishes.

"It's extraordinary, when you think about it," says Ralph Salerno, a former New York City supervisor of detectives and a consultant to congressional committees on organized crime. "Luciano forms the Commission around 1931, and for thirty years nobody talks. Some five thousand people across the country, all facing prison time, some faced with capital punishment, some being offered the opportunity to cooperate, and not one of them spoke. That's the power of *omertà*."

The legend grew, causing the Mob to be seen by many as an omnipotent international force. In the 1950s and 1960s, the Mafia was credited with, among other things, building Las Vegas, underwriting Batista's Cuba, delivering Kennedy's victory in the 1960 presidential election, and then helping to assassinate the man they supposedly elected. Never mind that most mobsters dropped out of school around the eighth grade, rarely left their own neighborhoods, and showed a proclivity for getting arrested and re-arrested. In the public mind, it was a highly sophisticated organization that controlled both church and state.

In truth, the Mob's authority has usually been aimed at the lower rungs of society. The victims, invariably, are working-class stiffs caught among corrupt unions, politicians and Mafia thugs eager to endear themselves to the powers that be. As the late godfather Paul Castellano once put it when describing to an associate the plight of the working man: "How many of them are so fucking stupid that they would knowingly try to fuck us? All right, now and then there's a guy who has delusions. A lunatic . . . He thinks he's got a whole union or a big politician protecting him. . . . But usually it's just sad-ass guys who make mistakes. . . . Do we let these sorry bastards ride? Hey, they knew the rules."

"I'll tell you about the Mob," says a veteran wholesaler at New York's Fulton Fish Market, long known as a classic Mob racket. "Down here, they operate just like the government, only more so."

Situated in Lower Manhattan in the shadow of the Brooklyn Bridge, the Fulton Fish Market is a throwback to an earlier era. In the predawn hours, the market is alive with commercial activity. Burly laborers "work the pallet," loading and unloading refrigerator trucks. Forklifts rumble across cobblestoned streets, fishmongers haggle over prices, and the salty aroma of fresh seafood permeates the air. Despite the fact that the market has shrunk by half in the past thirty years, it is still the nation's largest. Each year more than 125 million pounds of seafood, worth hundreds of millions of dollars, are bought and sold within the market's quaint five-block radius.

In 1987, the federal government declared the area a Mafia-run enterprise and vowed to return it to legitimate owners. Using civil RICO legislation, a judge appointed an administrator to oversee market operations. When public hearings were held last May to reveal the administrator's findings, witnesses wore black hoods and testified behind a screen, hoping to avoid Mob retribution.

The threat of violence has been an effective regulating factor in the market since the 1920s. In those days, Joseph "Socks" Lanza, a capo in the Genovese family, controlled all rackets through his role as business agent for Local 359 of the United Seafood Workers. The market became a world unto itself. Extortion, labor payoffs, gambling, and obstruction of justice became enduring traditions.

In 1984, a market worker who was hijacking fish trucks was shot twice in the head and left to die on a market street. A few years later, a local restaurateur parked his car in an unassigned location during market hours. He and a companion were pulled from the car and beaten with loading hooks and a hand truck. In the summer of 1990, when a worker who was banned from the market by one employer showed up to work for another, he was beaten with a lead pipe and wound up in the hospital. The incident occurred in a street crowded with workers and wholesalers. But when the cops asked around, there were no witnesses.

The mode of operation at the Fulton Fish Market is the same as that employed in other major Mob rackets, especially those in the garment trade, the International Longshoremen's Association (ILA), and the International Brotherhood of Teamsters. The Mob ensures there will be little or no competition. Inflated licensing fees and union pension funds are used to line the pockets of Mafia members. The climate of violence is so pervasive that even the city abdicated its responsibilities to a brutal form of underworld justice.

No one is claiming that the Mob has been eradicated from the Fulton Fish Market, but the government has finally established a presence. The city's Department of Investigation ran a sting operation on a group of illegal gun merchants in the market. Many fair-trade violations were cited, the violators were named in court documents and sanctions are being imposed. The City of New York was shamed into hiring managers and inspectors for the market.

Similar actions were taken against the ILA, the garment industry, and the teamsters. In the past three years, state and civil RICO suits have been filed and government administrators assigned. In the case of the teamsters, a 1989 civil racketeering suit resulted in a revolutionary change in leadership, with the union's national elections being opened to the rank and file for the first time in history.

"The big criminal convictions make the headlines," says Frederick Martens, executive director of the Pennsylvania Crime Commission. "But civil RICO has done more than all the criminal convictions put together to hit organized crime where it hurts most—at its economic base."

With recent government successes in criminal and civil litigation, there's little doubt the Mafia has been wounded. But it would be wrong to give all the credit to American law enforcement. The decline of the Mafia has come about as much through evolutionary changes in society as through the actions of cops and prosecutors. The unionized industrial economy of postwar America has given way to a high-tech economy. Businesses such as the Fulton Fish Market are becoming a thing of the past. Urban political machines—once wide open to Mob corruption—have lost power to interest groups and political action committees.

Throughout society, Italian Americans have assimilated. Forty years ago, a wayward working-class kid of Italian heritage might have considered the Gambino or Bonanno crime family as a career choice;

today he's more likely to think about Saint John's or Georgetown. Even those few who will opt for the criminal life do not feel bound by the rigid traditions of the past.

"These new guys just don't have it," says former FBI agent Pistone, whose testimony in various trials contributed to more than 200 indictments and 100 convictions. "When I was working undercover in the late '70s, circulating among the Mob, you had the last of a generation that still respected the old values. Maybe their parents or relatives were born in Italy. They hardly ever left the neighborhood.

"Then came the yuppie generation. They don't speak Italian or care about the old country. Their whole attitude is, 'What can the Mob do for me?' They don't have any loyalty to anybody but themselves. Because people think like that, the Mob has no future."

Of course, even if the old order continues to wane, it will not happen quietly. The decline of the five families in New York has already brought about a high degree of anarchy. Last December, while Gotti was in jail awaiting trial, the Gambino family waged war among themselves during a bloody seven-day period. There were at least five shootings in Brooklyn restaurants and on the street, resulting in numerous injuries to innocent bystanders. "Right now [the Mob] has more of an incentive than ever to start whacking people," says the media star of Mob informants, Henry Hill, who is himself a tempting target.

One former member who is well aware of the organization's continued willingness to use violence is Peter Chiodo. His testimony against his former *paisani* in the Lucchese family brought mixed results. During his long convalescence from gunshot wounds and the stress of taking the witness stand, Chiodo shed more than one hundred pounds. But Mafia hit men tried to murder his sister.

The shooting of Patricia Capozzalo, a mother of three and a PTA president at a local elementary school, was considered a major departure for the honored society. It violated an unwritten Mafia rule prohibiting the shooting of women and children and innocent family members. To some, it was further evidence of Cosa Nostra's fading code of honor, as well as its increasingly poor aim. Once again the hit men bungled the job. Capozzalo survived.

On the streets of big cities all across America, the new world order has been asserting itself for years. Colombians control the importation of cocaine, doling it out to Jamaican and Dominican retailers. The Chinese oversee the heroin trade, in which Hispanic and black American gangs serve as distributors. Of today's gangsters, Jamaican posses and Vietnamese hoodlums are considered to be the most violent. The old *paesano* Mafia exists mostly in the movies.

The new generation of gangsters presents a challenge to lawmen and journalists. Cosa Nostra had become a cottage industry, but its run is now probably ending. Exploring the new underworld will require added research and, most likely, a change of complexion on the block. Alone, white agents and investigators cannot do the job.

Privately, some cops and writers deride the new mobsters, citing the fact that their criminal reach does not compare with that of Cosa Nostra's. The old world mobsters, they contend, ran unions and industries. They had the power to corrupt cops and politicians and to compromise entire communities.

It is true that Vietnamese, Jamaican, and other ethnic criminal groups do not have a criminal structure to approach that of Cosa Nostra's—a structure that took fifty or sixty years to reach its pinnacle. It's of little comfort, however, that these emerging groups see themselves as outsiders in American society. Traditional Mob protocol, which states that cops and journalists could not be threatened or killed, was based partly on the Mob's identification with society at large. Many new crime groups, composed of impoverished and alienated immigrant youths, do not feel this identification, making wonton violence all the more likely.

One journalist who was willing to take on the new mobsters was Manuel de Dios Unanue. Born in Cuba, De Dios came to New York City in the early 1970s and became the crusading editor of *El Diario-La Prensa*, a New York City Spanish-language newspaper.

One of his targets was Hector Delgado, an Ecuadorian businessman and naturalized U.S. citizen who runs a string of travel agencies. In late 1990, Delgado was charged with running a money-laundering operation that funneled more than $200 million to Colombian drug cartels and with making $22 million in five years as his percentage—a profit margin that makes the Mafia's criminal rackets look like chump change. Delgado pleaded guilty to "structuring," circumventing a law requiring that a report be filed for cash transactions of $10,000 or more. He received probation and continues as a licensed money transmitter.

As the city's newspapers routinely speculated on who might be next to take over a Mafia crime family, De Dios exposed a vast criminal network that the press had all but ignored. Even the police scarcely knew of the Nine Kings, a mysterious group of drug traffickers and money launderers who masquerade as businessmen. De Dios wrote about them.

Last March, De Dios was seated at the bar of a Spanish restaurant in Queens. Two gunmen walked into the restaurant. One pressed a gun to the back of De Dios's head and pulled the trigger twice. The job was not bungled.

The blatant murder of a journalist is a relatively new phenomenon in the American underworld. The message it delivers is clear. In the new world order, society will not be allowed the courtesies accorded by Cosa Nostra's quaint code of ethics, which supposedly left room for the concept of innocent victims. Whether or not mainstream journalists and lawmen have the moxie to face the new reality remains to be seen.

In the meantime, *la famiglia* continues its decline from criminal reality to cultural myth.

II.

AMERICAN DREAM, AMERICAN NIGHTMARE

They say it's all about the money. They are, of course, correct. In the United States of America, the profit motive is king. And don't ever let anyone tell you otherwise. You especially know this is true when you see on television an extravagantly rich person—say, a Donald Trump—assure you that the choices they've made in life "are not about the money." They are either self-delusional, or lying. Most likely they are lying. Not often does anyone get rich in America unless they submit to the overriding principle that it is all about the money.

That's not to say there aren't other factors. Sex, for instance. In the universe of ways to get rich in the United States, sex is right up there with narcotics in its promise of sensual pleasure, danger, thrills, status, and the big payoff. Or so it would seem.

Few ever mastered the art of getting rich through the marketing of sex with as much flair and success as Jim and Artie Mitchell. They seemed to have it all. In the 1970s, they parlayed their status as pioneers in the adult film industry into a multimillion-dollar business of which the crown jewel was the O'Farrell Theatre in San Francisco, a world-renowned sex emporium. They had endeared themselves with the Bay Area's vibrant bohemian and libertarian elite. They were the

Merry Pranksters of Porn, lovable rogues whose reputation as pornographers was softened by the fact they were businessmen who brought a sense of familial camaraderie to the craft of smut mongering. Then, older brother, Jim, shot and killed younger brother, Artie, and the fun-loving image of the Mitchell brothers curdled like an after-dinner treat left out in the open too long, until its essential ingredients had congealed and lost their appeal.

Long before I was sent by Esquire *magazine to San Francisco to report on the shooting of Artie Mitchell, I knew of the brothers and their operations. I lived in San Francisco for ten months in 1984–1985, working as a security guard at the Embarcadero Center in the evenings while hustling for freelance journalism assignments during the day. I lived in the Mission District, which, at the time, was experiencing a huge influx of immigrants from Central America. My rent was reasonable, and I was able to subsist at a low level.*

One night, with a couple friends from my job, I went to the O'Farrell Theatre. The place was an extravaganza of nudity and sexual illusion. I visited the New York Room, which was one of many rooms with different themes. The O'Farrell was basically a strip club, but the Mitchell brothers had found a way to make it feel like a three-ring circus. They also seemed to have a sense of history; the club was rooted in the world of burlesque and stripping as a legitimate cultural phenomenon that had begun in the 1880s, when San Francisco was known as the Barbary Coast, a netherworld of licentious diversions. The Mitchell brothers were part of a long and proud tradition.

Seven years after I visited the O'Farrell Theatre, in 1991, I was living in New York City, a published writer with a first book that had been selected as a New York Times *Notable Book of the Year under my belt, a fact that carries some cache in the insular world of New York media. An editor from* Esquire *magazine—Bill Tonelli—contacted me and said he'd like to meet. We met for lunch. It was the kind of encounter of which there are dozens taking place on a daily basis in Manhattan—a writer and an editor meeting and getting to know each other. Tonelli asked me what, if anything, I was working on. I mentioned that I was considering doing a book on the O'Farrell Theatre in San Francisco. It would not be a crime book or a book about the porn business, per se, but rather a sex-positive book that encompassed a year in the life of a remarkable establishment. Tonelli thought it was a splendid idea for a book. We said good-bye to each other and expressed the desire to work together at some point down the road.*

Within days of my lunch with the Esquire *editor, I was off to San Francisco to meet the Mitchell brothers. Already, I'd had a phone conversation with Jim Mitchell and told him of my interest in doing a book on the O'Farrell Theatre. He was open to the idea. "Come on out," he said. "We'll show you around the place."*

On my first day at the O'Farrell Theatre, after meeting Jim and Artie, I could see something was wrong. Contrary to my previous conversation with Jim, he had no intention of allowing anyone into the inner sanctum of their business operations in the way I was suggesting. I'd been told the brothers were feuding, and it was obvious from the tension whenever they were in the same room that there was a bad energy loose within the universe of the Mitchell brothers. I returned to New York disappointed that my idea for a book was not going to materialize. Then, less than a week later, I got a call from a mutual friend of the brothers and mine.

"Did you hear what happened?" he asked.

"What."

"Last night, Jim shot and killed Artie."

Later that same day, the editor Tonelli called me and said with some urgency, "We want you to go back out there and do a piece on the shooting."

This was not the story I had intended to write about the Mitchell brothers. Tonelli said that Esquire *was going to assign someone to write the story; if it weren't me, it would be someone else. I felt that it was my obligation as a journalist to take the assignment.*

On the surface, Jim and Artie had achieved the American Dream. Their business ventures made them rich and famous beyond their wildest expectations. But the success they found in the American marketplace could not overcome the structural flaws in their relationship. In the end, the pressures of the porn business may have had less to do with their demise than the more primal strictures of blood and family.

For some, the level of success achieved by the Mitchell brothers represents a world beyond dreaming, something to be viewed in movies and on television, where riches and sensual pleasures abound, and "reality" is a fungible concept squeezed into thirty-minute time slots, with false narratives, fake survival games, and the illusory promise of fame and fortune.

In the early 1990s, the Asian community in New York City and elsewhere in the United States was in the throes of trauma. The 1989 uprising in Tiananmen Square in the People's Republic of China, which led to the massacre of citizen protestors by the Chinese military, set off a wave of undocumented migration from Asia. New York City was on the receiving end of a massive influx. Many of these desperate, undocumented immigrants resorted to using organized crime syndicates to smuggle them halfway across the world into the United States. Once they arrived, they were indebted to the smuggling overlords and at the mercy of gangsters. Representing the lowest rung on the ladder of assimilation, to this struggling generation of migrants the full measure of the American Dream as experienced by, say, the Mitchell brothers, was about as likely as a trip into outer space.

Over a five-year period, I covered criminal activities in Chinatown as if it were my regular beat. I wrote a book, Born to Kill *(1995), about the arrival on the scene of a Vietnamese gang, and also a number of articles mostly from the point of view of people in the community who were being exploited and victimized. The underworld activity was made more insidious by the fact that the New York Police Department didn't have much of a grasp on what was happening in Chinatown, and the media was generally indifferent, except to occasionally report on gang shootings and violent extortions in the most sensationalized way possible.*

I cultivated sources and pitched many story ideas to magazines during this period and encountered mostly a lack of interest. The media in general was far more interested in nostalgia for the Mafia, a story then centered around the prosecution of Mafia boss John Gotti, than they were about a contemporary crime phenomenon that was having a traumatizing impact on an entire generation of immigrants. The Village Voice *was the only media outlet I could find that offered the opportunity* to address some of these issues with the kind of depth and complexity that was required.

The final piece in this section is an article I wrote for the op-ed page of the New York Times upon news of the death of George Whitmore Jr. I got to know George while researching and writing The Savage City (2011). Whitmore's ordeal was a significant part of that book's narrative structure. I am still touched by having known George Whitmore, still outraged by what he experienced in his life, and will forever be astounded by how many citizens are blind to the racism and injustice that infects the U.S. criminal justice system on a daily basis.

The pursuit of the American Dream is a potent opiate, both a powerful motivational elixir, with potentially hallucinogenic qualities, but also a disease-ridden whore. It is a journey that can lead to astounding levels of achievement and success, or result in marginalization, exploitation, and the destruction of the human spirit. In the desire to reach the promised land of acceptance as a fully endowed citizen of the commonwealth, or to attain material comfort and/or prosperity, some will make it, and some will not. Whether striving at the highest levels of attainment or down at the bottom wallowing in the mud, the desire to survive and thrive is a harvest that occasionally bears the same bitter fruit: dead bodies.

1.

CAIN AND ABEL IN THE SKIN TRADE

Esquire, June 1991

Jim and Artie Mitchell were sexual revolutionaries, rich hippie pornographers, San Francisco righteous dudes, brothers to the end.

In a city accustomed to spectacular endings—where ritualistic cult killings, political assassinations, savage whims of God, and run-of-the-mill urban mayhem have all been absorbed into the local lore—it was still a shocker. PORN KING SLAIN, BROTHER ARRESTED read the headline in the February 28 *San Francisco Chronicle*. Outside the Bay Area, the shooting of one pornographer by another might not have elicited much surprise. It is generally a sleazy business, the common wisdom goes, where guns and indecency are standard issue. But here, at least, the Mitchell brothers and their theater had done a great deal to dispel the stereotypes.

A career such as theirs could have started only in San Francisco, and only in that adventurous, gentle time immediately following the Summer of Love. Certainly, there is no other place in America where a pair of pornographers would have been seen so indulgently; the brothers were, to many, simply very naughty boys who provided a bit of local color and controversy. Even along the licentious avenues of New York City, no such quarter would be extended to smut mongers—no tour buses would deposit foreign visitors at Times Square's peep shows, as they did at the Mitchell brothers' establishment.

In the years since the late 1960s, Jim and Artie presided over a burgeoning empire that extended far beyond their city's boundaries. Beginning with their production of *Behind the Green Door*, the landmark 1972 skin flick starring Marilyn Chambers, the Mitchell brothers' name became widely synonymous with "quality," at least to the extent that such a thing existed at all in the business. They made dozens more movies over the years and opened a half dozen sex-show emporiums in San Francisco and Los Angeles.

The flagship of their empire, the O'Farrell Theatre, is located in one of the city's toughest neighborhoods, but its outer walls are adorned with elaborate, colorful murals depicting jungle and underwater scenes. Inside, the plush red carpets, cleanliness, and state-of-the-art lighting and sound equipment are a far cry from the dreary, sticky-floored porn parlors found in most cities.

While the performers strutted their stuff in the various showrooms downstairs, upstairs in the office, Jim, Artie, and a collection of friends and colleagues could usually be found drinking beer, shooting pool, hatching all kinds of outlaw schemes. The Mitchell brothers' coterie included an assortment of celebrated counterculture types, such as the late Black Panther leader Huey Newton and writer Hunter S. Thompson. On the wall above his desk, Jim had a framed letter from Abbie Hoffman, thanking the brothers for their generosity during a visit to the theater in the 1970s.

A number of book ideas to document this unusual empire have been hatched, including one by Thompson, who spent almost a year at the O'Farrell ostensibly working as the night manager. (His book has yet to be published, but those close to the theater remember his months there as one of the O'Farrell's more ribald periods.) The brothers' circle also included Warren Hinckle, the rabble-rousing, eye-patch-wearing newspaper columnist. Hinckle figured prominently in the theater's most celebrated bust, the 1985 arrest of Marilyn Chambers for allegedly allowing a customer the privilege of "digital" penetration during her striptease act. Over the next week, Hinckle wrote a series of articles ridiculing the police department, which had used thirteen officers and a dozen or so backups to arrest the unarmed—and unclothed—porn queen.

Hinckle's columns touched off public outrage, not at the brothers but at the police.

So I wasn't the first journalist to be seduced by the goings-on at the theater. In mid-February, I arrived in San Francisco to spend the better part of a week with Jim and Artie, in hopes of writing a book at some point on them and their operation. Jim had read and liked *The Westies*, a book I'd written about a group of Irish gangsters in New York City. Earlier we'd talked on the phone a few times; he seemed open to the idea of my spending time there and writing about them. "I have to check this out with my brother, Artie," he said, "but, yeah, come on out."

The last time I saw Artie Mitchell was in the middle of the afternoon, and he was rolling a joint. Carefully. The city had been suffering through one of those periodic dry spells when the gourmet herb that grows in nearby Humboldt County had yet to be harvested. Since Artie had a reputation as something of a connoisseur, he wasn't about to waste the last of his stash. It was a tight, lean joint.

The office at the O'Farrell Theatre, the brothers' base of operations since the day it opened in 1969, is up a flight of stairs. In the center of the room is a pool table. An old jukebox stands against one wall. A refrigerator in the corner is usually stocked with beer, and a selection of newspaper clippings relating to the theater have been framed and hung haphazardly around the room. Most conspicuous, though, is a bank of six surveillance monitors that dominates one wall. One of the monitors constantly reveals a gathering of nude and partially clad women lounging in a dressing room down the hall.

Even though he had precious little marijuana left that afternoon, Artie passed his joint around the office without hesitation. With his scraggly brown beard and equally unkempt shoulder-length hair (a baseball cap hid the fact that he was as bald as a Kojak on top), forty-five-year-old Artie cut a raffish figure. He usually had a mischievous glint in his eyes, in keeping with his nickname, Party Artie.

Jim, on the other hand, though he possessed a gentle voice and gracious manner, seemed stern next to his brother. At forty-seven, he, too, was bald on top, but his remaining hair was neatly trimmed and starting to gray. Though he presented himself more conservatively than Artie, the family resemblance was strong. In the early years, when both wore glasses and mustaches, they looked like twins.

It was Artie who gave me an upstairs tour of the theater, gleefully taking me down hallways and around corners, past seemingly oblivious naked performers.

From the rafters, where the light and the audio technicians were positioned, we could see inside the New York Room, where a dancer shimmied her way down a long stage that reached out into the audience, a rather traditional strip act. The Ultra Room was set up like a nightclub, with customers sitting at tables in front of a semicircular stage. The curtain opened to reveal a shower, where five women hosed and fondled one another, then walked out into the audience dripping-wet. Elsewhere in the theater, in the Kopenhagen Lounge, customers sat in the dark with red flashlights, which they shone on the performers as they danced and simulated sex acts.

Back in the office, Artie reached into the refrigerator and pulled out a nonalcoholic beer. When I asked why, he replied, "They say I'm an alcoholic. They say I've got a problem." He took a hit off a joint and held the smoke there in his lungs. There had been a touch of sarcasm in his voice. Jim, perhaps sensing something in his brother's tone, suddenly excused himself from the room.

In the months before that afternoon, those acquainted with the brothers had become even more aware than usual of the tension between them. It was the worst kept secret in San Francisco. Their relationship had always been fractious—the legal trouble and other distractions inherent in their business, along with each brother's divorces and reconciliations, saw to that. Lately, the tension centered mostly on Artie's social habits. In late 1990 and on into this year, he had been drinking heavily and getting stoned more than ever. Jim frequently expressed his concern about Artie to his friends, and no one doubted Jim's wish to get Artie into a rehab center for the younger brother's own sake. But Jim had also recently begun pressuring Artie to divest himself of his share of the business. Still, no one who knew them well would have believed that their disagreements would come to a bad end. Especially not to the particular bad end that awaited them.

When I finally got Jim Mitchell to sit down and discuss the details of my book proposal, I was surprised to find that he was now reluctant. Until then he seemed to like the idea of having a book written about the place. But as I explained my plan—to chronicle a year in the life of the O'Farrell Theatre—he became increasingly more uncomfortable and distracted. "Why would we want to call attention to ourselves like that?" he finally asked, adding mysteriously, "We have secrets, things I'd rather not have aired in public."

One week after I last saw Artie Mitchell savoring toke after toke of northern California's finest, he died in his home in Corte Madera, shot three times. The clincher was a .22 caliber bullet that entered through his right eye and pierced his brain. One block away from the house, police stopped and arrested Jim Mitchell, who was carrying a .22 rifle and a fully loaded .38 caliber handgun. Before the week was out, Jim would be charged with the premeditated murder of his brother.

The house on Mohawk Avenue where Artie Mitchell lived and died is a white stucco ranch house with sky-blue shutters and a picket fence. From the front window, you can see Mount Tamalpais, the highest point in Marin County. It is an unassuming house in a clean, middle-class neighborhood, not what you'd expect for the home of a "porn king." Jim Mitchell lived across the Golden Gate Bridge in San Francisco—about thirty minutes by car—in an equally nondescript house in the Sunset District.

Although their business had been successful from almost the start, Jim and Artie never strayed far from their working-class roots. They grew up in nearby Antioch, at the time a dusty village of about 7,000 people, located on the Sacramento River Delta. Their mother, Georgia Mae, who would eventually hold an interest in her sons' business, was once a schoolteacher. Their father, who died in 1973, was a professional gambler and grifter who sometimes handled security at local card games. "We were raised to be torpedoes against the state," Artie used to say.

When the Mitchell brothers first began producing grainy, ten-minute skin flicks, or "loops," in the early 1960s, the porn business was nearly invisible. What little industry there was existed in New York, the domain of men whose idea of what sex films should look like had been formed decades earlier. As with nearly everything in American culture, the 1960s brought big changes. An early, unmistakable sign of change in the porn business was *Behind the Green Door*, the first and one of the most profitable feature-length (seventy-two minutes, as opposed to its quickie forebears) "erotic" films. It cost $60,000 to make—a fortune for a porn flick at the time—but is reported to have grossed $50 million to $60 million, including bootleg versions.

Along with its higher-than-usual production values, the movie brought the promise of an entirely new, young sensibility to the industry. The star was nineteen-year-old Marilyn Chambers, whose angelic features had just graced boxes of Ivory Snow. She didn't look anything like the leather-bound prostitutes or aging vixens who populated most porn films up to that time.

A young Jim and Artie Mitchell can be seen briefly in the film as a couple of hoodlums who abduct Chambers and bring her to a plush boudoir, where she is ravished by a succession of lesbians, a black stud, and three men seated on trapezes. The movie retained the traditional slow-motion shots of ejaculating male members, but it also took the time to focus on Chambers's seemingly genuine orgasms.

Throughout the 1970s and into the 1980s, the brothers put their unorthodox stamp on film after film, including *Autobiography of a Flea*, *Resurrection of Eve*, and *Sodom and Gomorrah*, which, with a budget near $350,000, is believed to be the most expensive such movie ever made.

"The Mitchells were unique," says Jared Rutter, former president of the now-disbanded X-rated Film Critics Association. "Their product seemed to come out of the sexual revolution of the 1960s and early 1970s. There was an emphasis on actual lovemaking. It was very Bay Area. Generally, they were seen as eccentrics by the rest of the business."

While they were filming, the division of labor between Jim and Artie was often ad hoc. Jim had taken a few film classes at San Francisco State University and seemed more interested in the creative process, so he would usually direct. Nonetheless, there were inevitable disagreements.

Former porn star George McDonald, who appeared in more than twenty movies for the Mitchells in the early 1970s, remembers an almost comic lack of professionalism, despite the brothers' reputation for putting out a relatively polished product.

"There were a lot of sharp words on the set," says McDonald. "Sometimes it was funny. I'd be sitting on a bed naked, waiting for a scene to begin. Jim would be on one side of me and Art would be on the other, and I'd be getting conflicting directions on what they wanted. I'm sitting there trying to get it up and keep it up and I'd say, 'Couldn't you guys have worked this out ahead of time?' "

The Mitchell brothers changed the world of pornography, but they had been outstripped by changes. Their theaters and international film distribution sideline were made all but obsolete by the widespread availability of videos. Consumer demand did not materialize for the ambitious, big-budget porn films they wanted to continue making.

Their success had brought the brothers lots of attention, but more and more it was unwanted. They were forever defending themselves against obscenity and prostitution charges, mainly in connection with the inventive live shows that came to be their theaters' main draws. Last year, one of their most profitable movie houses, located in con- servative Orange County, closed down, the victim of a relentless anti- porn crusade. Although the success of their operation over the years had exceeded their wildest expectations, Jim and Artie used to laugh at newspaper accounts that estimated their worth at $50 million. In 1988, even before their Orange County theater closed, accountants set the value of the corporation at $1 million.

Their business matured into a compact enterprise that practically ran itself, leaving Jim and Artie with time for other concerns. Over the years, Artie had married three times and Jim twice, and they had nine children between them. For a while, they ran a commercial fishing venture together, and at dawn they would rise with the children and spend the day out on a trawler.

"They were two of the most normal, family-oriented guys you could ever meet," says Susie Bright, a friend of the brothers who publishes *On Our Backs*, a San Francisco–based lesbian sex and lifestyle magazine. "Jim was like Dad; Artie was like everybody's favorite uncle." Bright, thirty-three, is the typical kind of bohemian character the O'Farrell Theatre has always attracted. Her perky, in-your-face sexiness, combined with her stereotype-defying manner, she believes, is precisely why the brothers were so supportive.

"The idea of a lesbian sex magazine was right up their alley," says Bright. "It totally fit with their mission of fucking with the status quo, of doing something as pornographers that was innovative, revolutionary."

By then, however, their role as revolutionaries was mainly in an advisory capacity. Their business had become as middle-aged as they were.

"The brothers won a lot of legal battles," says Warren Hinckle. "They'd stayed out of jail. After the Marilyn Chambers victory, they seemed to get bored with the business. Jim started looking around for other things to occupy his days.

"And Artie? Well, Artie started looking around for a good time."

The stories of Artie Mitchell's wild behavior had always been part of the brother's official legend. If he pulled out a gun and started firing around the office, well, that was just Artie. In his sober moments, he had such a charming, outlandish sense of humor that it was hard for some friends to take his darker side seriously.

But beginning in late 1990, Artie's antics—once so rakish and infectious—developed a nasty edge. At the many lavish holiday parties the brothers would throw at the top of the theater, Artie had begun to go too far, groping women and insulting guests for no reason. An affidavit filed by one of Artie's ex-wives during their bitter child-custody battle claimed he was "frequently under the influence with the children" and that he used cocaine, heroin, and psychedelic mushrooms. Three weeks before the shooting, Artie had walked into Maye's Original Oyster House in the middle of the afternoon waving a loaded .38 caliber pistol.

The last time George McDonald saw Artie was on Valentine's Day. That night, up in the office, Artie was in a bad way.

"He was slugging off a bottle of Stolichnaya," McDonald remembers. "He was shooting pool, then he turns to me for no reason and says, 'You know, me and my brother, we never liked you. In fact, get the fuck outta here.'

"I tried to ignore him, walked over and handed him a joint. Then I realize he's gonna take a swing at me with the pool cue. I think, *Oh, Jesus, is it really gonna come to that?* So I duck. But I realize he's so drunk he can't stop his momentum. He's gonna come around a second time. Finally, he caught himself. Ten minutes later, he's curled up in the fetal position, snoring."

Artie enjoyed the freedom to intoxicate himself regularly and misbehave partly because big brother Jim was the responsible one, the one who would keep the business running smoothly. He was also the one their friends would call with tales of Artie's sometimes frightening wildness. By late last year, however, Jim seemed to have grown weary of his role as his brother's keeper.

"One night, I was with Artie and Jim at a little party we had for a local boxer and a bunch of boxing writers," recalls Bob Callahan, a Bay Area journalist and friend of the brothers. "And Artie was drunk and making an ass of himself, trying to pick a fight with this boxer. And I could see Jim was just heartbroken. You know, he never showed his emotions much. But he just looked at me and said, 'God, it drives me nuts to see my brother like that. I built an empire with this guy, and now he's like a Telegraph Avenue street babbler. He doesn't understand how fucked up he is. He's got to go into a hospital.' And that's when I knew Artie was really getting to him."

In fact, Mitchell family discussions of Artie's problem had often concluded with the thought that if he could only be coaxed away from the scene upstairs at the theater, he might finally seek medical help. It was under these pressures that the brothers had begun to dissolve their partnership. They had even gone so far as to begin the paperwork with Dennis Roberts, their attorney.

Jim also began looking for new challenges away from the theater. One outside endeavor he got involved with—sans Artie—was *War News*, an impromptu anti–Gulf War newspaper that their buddy Hinckle was to edit and publish. At significant cost to Cinema 7, their joint-business entity, Jim had agreed to bankroll the project. Staff members were amazed at the energy Jim was devoting to an enterprise that most considered a lark. When I spoke with Jim in mid-February, he seemed consumed by the *War News* project. He had even bought a defunct restaurant in North Beach to serve as headquarters for the paper.

"This is it," he said dramatically as we downed a couple beers. "A lot of us are pushing fifty. This could be our last chance to do something worthwhile."

A few days later, the publication of the first issue coincided with a series of heated phone conversations between Jim and Artie. As the afternoon wore on, Artie got increasingly angry over the fact that when it finally came time to terminate their twenty-two-year partnership, Jim had chosen to do it through Roberts, their attorney, rather than face-to-face. According to Julie Bajo, a former dancer at the theater and Artie's last girlfriend, Artie threatened Jim over the phone that evening, suggesting that if he were not "treated fairly" in their business settlement, he would come over to Jim's house and "blow away" Jim and his girlfriend.

Reportedly, Jim's girlfriend took the threats seriously and suggested they call the police. Jim said no; he could handle it himself. Alone, he hopped into his late-model Ford Explorer and headed for the Golden Gate Bridge.

Only Jim Mitchell knows what thoughts raced through his mind as he drove for thirty minutes though Marin County along Highway 101. Nothing in his life up to that point suggested a man capable of killing anyone, much less a brother to whom he had been thoroughly devoted.

When he arrived in Corte Madera, Jim parked his car on the street behind his brother's house. He slashed two tires on Artie's van with a pocketknife. At approximately 10:15 p.m. he entered the house, where Artie and Julie slept in a back bedroom. Once inside the front door, Jim immediately opened fire with a .22 caliber rifle.

Artie and his girlfriend head the gunshots from their bed. Julie grabbed the telephone, crawled into a closet, and dialed 911. Artie shouted, "Who's there?" and then headed—unarmed—into the hallway.

Then Jim fired, hitting Artie three times, in the stomach, arm, and right eye. The Marin County medical examiner said the fatal shot had come from nearly twenty feet away. The entire rampage took two minutes. A total of seven bullets had been fired.

Outside the house, a Corte Madera policeman who had been summoned by Julie's call found Jim Mitchell trying to get away. He had "the most desperate look I've ever seen on a human being in my career," the arresting officer later told the grand jury.

"Sure, we all knew they had differences and arguments about the business," says Warren Hinckle, echoing the sentiments of many. "But there's no way it was a planned act. If Jim had planned to kill Artie, he would have really planned it. He isn't stupid. The brothers were Okies in a way. It's possible Jim went out there with a gun to scare Artie. Fire a few shots in the house and try to get Artie to straighten up. It may not make sense to you or me, but it's the logic they would have used. Okie logic."

"So far," insisted Marin County deputy district attorney Charles Cacciatore two weeks after the shooting, "the circumstantial evidence suggested cold-blooded fratricide." The district attorney's theory was that there might be some tie between the shooting and the financial aspect of their agreement to dissolve the partnership.

Jim Mitchell's defense team, Dennis Roberts and New York lawyer Michael Kennedy, a longtime friend who has also represented Ivana Trump and Jean Harris, scoffed at that. Admitting that Jim had pulled the trigger, Kennedy told reporters outside a Marin County courtroom, "This was not a premeditated, malicious murder. It was at most a situational, aberrational, accidental killing." Most of those who knew the brothers agree with Hinckle and Kennedy that the idea of Jim planning to kill Artie is preposterous. Still, considering that Jim got into his car armed with two guns and drove for thirty minutes before he begun shooting, the lawyer's argument does little to console the brothers' friends or solve the dark mystery that surrounds the event.

After the initial shock of the shooting, friends and associates immediately began to worry about Jim, who had been jailed. Word was out that he had gone into a deep depression and was possibly suicidal. Later, after he pleaded not guilty to the crime of having murdered his brother, he would be called a "serious threat to society" and denied bail.

At the memorial service for Artie, on a gray, windswept day, friends and family gathered at a funeral home in Antioch, the town of the brother's birth. One recent exploit the brothers shared came to most minds: In March 1990, one year before the shooting, Artie and Jim were at Ocean Beach, on the city's western shore, and while swimming Artie got caught up in a riptide and was carried out to sea. Paddling a surfboard through rough water, Jim and some lifeguards saved Artie from drowning.

Friends and family members spoke at the service, and they seemed to be mourning not just Artie but Jim, too. "I love Uncle Jim," Artie's seventeen-year-old daughter, Mariah, said. "I don't blame him at all. No matter what, he's my uncle and I love him."

Artie and Jim's cousin, the Reverend Bill Mitchell, presided over the ceremony and read a statement from their mother, Georgia Mae. "I know Jim loved Art," it read. "He took care of him all their lives."

POSTSCRIPT: At trial in 1993, Jim Mitchell admitted shooting Artie, but claimed that, as a result of his brother's erratic behavior, he had "snapped" and was not fully cognizant of his actions. He was found guilty of "involuntary manslaughter" and sentenced to six years in prison. After serving less than three years at San Quentin prison, he was released in October 1997 and resumed his overseer role at the O'Farrell Theater.

There were three books published about the Mitchell brothers, and, in 2000, Showtime aired *Rated X*, a movie about the brothers directed by Emilio Estevez, with Estevez starring as Jim Mitchell and Charlie Sheen as his brother, Artie Mitchell.

On July 12, 2007, Jim Mitchell, age 63, died of a heart attack at his home in west Sonoma County.

2.

SLAVING AWAY

The Village Voice, February 5, 1991

Chinese Immigrants Oppressed at Home, Exploited Here.

On Eldridge Street, a sharp winter breeze rustles the debris that has accumulated alongside beat-up metal dumpsters and garbage cans. A few blocks to the west, in the heart of Chinatown, the restaurants and other commercial buildings have been spit-shined for the tourists. But here on Eldridge Street, the buildings are dilapidated, and long-standing restaurants and laundries are nearly indistinguishable from four- and five-story residential walk-ups.

Down the front steps and in the basement of one anonymous tenement is a sprawling, cluttered living quarter, once home to nearly two dozen Chinese immigrants. Further down a dark hallway, deep into the basement of the building, is a maze of low-ceilinged cubicles measuring perhaps five feet by ten feet. Each cubicle is furnished with only a homemade bunk bed haphazardly put together with unfinished wood. The rooms are dank and filthy. There are no windows. The lack of air is stifling.

Throughout the rooms and hallway there is evidence that the occupants have left in a hurry—scattered clothing, a calendar on the wall from a local Chinese restaurant, cigarettes left in ashtrays. In one cubicle, a pair of men's underwear hangs neatly on a hanger perched on the back of a door.

Outside, around the corner on Hester Street, similar conditions prevail. Here, a seven-story walk-up was recently cleared out when an anonymous phone caller informed the fire department about the dwelling's primitive conditions. Fire officials found each of the five floors occupied by some fifty people, all living in makeshift cubicles that were even more cramped than those on Eldridge Street.

Once again, the occupants—in this case "illegals" from Fujian Province in southern China—scattered quickly. Among the items left behind on the third floor was an unpaid phone bill totaling $1,351.84.

For every deserted Chinatown building like the ones on Eldridge and Hester Streets, there are perhaps a dozen more within a few blocks' radius that are fully occupied. In most, the tenants are illegal aliens, ready to move fast when housing inspectors or the fire department pay an unexpected visit. Alone, with no understanding of the English language or the byways of American culture, they represent the undocumented Chinese, growing in vast numbers each year. Now, an estimated 30,000 illegal Chinese live in New York City. Traditionally, their presence has always been tolerated in the Chinese community; their willingness to work "off the books" has fueled the underground economy.

But these days the presence of the illegals has created a crisis in Chinatown, taxing community groups and bringing about troubling accusations of exploitation, both within the community and beyond. The squalid living conditions tell only half the story.

Like generations of Chinese immigrants who came before, most new illegals will find work in the restaurant and garment trades. They will work long, arduous hours for low wages, and they will do so without many of the benefits on which most Americans rely—worker's compensation, overtime pay, medical insurance. But unlike those who came before, these undocumented aliens will spend years working before they accumulate anything even remotely resembling a savings.

That's because many of them owe huge fees—anywhere from $10,000 to $40,000—to be paid to the smugglers who provided fake documents and secured their passage, usually through Central America and Mexico, sometimes through Canada. Part or all of the fee will have been fronted by a relative, an informal credit association, or the smugglers themselves. U.S. immigration officials estimate that since 1980, as many as 50,000 Chinese have been smuggled into the metropolitan area from Fujian Province alone.

Upon arrival in the United States, the smuggled aliens work to pay off their debt. The consequences for those who don't pay are sometimes enormous.

In early January, police arrested thirteen people—all illegal aliens from Fujian Province—for kidnapping and torturing Kin Wah Fong, a thirty-year-old restaurant worker also from Fujian. Fong had refused to pay his smuggling debt. He was snatched from the restaurant where he worked and taken to an apartment in the Bronx, handcuffed to a bed for twelve hours, and beaten with a claw hammer. "They also put him on the phone with his family and he begged them to come up with the money," Lieutenant Joseph Pollini of the New York Police Department's Major Case Squad told *Newsday*. "He thought that at any moment they might terminate him."

One week later, Pollini's squad rescued four more Fujianese who had been kidnapped on Christmas Day and taken to an apartment near the Brooklyn Navy Yard. There abductors demanded money still due from a $20,000 smuggling fee. For twelve days, until they were discovered, three of the illegal immigrants were handcuffed to a bed. The police found a fourth crammed into a small sink cabinet.

Despite the recent spate of kidnappings, the more common way for smuggled immigrants to pay off their debt is somewhat less sensational, though no less demeaning. It's a payment described as "debt bondage" by the international Anti-Slavery Society, a 150-year-old human rights organization affiliated with the United Nations, and it amounts to a modern form of slavery.

"We've never seen anything like this in the Chinese community before," says Pete Kwong, author of *The New Chinatown* and a professor at State University of New York at Old Westbury. "Living conditions are worse than ever. As for wages and working conditions, they've always been bad. But now it has become like slavery competing against slavery."

It is the profitability of "debt bondage" that distinguishes Chinatown from other immigrant communities with sizable undocumented populations. Compared to the $50 to $1,000 the average Central American refugee pays to be smuggled into the United States, the $30,000 fee paid by some Chinese illegals is staggering. Whereas a Nicaraguan, Haitian, or Dominican illegal might work months to pay off his or her debt, an alien smuggled in from Hong Kong, Taiwan, or Mainland China will work up to five or six years.

Another factor that distinguishes the problem in the Asian community is Chinatown itself. Unlike many ethnic ghettos that lack jobs and capital, Chinatown is geared toward a thriving business and political elite. Although it has changed somewhat in recent years, the work force is still controlled by the many tongs, or "family associations." Each association's power is based partly on its ability to provide cheap labor; it is in its own interest to do so.

Add to the demand for illegal labor the nature of the illegals themselves. Many lack formal educations and come from the poorest regions of China. Some yearn for the kind of freedom they associate with Western culture, or *Kam San*, the "Golden Mountain," as America is known to many Chinese. Some are told of the hardships that await them, but their desire to emigrate is paramount.

"Many of these people think that America is the land of milk and honey, that New York is paradise," says James Goldman, a senior agent with the U.S. Immigration and Naturalization Service (INS). "What some of these aliens go through to get here would turn your stomach."

Born and raised in the South of China, "Yin Lee" was working in a wristwatch factory in her native city, making the equivalent of $270 a month. In late 1989, she decided to come to the United States because there was "no freedom, no people's rights" in her home city. For a fee of $2,000, arrangements were made for her to fly to Hong Kong and then to Panama. She had no idea who the arrangements were made with, only that the money was put up by her relatives.

With jet-black hair, doleful eyes, and broad, delicate features, Yin does not look like someone who has just been through a hellish ordeal.

In her mid-twenties, she looks perhaps a few years older than she is. There is an openness about her, an innocence even. She agreed to talk about her experience only if her real name was not used. For the purposes of our interview, she spoke through an interpreter.

Once in Panama, Yin was to pay an additional $3,000 for a fraudulent visa that was supposed to get her into the United States. But within weeks of her arrival, complications ensued. In December of 1989, American troops invaded Panama in search of Manuel Noriega. Yin was stranded for the next seven months.

Speaking neither English nor Spanish, Yin worked in a Chinese restaurant and lived in a cheap hotel, waiting for the false documentation she needed to get out of Panama. After she had been there a few months, she was raped by a Chinese man who lived in her hotel.

"The guy says to me, 'You want sex?' " remembers Yin. "I could do nothing. Afterwards, I tell no one. Too scared."

Yin believes the man was connected with a professional smuggling ring, perhaps himself a "Snakehead," as Chinese smugglers are known, or maybe simply a businessman who profited in some way from the smuggling racket. Either way, he seemed to know a lot about her situation. He knew, for instance, that she was unmarried, alone, and had no family in the country. He also knew she was in the process of being smuggled.

Weeks after the first incident, Yin was raped again by the same man. Then again. As she tells her story now—months after the fact—her voice is steady and determined, her face betraying little emotion.

At the time, Yin was depressed and lonely. Outside the window of her tiny room, a war raged and U.S. troops patrolled the streets. She was too terrified to tell anyone what had happened.

Eventually, Yin secured passage out of Panama to the Bahamas. Traveling with six other Chinese aliens, she arrived in Nassau with no documentation. Though she had half expected as much, Yin's hopes were crushed when Bahamian customs officials would not let her in the country. She was put back on the plane destined to return to Panama.

On the return flight, Yin's plane developed mechanical problems and was forced to touch down unexpectedly in Miami. When she tried to get through customs, she was taken into custody by U.S. immigration officials and charged with lacking a proper visa or passport.

Although she spent the next two months in a detention camp outside of Miami, Yin was overjoyed to be in the United States. She called her uncle in New York, who was able to put up money to get her an immigration lawyer. Because she was from the People's Republic of China, she was able to apply for political asylum. In the meantime, she was paroled and released to her uncle's custody.

According to immigration officials and members of the Chinese community, familiar with the plight of today's illegals, Yin's experiences are both typical and unusual. Sexual abuse is not uncommon. And the route taken by Yin through Panama is a well-worn path. Following the U.S. toppling of Noriega, immigration officials were estimating that as many as 35,000 Chinese had been stranded there without documentation.

What is unusual about Yin's odyssey is the price. By the time she arrived in New York, Yin had run up a total debt of about $10,000, which included the smuggler's fee to Panama and money for a lawyer. This price, well below the $30,000 to $40,000 fee paid by many Chinese illegals, was mitigated by the fact she did not have to pay a snakehead to smuggle her into the United States. That came about merely through an act of luck, or, as Yin calls it, "an act of Buddha," when her plane, unexpectedly, had to land in Miami.

Now that she has arrived in Chinatown, Yin's primary concern is finding a job. Along with thousands of other Chinese women, the garment business is her most likely bet. (If she were male, it would be the restaurant businesses or construction.) Though Yin's prospects for work are good, the conditions are likely to be deplorable.

Wing Lam, program director for the Chinese Staff and Workers Association (CSWA)—a nonprofit labor rights group dedicated to "securing dignity for Chinese workers"—says that with the recent influx of illegals, wages and working conditions have spiraled downward. Lam estimates an average restaurant kitchen helper might make $1,100 a month working twelve hours a day, six days a week.

Despite the prospect of wages and working conditions only slightly better than what she left behind in China, Yin Lee seems relieved to be here. "After all that has happened already," she says, "how can things not get better?"

In Corona, Queens, where the Number 7 subway that runs through the neighborhood is known as "the Orient Express" because of the area's burgeoning Asian population, the days are long. In an alley off Forty-Fourth Avenue, below the elevated Long Island Railroad tracks, a typical garment "sweatshop" is in full operation. Inside a nondescript redbrick warehouse, a few hundred women toil over sewing machines and steam presses on a chilly afternoon.

Joe Halik and Charles DeSiervo, supervising agents with the New York State Department of Labor's Apparel Industry Task Force, climb the steps to the first floor. Since the task force was begun in October of 1987—after a state investigation revealed widespread abuse in the apparel industry—Halik and DeSiervo have made daily visits to sweatshops in Queens and Chinatown.

As the two stroll through the factory, the women keep their eyes on their work. They've seen Halik, DeSiervo, and other members of the task force on many occasions, and they know they have nothing to fear. Unlike the INS, labor inspectors are not concerned with the immigration status of the workers. Their job is simply to make sure the working conditions meet state law.

The warehouse is cluttered with mounds of cut fabric. The sewing tables are situated next to one another in row after row. Overhead, dingy fluorescent lights, many burned out, hang from the ceiling. Some women wear white surgical masks to keep from breathing in dust; almost all are Asian, with a few Hispanics mixed in.

The most common violation Halik and DeSiervo find is an employer who has not paid overtime when, in fact, most women work ten- and twelve-hour shifts. Inevitably, the undocumented aliens aren't even on the books.

For the employer, the benefits in using such labor are clear and compelling. If owners aren't caught by state inspectors, they can pay the worker below the $3.80 minimum hourly wage and avoid paying Social Security, payroll taxes, and insurance benefits. Also, the docile nature of an undocumented work force living in fear makes it a lot easier for the employer to call the shots.

"The worst thing," says DeSiervo, "is seeing five- and six-year-old kids working alongside their mothers."

Task force statistics show that in the last two years, they've closed down thirty-three shops, usually for the most basic requirement: failure to properly register with the Department of Labor. Halik and DeSiervo have seen dozens of shops open and close within a matter of months, in classic fly-by-night fashion. Says Halik: "It's an ongoing cat-and-mouse game."

A recent report by CSWA predicts that if conditions continue on their current path, women working in the sweatshops can expect declining wages and longer hours in the year ahead. Right now, some women are earning a daily wage of twenty dollars, half of what they might have made a year ago. The report concludes: "Sweatshops reminiscent of the early twentieth century have come back in a big way."

As bad as conditions are, things could be worse. For someone with a smuggling debt, a bad job is better than no job at all. Especially for women, the options are limited. Mostly, there are only the sweatshops, or, for some, the sprawling Asian sex trade—an occasional form of employment for young, desperate women with a debt to pay.

In Chinatown, an ethos of insularity prevails. Fear and ethnic pride makes most residents reluctant to put forth a negative image of the community. Chinese Americans have long been perceived as the "model minority" by many non-Asians, an image carefully cultivated by the community's business and political leaders. But the oppressive system of indentured servitude both undermines and, ironically, underscores that image by supplying cheap labor that makes it all possible.

In the last decade, numerous advocacy groups like the CSWA, Asian Americans for Equality, and the Center for Immigrants Rights have been trying to challenge the established order in Chinatown— one that was essentially transplanted from feudal China in the late nineteenth century. Even some business leaders have spoken out, like Yee Kam Yeung.

Last April, Yeung decided to "disassociate" himself from the Fujianese American Association, after having been a member since 1973. The association is believed by many law enforcement officials to be a conduit in the smuggling process. One of the association members is Cheng Chui Ping, aka Sister Ping, a Fujianese woman cited in a recent New York *Daily News* report as the "empress of alien smuggling." She and her husband are two of only twenty members to have donated $10,000 or more to the association's $1.6 million building fund.

Even before he left the Fujianese Association, Yee Kam Yeung had become a vocal critic. When he left, he did the unthinkable: He began his own association, the United Fujianese of America, located on Canal Street.

In Chinatown, few undertakings are more perilous than trying to start your own renegade association. One evening last September, Yeung says he was visited in his offices by four Chinese males who put a gun to his head and pistol-whipped him—an incident later reported in the local Chinese press. One of the men allegedly warned Yeung: "Don't fool around in Chinatown."

"I believe my life is in danger," said Yeung, who nonetheless agreed to be interviewed.

Seated in a Manhattan coffee shop far from Chinatown at one o'clock in the morning, the fifty-two-year-old community leader frankly admitted that there is a problem of indentured servitude among the Fujianese. He knows the appalling conditions under which many of the new illegals are forced to live. In association newsletters he has called for an amnesty similar to the one granted by President Bush in 1989 following the upheavals in Tiananmen Square.

The very fact that Yeung was willing to talk with a journalist about the problems in Chinatown puts him at odds with members of the business community who, activists contend, implicitly condone the phenomenon of indentured servitude. Yeung claims that the beating he received was partly a result of this calling for the amnesty, which many in the community feel would ameliorate the current crisis.

The violence directed at Yeung underscores another fact of life in Chinatown. Local police and the feds believe that the Fuk Ching, a New York-based gang made up of Fujianese, plays a major role in the hugely profitable alien smuggling racket. It was Fuk Ching gangsters who kidnapped and tortured Kin Wah Fong in the Bronx two weeks ago. A recent fatal shooting at a Chinese travel agency on Bowery is also believed to be related to the smuggling rings. Cops are finally beginning to get a handle on what community organizers like Yeung have known for years: that muscle provided by Fuk Ching gangsters is the intimidating factor that makes indentured servitude possible.

As the February 15 New Year approaches, ushering in the Year of the Ram, Chinatown continues to grow. Community and immigration officials point to 1997 and the repatriation of Hong Kong with mainland China as the cause of increasing immigration. In the year ahead, already scarce jobs and housing may become even more rare.

For Yin Lee, who traveled halfway across the world and through a war to get here, the future is uncertain. On the day of our interview, she had just come from a Manhattan abortion clinic. Living with the humiliation of having been raped, she neglected to reveal her secret to anyone until it was almost too late. Now four-and-a-half months pregnant, the doctor had warned her that it would be a potentially dangerous operation.

Despite everything, Yin was hopeful. Sitting in the bustling midtown coffee shop, she spoke idealistically of going to school to learn English. Today, her $10,000 smuggling debt was far from her mind; the fact that she might be working twelve hours a day for a wage of twenty or thirty dollars hadn't registered. She talked with such animation and intensity that she barely touched her tuna salad sandwich. "I don't really like it, anyway," she explained, smiling politely. "When I was in the detention camp in Miami, that's all they had—American food."

Days later, Yin borrowed more money to finance her abortion. Following the operation, she was recuperating well. Although she had lost a few pounds and was feeling weak, her idealism remained intact. Soon, she would go looking for work.

3.

FORGET IT, JAKE, IT'S CHINATOWN

The Village Voice, February 28, 1995

For decades, cops have found the Asian community to be inscrutable—
with lethal consequences. Can they change?

hong Hui Chen did not have to die.

In September 1993, when the nineteen-year-old student at Seward Park High School in New York City was kidnapped by gangsters, Chen's parents did what they thought was the right thing. They went to the police.

Chen's father, Bi Lin Chen, was aware of the dangers involved. He was there the night his son was pistol-whipped and snatched from the family's tiny takeout restaurant at 371 Grand Street, on the northeastern edge of Chinatown, in Lower Manhattan. The abduction had taken place during a terrifying kidnap-for-ransom spree that was sending shockwaves through the city's Asian community. In the previous two weeks, there had been nearly a dozen kidnappings in Queens, Brooklyn, and Manhattan, most of them perpetrated by the Fuk Ching Gang. Targeted by the feds because of their involvement in the *Golden Venture*—the huge freighter that dramatically ran aground off Rockaway Beach, spilling nearly 300 illegal stowaways into the ocean, with ten drowning or dying from hyperthermia—the Fuk Ching were desperate. Previously, they only kidnapped undocumented immigrants who were smuggled into the country and had outstanding debts to pay to their "Snakehead," or smuggler. But Chong Hui Chen was a legal resident with no known gang affiliation, and no outstanding debts.

Bi Lin Chen and his wife, Mei Yu Yang, were contacted by the kidnappers, who demanded $80,000 in ransom or their son would be killed. The kidnappers specified a drop site in Flushing.

On the night Bi Lin Chen agreed to meet the kidnappers, he was trailed by a unit from the NYPD's Major Case Squad. According to Chen, the police bungled the case from the start. Though the gangsters had warned that if they saw police in the area they would kill Chen's son, the cops showed up that night wearing easily identifiable bullet-proof vests and parked only half a block away from the drop site. The stakeout team waited for a while, but eventually left their posts and returned to headquarters because their shift was over for the night.

The ransom was never picked up. Three days later, Chong Hui Chen's body was found dumped near the Belt Parkway on the outskirts of Brooklyn. He'd been stabbed twenty times.

Bi Lin Chen and Mei Yu Yang were in a state of shock. Following the incident, the grieving father was quoted in the New York *Daily News* saying, "We put out faith in the police. Now our son is dead and our family is ruined."

In the months that followed, the parents' grief turned to anger. Late last year, Bi Lin Chen and Mei Yu Yang filed a civil lawsuit in State Supreme Court charging that the NYPD and the City of New York with gross negligence. The police department is contesting the suit. Citing the mental anguish and torture their son suffered between the time of his kidnapping and the time of his death, the plaintiffs are asking for damages totaling $21 million. None of which will bring back their son.

In itself, the murder of Chong Hui Chen was tragic enough, but there is evidence to suggest it is part of a pattern of ineptitude on the part of the NYPD when dealing with Asian gangs—a pattern that is itself the result of deep-rooted attitudes, which have always dictated the way law enforcement deals with underworld crime in Chinatown.

Late last year, the city settled out of court with Ying Jing Gan, the widow of a Vietnamese merchant who was murdered on a busy Sunday afternoon in March 1991. Gan's husband had been cooperating with the police in an ongoing robbery investigation involving the notorious Vietnamese gang, Born to Kill (BTK). Inexplicably, he was left unprotected—to be shot in the head by a BTK assassin while working in a clothing store near Canal Street. The widow's lawsuit contended that her husband was murdered because of a long-standing indifference on the part of law enforcement to the realities of gang violence in the Asian community.

Not surprisingly, these recent examples of alleged police ineptitude have proven embarrassing to the NYPD and potentially costly to the city. As a result, certain steps have been taken. Department press officers point proudly to the fact that nearly 1,100 applicants for the most recent police entry exam were of Asian descent, the product of a concerted recruitment campaign. And last May, the NYPD appointed Thomas M. Chan captain of Chinatown's Fifth Precinct—the first Asian-American captain in the city's history—a move designed to give the appearance of a department better equipped to confront a crime problem that has bedeviled law enforcement for at least the last three decades.

As many Chinatown merchants and residents know all too well, appearances can be deceiving. Even before the death of Chong Hui Chen, it might have seemed as if law enforcement was being unusually diligent in its pursuit and prosecution of organized crime figures in Chinatown. Beginning with the successful prosecution of the BTK in early 1992, there have been at least four major RICO trials involving Asian gangsters. This trend continued when thirty-three alleged members of the Flying Dragons, one of Chinatown's oldest gangs, were arrested in November 1994 and charged on multiple counts of murder, heroin trafficking, arson, illegal gambling, extortion, and robberies that stretched from Manhattan into Brooklyn and Queens. More recently, a trial involving two powerful Chinatown tongs resulted in the January 1995 conviction of forty-year-old Clifford Wong, a well-known businessman and tong leader.

Taken together, these criminal indictments and prosecutions involve more than 200 assorted gang members and racketeers. Law enforcement spokespersons contend that the high volume of prosecutions is a clear sign that they are winning the battle against organized crime in the Asian community. Many in the community, however, see these sprawling RICO cases as a clear illustration of law enforcement's inability to respond to criminal patterns until they have already become deeply entrenched, sometimes reaching epidemic proportions.

"All these federal racketeering cases come after that fact," says Shiauh Wei Lin, a Chinatown attorney who has represented local residents in their grievances against the NYPD. Echoing the sentiments of others in the community, Lin asks, "Why can't something be done before dozens of merchants are extorted by the gangs? Before so many innocent people are intimidated and kidnapped and killed? Before hundreds of young males are drawn into the gang life and wind up either dead or in jail for the rest of their lives?" It has long been the contention of Chinatown residents that when it comes to gang activity and organized crime, the police are the last to know. The most obvious and egregious example was the case of the *Golden Venture*. To law enforcement and the mainstream media, it was as if the wholesale smuggling of aliens had only then reached its apex with the terrible tragedy in the waters off Rockaway Beach. Most people in Chinatown knew better. For at least the previous six or seven years, untold thousands of immigrants have been smuggled into Chinatown, Flushing, Sunset Park, and other Asian enclaves as they still are today. Once in the city, these undocumented migrants struggle to pay off their smuggling debts by working at paltry wages in restaurants, sweatshops, and brothels while living in tiny cubicles.

To the criminals who oversee this modern form of indentured servitude, the high profitability of alien smuggling has helped lay the foundation for an array of intertwined criminal rackets. Even with all the recent prosecutions, mainstay businesses like gambling, extortion, prostitution, and heroin smuggling continue to flourish, while living, health, and work conditions for many of the community's newest immigrants are as bad as anything that existed a century ago.

The reason Chinatown's criminal underworld has remained so durable over the decades certainly cannot be blamed entirely on law enforcement. But just as the area's various rackets have persisted through years of social evolution, so have police attitudes toward Chinatown.

Like many of the city's non-Asian residents, cops have long subscribed to the theory that Chinatown is a hopelessly enigmatic netherworld that can never be understood by anyone who isn't Chinese. In the past, this resulted in allowing designated tong leaders to resolve sometimes-violent gang disputes without the interference of "outside forces." It might even have meant certain officers would be paid to stay away, through cash payoffs and gratuities. While many agree that the grafts have diminished if not disappeared entirely, what lingers on is the attitudes those practices engendered.

"Despite what you read in the mainstream press, the police have never really taken Asian gangs seriously," says forty-year-old Steven Wong, a Chinatown activist who has had numerous dealings with both local and federal law enforcement. "They either don't know or don't care about the damage the gangs do to the community. All they care about is the impact they create in the media."

Ten years ago, Wong played a key role in one of the best-known gang prosecutions in Chinatown history. Posing as a local gangster with Mafia connections, Wong infiltrated the United Bamboo, an international gang with strong ties to the Taiwanese government. Born in Hong Kong and raised in Chinatown, Wong was able to give the impression he was a tough, steely-eyed gang veteran. In truth, he was nothing more than a former taxi driver fed up with seeing the community's relatively small criminal element run roughshod over the neighborhood's mostly hardworking, law-abiding citizenry.

Wong's high-risk infiltration of the gang was conducted in conjunction with a special FBI-NYPD task force. But the fact that he was a legitimate citizen and not a criminal facing charges like most confidential informants was anathema to the police investigators. "Because I wasn't a cop or a criminal, they never trusted me," says Wong. "The cops called me a cowboy. The FBI tried to say I had political motivations."

Eventually, the investigation culminated in a long federal trial in which Steven Wong, the main witness for the prosecution, faced two weeks of sometimes-merciless cross-examination at the hands of eleven criminal defense attorneys. In 1986, eleven members of the United Bamboo were convicted on RICO charges. Afterward, many of the investigators received commendations and promotions within their various agencies and bureaus. Wong disappeared, his life in serious peril. After laying low for a few years, he returned to Chinatown, where he now works as a community advocate and part-time journalist for *Sing Tao*, a Chinese-language daily newspaper.

"They say the Chinese don't cooperate with the police because of Chinese history," explains Wong, referring to a commonly held belief that Chinese attitudes toward the police are formed in the People's Republic of China, where the police have always been a corrupt and sometimes brutal instrument of the state. "I don't agree. Chinese people distrust the police because of how they are treated, and have always been treated, by the police here in the United States."

To illustrate his point, Wong relates a story from his childhood. As a youngster in Chinatown, he once brought home an essay from school in which he proclaimed his desire to be a police officer when he grew up. Like many Chinese parents, his mother and father were dead set against the idea. "I'd rather you join the triad," said Wong's father, referring to the secret criminal societies first formed in sixteenth-century China. "This way, if you are a crook, you are an honest crook. You're telling people you are a bad guy, instead of doing it the devious way by being a police officer."

Wong's father took him downstairs to a Chinese coffee shop, where they waited until two cops came in. "Watch this," Steven was told. The two Caucasian officers ordered coffee, then rice and noodles, then bottles of beer. They ate voraciously, made lots of noise, then stood up and arrogantly walked out without paying.

The point Steven Wong's father was trying to make to his son was one most people in Chinatown knew. Decades of low level payola and more serious forms of graft made Chinatown an attractive beat for cops on the take.

The fact that local merchants and tong leaders routinely paid off police officers was something most cops grew accustomed to, but one thing the police have never been able to understand is why those same merchants also pay money to the gangs.

Protection money is still paid by most Chinatown merchants, for reasons that are as clear as a broken store window, a threatening late-night phone call, or a blow to the back of the head. "They pay because they don't want to be harassed," says Steven Wong. "Or to have their store robbed on a regular basis. Or be killed. They know the police cannot protect them."

Cops have always maintained that merchants paying extortion money to hoodlums only perpetuates the gang problem. In the minds of some officers, this, in fact, makes the merchants part of the crime problem.

One cop in a better position than most to understand the complicated relationship that exists between the police and the community is Thomas Chan, the Fifth Precinct commander whose promotion has been widely heralded. Chan was born in Chinatown and grew up in the Alfred E. Smith Houses on Catherine Street. From his youth, he remembers the police as a forbidding presence. "Overall," says Chan, "people in Chinatown didn't want to have anything to do with the police unless they had to."

Seated in his office inside the hectic Fifth Precinct station house on Elizabeth Street, Captain Chan cuts an attractive figure. He is articulate, friendly, and projects an air of earnestness and sincerity. Although he has been with the department a mere twelve years, his rise has been meteoric.

As the first Asian-American precinct commander in the history of the NYPD, Chan is understandably glowing in his assessment of the department's commitment to establishing a more user-friendly profile in the community; his promotion, he feels, is a product of that commitment. But Chan also has been around long enough to know that in order to satisfy his department overseers, he, like any other precinct commander, must show himself to be adequately tough-minded in his dealings with local troublemakers.

One activity that has always created bad blood between local residents and the police is the sale of counterfeit merchandise. In October and November of 1994—apparently unbeknownst to Captain Chan—the NYPD conducted a series of counterfeit raids in a commercially dense section of Canal Street. The raids were brought about by a legal action on behalf of Ralph Lauren, Guess, Timberland, and other popular manufacturers. Although the raids were not carried out by officers from the Fifth Precinct, the residue from these rids is something local cops will have to deal with for months to come.

It's certainly no secret that counterfeit watches, leather jackets, perfume, and other goods are routinely sold on Canal Street. Most merchants would not dispute the claim. The merchants' complaint—aired in a series of interviews at the law offices of Shiauh Wei Lin—was not that the raids took place, but the manner in which they were conducted.

The raids culminated one morning when some twenty officers from a special midtown counterfeit squad descended on a number of stores near the intersection of Canal and Broadway. Most of the stores had been raided before, so the merchants were familiar with the routine. This time, the police followed a different procedure. "They came in like it was a war," says one store owner.

Gates were pulled down so that onlookers on the sidewalk could not see what was happening inside. The merchants claim the cops were laughing with one another, trying on jackets, and loading merchandise into plastic garbage bags without looking to see what was counterfeit and what wasn't. One officer removed a videotape from a VCR on which their actions would have been recorded through a security camera mounted on the wall. No receipts were given, nor was any attempt made to itemize what was being seized. One merchant claims police confiscated $20,000 worth of *legitimate* merchandise from his store. These counterfeit raids are a classic example of the kind of clumsy community relations that have contributed greatly to the NYPD's negative image in Chinatown.

The intersection where these raids took place has long been a nexus of gang activity. For years, these merchants have been extorted by members of both the BTK and a faction of the Ghost Shadows.

Most work twelve-hour days, seven days a week. What money they make usually goes into overhead, city and state taxes, and fines of one kind or another for allegedly selling counterfeit.

"These people struggle to survive," says Shiauh Wei Lin, who is considering a class action suit against the NYPD to find out where the merchandise goes after it is seized. "They cannot afford to take a hit like this."

Asked about the raids in his Fifth Precinct office, Captain Chan opts for the role of the dutiful commander. Unequivocally, he supports the action of the NYPD and expresses little sympathy for the merchants. "It is incumbent upon these people to know whether or not they are selling counterfeit merchandise," explains Chan. "They are jeopardizing themselves and their stores when they do this."

Aside from the issue of counterfeit, however, is the question of whether or not the raids were conducted in a manner that was counterproductive. As Chan knows, merchants in the Canal Street area are a tight-knit group, recent Vietnamese and Chinese immigrants who depend on one another for security. One day, local officers may return to this intersection to investigate a violent robbery or a gang murder, and they will be asking for cooperation. These merchants, remembering their treatment at the hands of the police, will be reluctant—if not hostile. The police will walk away, perhaps cursing under their breath about those inscrutable Asians who, for historical and cultural reasons, never cooperate with the police.

Asked about this, the captain either does not comprehend the question or chooses to sidestep the issue. "If any of the merchants are not happy," says Chan, "we can meet with them and give them additional information and inform them what the laws are. My doors are always open."

Captain Chan can certainly expect a steady stream of overtures from the local populace, many of whom will presume a higher degree of sensitivity toward the community from him than that of his Caucasian predecessors. So far, he has been well received by the established business and community associations, though he gets lower marks from community activists, street-level merchants, and others whose standing within Chinatown's sometimes rigid economic caste system is less exalted. As for Asian-American police officers, there is a similar split.

"I think Tommy Chan's promotion is a big step forward, at least symbolically," says Detective Bruce May, president of SCALE (Supreme Council of Asians in Law Enforcement), a recently formed umbrella organization that includes Asian officers at the city, state, and federal levels.

"Tommy Chan is a nice guy, very intelligent," says another Chinese-American detective. "But don't kid yourself. He's one person. For the department at large, I don't think his promotion means anything."

"Andy Chow" is a veteran officer assigned to a prestigious citywide unit. He was raised in Chinatown. Like other Asian-American officers not affiliated with SCALE or any of the other official police fraternal organizations, Chow's feelings reflect a deep-rooted bitterness expressed in varying degrees—almost always off the record.

In contrast to recent recruitment efforts in which the NYPD claims to offer a fair working environment for Asian Americans, Chow feels the department is still a white male-dominated universe mired in an outdated, racially motivated system of approval. "The job is rigged. Everybody knows it. Advancement is not based on performance. It's who you know, who you drink with." Chow claims to know one sergeant who got ahead because he mowed his chief's lawn. "I'm telling you, it's who you know and who you blow."

"The department is afraid to be fair with minority officers," adds Chow. "They're afraid it will bring down the morale of the department overall. Chinese, Hispanic, black officers know this. That's why they're reluctant to try to do anything to rock the boat. The odds against them are too large."

Chow laughs when asked whether or not law enforcement is prepared to deal with the complexities of Asian organized crime and the gangs. "Every now and then, some Caucasian officer comes forward and declares himself an expert on the subject. It's a joke." Chow claims that there are very few officers in the department who speak fluent Foujou, the dialect spoken by Fujianese immigrants—and Fuk Ching Gang members. Language has always been a primary stumbling block for law enforcement when dealing with Asian gangs and their victims.

Disdainfully, Chow mentions a recent move by the NYPD to send ten to fifteen officers to a language-training course to learn the dialect.

"Foujou is a very difficult language even for fluent Cantonese and Mandarin speakers," says Chow. "You need to speak it every day. Now they're going to send a group of mostly white cops to a class to learn Foujou? C'mon! Maybe they learn how to count to ten, maybe they can say hello and order a meal. But they can't communicate with the community. They don't know jack shit. But this is typical of the job. They think they can put a Band-Aid on a major head wound."

In November 1994, at a press conference to announce the indictment of the Flying Dragons, Mary Jo White, the U.S. attorney for the Southern District of New York, declared, "With today's indictment, the last of the major Chinatown gangs has been prosecuted and dismantled." Aspiring young gangsters throughout Chinatown might have chuckled at the irrelevance of White's proclamation.

In fact, some journalists and law enforcement analysts have for years been warning of a new incursion of Asian criminals into New York. In 1997, Hong Kong will be coming under the domain of the People's Republic of China, and that city's large triad-based underworld has begun to move money and manpower into Canada and a number of other U.S. cities. In the recently completed federal trial that resulted in the conviction of Clifford Wong, it was alleged that the Tsung Tsin Association, one of Chinatown's wealthiest tongs, has already established itself as a beachhead for the Sun Yee On, an international criminal brotherhood based in Hong Kong.

With a fresh set of players arriving to stake their claim to local rackets, law enforcement can expect the area's multilayered Asian crime-scape to become even more challenging. In the past, an inability or unwillingness on the part of police to vigorously address criminal developments as they unfolded has helped make it possible for a vast underworld to evolve. A tradition of police indifference has helped make it possible for established gangs to constantly regenerate, ensnaring hundreds of Asian youths and making life for the community's street-level merchant class a sometimes perilous struggle.

Now the local police establishment and some federal law enforcement agencies claim to have gotten themselves up to speed, with more Asian officers and increased manpower focused on a violent underworld that stretches far beyond New York to communities in Hong Kong, Europe, Canada, and numerous U.S. cities. It may be some time before this claim can be fairly evaluated, but given the tragic human consequences for Ying Jing Gan, the parents of Chong Hui Chen, and other Chinatown residents who have been on the receiving end of police screwups in the past, it is a claim that cries out for careful and continued scrutiny.

4.

WHO WILL MOURN GEORGE WHITMORE?

The New York Times, October 13, 2012

In 1964, a black teenager confessed to a double
homicide he didn't do.

I received news this week of the death of George Whitmore Jr., an
occurrence noted, apparently, by no one in the public arena.

That Whitmore could die without a single mention in the media is
a commentary on a city and nation that would rather bury and forget
the difficult aspects of our shared history.

Forty-eight years ago, as a New York City teenager, Whitmore was
initiated into an ordeal at the hands of a racist criminal justice system.
For a time, his story rattled the news cycle. He was chewed up and spit
out: an ill-prepared kid vilified as a murderer, then championed as an
emblem of injustice and, finally, cast aside. That he survived his tribu-
lations and lived to the age of sixty-eight was a miracle.

I first met Whitmore in the spring of 2009 while doing research for
a book that posited that his experiences constituted an important sub-
narrative to the racial turmoil of the 1960s and early 1970s.

Finding him was not easy. I eventually tracked him down in Wildwood, New Jersey, nor far from where he'd been born and raised. I
found a man who was broken but unbowed, humble, with glimmers of
an innocence that had been snatched from him a long time ago. For a
time in his adolescence, he'd been infamous. By the time I found him,
he was anonymous, and that was okay with him.

Back in April 1964, like a horrifying urban-jungle version of *Alice's Adventures in Wonderland*, Whitmore began a nearly decade-long ramble through the justice system that still boggles the mind. It started on a misty morning when Whitmore, nineteen years old, African American, raised in poverty, and a grade-school dropout, was taken by a handful of New York City detectives into the Seventy-Third Precinct station house in East New York, Brooklyn. After a twenty-two-hour interrogation by numerous detectives—all of them white—he was coerced into signing a sixty-one-page confession detailing a series of horrific crimes, including, most notably, a brutal double murder of two young white women on the Upper East Side of Manhattan.

The case had become known in the media as "The Career Girl Murders." The killings took place on the same day—August 28, 1963—and perhaps the exact time that the Rev. Dr. Martin Luther King Jr. delivered his "I Have a Dream" speech at the March on Washington for Jobs and Freedom.

The confession was front-page news. The Brooklyn cops who were involved congratulated themselves; one was given a special award for exemplary work. But the confession was a fraud. To most objective observers, it didn't seem likely that Whitmore could have committed the murders. At his arraignment, he told the judge that he'd been coerced into admitting guilt. Few cared: He was a disposable Negro who'd been raised in a shack alongside a junkyard in Wildwood—a "drifter," described in one account as "possibly mentally retarded." He was indicted, imprisoned, and declared a monster.

America was just on the cusp of the civil rights revolution; it was a time of pernicious institutional racism. A black kid had been railroaded, and he wasn't the first nor would he be the last. But the detectives had made the mistake of pinning on him the city's most notorious open murder case, which brought about a higher level of scrutiny than the average homicide.

The case quickly began to fall apart. The detectives claimed that they had found a photo of one of the career girls in Whitmore's wallet when they arrested him. He'd told them he'd found it at the murder scene and stolen it, they said. None of it was true. (He did have a photo on him, but it was not of either of the victims.) On the day of the murders, witnesses had seen him sitting in an empty catering hall in Wildwood, where he was working at the time, watching King's speech on television.

Despite a mounting belief among some civil rights activists associated with the NAACP, and a few intrepid journalists, that Whitmore was innocent, he remained in prison, facing two death sentences. Depressed, frightened, and alone, he pondered his imminent demise at the hands of the state. He asked other inmates, "If you were going to be put to death, which would it be? The chair? Lethal injection? What's the least painful way to die?" A teenager, having committed no crime—ever—at that point in his life, pondering what means of execution he would choose: This was his reality.

It would take nine years for Whitmore to clear his name. It wouldn't have happened without the help of many lawyers, a few newspaper reporters, and the civil rights activists. Though the "Career Girls" murder charges were dropped early on—and the actual killer, Richard Robles, was eventually tried and convicted—Whitmore had also been forced to confess to another murder charge, and the assault and attempted rape of a woman in Brooklyn. There followed a numbing cycle of trials, convictions, convictions overturned, retrials, and appeals. Whitmore went from being a nobody to being a perceived murderer to being a terribly "wronged man" and back to being a nobody. In prison, he learned to make rotgut hooch and, trying to dull the pain, became an alcoholic.

In April 1973, he emerged triumphant. A few weeks before all the charges against him were finally thrown out, CBS broadcast a highly promoted movie-of-the-week based on his ordeal. The movie, *The Marcus-Nelson Murders*, based on a book by the *New York Times* reporter Selwyn Raab, was produced and written by Abby Mann, an Academy Award–winning screenwriter. Whitmore was paid a pittance for his cooperation. In the end, the movie is best remembered for having introduced a character named Detective Theo Kojak, played by the actor Telly Savalas. Mr. Savalas and Kojak would go down in the annals of TV history. Whitmore watched the movie from the medical ward at the Green Haven state prison in Dutchess County.

Nine years after his name was finally cleared and he'd been released from prison, Whitmore won a settlement of half a million dollars from the City of New York. But it was too little, too late. He'd been crushed by the system, his self-worth obliterated in ways that could never fully be put back together. He squandered the money he'd been awarded through bad business ventures and at the hands of devious friends and relatives.

By the time I found Whitmore, he was back living in poverty similar to what he'd known in those years before he was led into that police station in Brooklyn back in 1964.

Meeting Whitmore was eerie for me. Though he was sixty-five years old at the time, I could still see that nineteen-year-old kid who had been so horribly wronged all those years ago. You could see the pain in his face. In one of our first meetings, in the backyard of his tiny rented house on Route 9, I took a photo of him. You can look in his eyes and almost hear him asking the question, "Why me?"

Over the next two years, I frequently made the drive to Wildwood from Manhattan, a three-and-a-half-hour jaunt along the Jersey Shore. I'd take Whitmore to the market to buy groceries to fill his empty kitchen cabinets and refrigerator. Then we'd sit and talk.

Going over the past was painful for him. I tried to catch him early in the day. After he had his first couple of drinks, he was lucid and charming. He remembered his ordeal with such detail that it could send a chill up your spine and bring you to tears. After a few more drinks, he would lose focus, get sloppy, and sometimes become ornery and difficult.

When the book was finished, I delivered a couple of copies to Whitmore. He held it in his hands, felt its heft and smiled with pride. Since adolescence, he had had poor eyesight, and I'm not sure he ever learned to read. But after he'd taken a few minutes to look at the pictures in the book and flip through its pages, seeing the familiar names and descriptions of events, he wept at the memory of his lost youth.

In recent months, I'd fallen out of touch with Whitmore. Knowing him, and attempting to assume a measure of responsibility for his life, was often exhausting. While I had come to love him, the drunken phone calls, the calls from hospital emergency rooms and flophouses, and the constant demands for money became overwhelming. When people who claimed to be friends of his starting calling me and asking for favors, I decided to back off. But when I received a cryptic e-mail from one of his nephews, informing me that Whitmore had died on Monday, I was overcome with sadness and regret.

Whitmore never saw himself as a race activist. In the 1960s and 1970s, from prison and on the streets, he watched the civil rights movement and the Black Power movement at a wary distance. He did not judge people by their skin color. He knew he had been the victim of a grave injustice, but he did not assume that the detectives who framed him, or his slow torture at the hands of a rigged system, were motivated by racial prejudice

By staying strong for all those years—by not taking a plea deal, as he had been offered numerous times—Whitmore forced the justice system to come to terms with the injustice that had been done to him. His ordeal was a key factor in the abolition of the death penalty (except for cases involving the killing of a police officer) by the state legislature and Gov. Nelson A. Rockefeller, in 1965, and in the U.S. Supreme Court's decision in the 1966 case *Miranda v. Arizona*, which broadened the rights of criminal suspects under interrogation. (The death penalty was restored in New York in 1995, but it was ruled unconstitutional by the state's highest court in 2004.) Whitmore's plight turned the wheels of justice, however painfully and incrementally.

Yet there are no plaques in honor of George Whitmore Jr., no schools named after him, or any civic recognition of his humble fortitude. His name should be known to every student in New York, especially kids of color, but it is not part of the curriculum.

This week, a flawed but beautiful man who offered up his innocence to New York City died with hardly any notice. To those who benefited from his struggles, or who believe the city is a fairer place for his having borne them, I ask: Who grieves for George Whitmore?

III.

NARCO WARS, AT HOME AND ABROAD

*A*nd now a word about law enforcement.

In the course of my career as a writer, I have encountered or interviewed hundreds of patrol cops, detectives, federal agents, U.S. marshals, border patrol agents, district attorneys, federal and state prosecutors, and other representatives of the U.S. criminal justice system. Any relationship I might have with these people is shaped, of course, by the fact that I am a journalist and they are representatives of the system. To many in law enforcement, and some in the media, the journalist-cop relationship is and always will be an adversarial one.

For any cop or prosecutor to speak with me on the record, they must first have authorization from their department's press office. If a cop has been authorized to speak with a reporter, it's usually so that he or she can get their version of events out there. The cop and his bosses are interested in shaping the flow of information to the public, or giving the impression that they are on top of things even when they are not. Having been involved in writing about crime for as long as I have, I have cultivated a network of lawmen who will talk honestly with me—off the record. As a rule, cops or agents who are recently retired make the best sources, because they can speak more freely and with a higher degree of insight and objectivity. Since they were once part of the system, they know how things operate, and now that they are no longer beholden to the propaganda dictates of the job, they sometimes have a lot to get off their chests.

Generally, I like cops and get along well with them, though I sometimes have problems with particulars of the policies they are entrusted to carry out (as do some cops, by the way, though you are unlikely to hear them express it publicly.)

Most people in law enforcement take their job seriously and conduct themselves with an adequate level of professionalism and respect. This varies in different jurisdictions depending on the competency of the training, quality of supervision, and the historical forces that have shaped the attitudes of a particular police force or prosecutorial agency.

Law enforcement can be a high intensity endeavor. Our culture tends to glorify the forces of law and order, so that some on the job crack under the scrutiny, or become drunk with the power and authority that has been bestowed upon them. In my time as a journalist, I've come across some who deviate from the norm of basic professionalism. They tend to fall into one of three categories:

1) The blowhard self-promoter, a cop or prosecutor who is driven by ego and self-aggrandizement. Public servants in disguise, this breed of lawmen are driven primarily by the desire to advance their profile in the media and the hope that, soon, they will land an agent and/or book deal. If it's a detective or federal agent, they are angling for a cushy job as a consultant on a TV series or movie, or dreaming that one day they will meet Robert De Niro or Al Pacino. If it's a prosecutor in the office of the U.S. attorney or district attorney, they are laying the groundwork for a career in politics that they hope will one day take them all the way to the White House (see: Rudy Giuliani).

Being based in New York, I have encountered many cops and prosecutors who fit this profile, and others who hope to one day fit this profile. They are sometimes entertaining or charismatic figures who are masters at manipulating the media and playing the system. They are also, quite often, a danger to the concept of fairness and justice. In some cases, they will trample on due process, withhold evidence, frame people, or engage in all manner of malfeasance if it is to the benefit of their careers.

2) The lazy bureaucrat. *It is true that you may find this breed in almost any sector of government employment, but in law enforcement laziness and slovenly investigative work can lead to wrongful indictments and convictions, ruined lives, and an incalculable loss of faith in the American system. Not only that, but the lazy lawmen or prosecutors—like all lazy bureaucrats—spend more time trying to cover up for their shoddiness than they do on their actual jobs.*

3) The outright corrupt agent of the law. *Movies and TV shows have led the public to believe that for a cop to be corrupt, he or she must be blowing people away, working in consort with gangsters or drug lords, or absconding with hundreds of thousands of dollars. Generally, corruption in law enforcement is far more mundane. It starts with an attitude that the biggest threat to proper police work is "liberals" and that the "liberal media" is out to get cops. Cops and prosecutors in this camp are unable to separate their personal politics from their job, and it affects their relationship with the public. Everything comes down to us versus them. Racism, excessive use of force, bullying and rude behavior, disrespect for community members—these are the true hallmarks of corruption in law enforcement. With attitudes like these, it is a short distance to planting and falsifying evidence, lying on the witness stand, doing whatever it takes to make a case, even if it violates the law.*

In the twenty-plus years that I have been writing about crime in America, I have seen the relationship between the public and law enforcement deteriorate. The irony is that during this time period, crime in most major cities in the United States has gone down dramatically. State and federal prison systems throughout the country are bursting at the seams. The United States locks up its citizens at a rate ten times higher than the next highest industrialized nation. The consequence of this spiraling process of incarceration, where people are locked up and put through the system as a form of social control, breeds distrust and hostility.

The primary reason for this bad blood between the police and the public is not hard to pinpoint—the U.S. war on drugs.

Of all the subjects I've written about, it is hardest to maintain objectivity when writing about U.S. narcotics policy, both at home and abroad. The narco war is such an unmitigated and costly failure, and has wreaked so much havoc on the criminal justice system, that what seems to be called for is not old-school, two-sides-to-every-story type journalism, but flat-out advocacy journalism from the point of view of decriminalization and reform.

I am not necessarily a legalization advocate, nor do I pretend to know of a magic solution that will stanch the flow of narcotics into the United States and/or alter the drug consumption habits of U.S. citizens. But I do know that the course the United States has been on for forty years, since the War on Drugs was first launched by President Richard M. Nixon in 1971, has been a disaster. It has led to a system in which narcotics cops are rewarded for high numbers of arrests, and so they invariably go where those arrests are easiest to make—poor communities primarily populated by people of color. It is the main reason our prisons are disproportionately populated with black and brown-skinned people.

On an international level, the drug war has polluted our relationship with countries around the globe. Though everyone knows that the United States is overwhelmingly the primary marketplace for illegal narcotics from around the world, the U.S. government often bases its relationship with other nations—and its willingness to supply economic aid—based on whether or not they fall in line with U.S. drug policies. Successive U.S. administrations have demanded that countries like Colombia and others in South America engage in vigorous eradication programs, often causing a rift between the governments in those countries and their own people. In Mexico, the United States has sponsored and financed the militarization of the war on drugs, adding fuel to a fire that has raged for years and engulfed the lives of an entire generation.

The corrupting consequences of the War on Drugs have been almost beyond calculation. Over the last forty years, the number of people who have been killed, incarcerated, and had their lives shattered in the effort to keep people from selling and using a product they clearly want to use makes the thirteen years of alcohol prohibition, from 1919 to 1932, look like child's play. Perhaps some day in the future, U.S. citizens will look back on this era of the narco war as a violent folly and have as difficult a time explaining it to their children and grandchildren as previous generations have had trying to explain the Roaring Twenties. Both of these eras of prohibition have succeeded in giving rise to an underworld criminal structure and framework for organized crime that has left a legacy of corruption and violence for the generations that followed.

And yet, politicians and civic leaders in the United States seem incapable of having a rational, mature conversation about national narcotics policy. It rarely comes up as a topic in presidential debates. Each year, Congress authorizes, on average, $40 million in expenditures on various anti-narco initiatives, the overwhelming majority of that spent on costly international and domestic investigations, special task forces, raids, seizures of drugs and property, arrests, prosecutions, and other law enforcement activities in the most expensive domestic "war" the United States has ever waged.

The decline in narcotics use in the last forty years has been negligible. Illegal drugs are now easier to get, and cheaper, than ever before. A failed policy is a failed policy. The inability of the United States to alter the direction of this ongoing fiasco has brought about an incalculable level of social devastation. As long as this continues to undermine the relationship between the people and the social system under which we live, it is a subject that, as a concerned citizen and as a storyteller, I plan on revisiting over and over again.

1.

DOPE

Playboy, December 2009

**Lee Lucas rose through the ranks of the DEA the old-fashioned way—
employing shoddy evidence, partnering with thugs, and abusing the
authority of his position.**

Geneva France remembers vividly the day a task force of federal narcotics agents came pounding at her front door. It was 6:00 a.m. and
she was about to get her kids ready for school. Her third child, twenty-
one months old, was barely out of the crib. Once she woke the kids
and sent them off, France would head to her part-time job at a nursing
home, where she emptied bedpans and cleaned and fed old people for
a living. Just twenty-two years old, an African-American single mother
struggling to raise three children on a subsistence income, she had a
difficult enough life without a swarm of lawmen arriving at her house.

"It's the sheriff's department. Open the door or we'll kick it in."

France opened the door. A stream of cops flooded through, in uniform and carrying guns. They fanned out around the house, opening
drawers and turning everything upside down.

"They went rambling," France recalls. "They weren't searching for
anything in particular, so I didn't know why they were there until one
of the officers asked me, 'Where's the drugs?' "

"Drugs?" she said. "What drugs?"

A female cop made her stand against the wall and spread her legs.
France was searched, cuffed and told, "We're taking you in."

"One of those officers threw my baby on the sofa, and the baby started crying. The female officer said, 'We're taking your kids to child welfare.' I said, 'The hell you are.' "

Luckily for France, her sister Natasha was there. Natasha lived at the residence and was eighteen, old enough to serve as legal guardian. Natasha missed school that day to stay with the kids so they would not be seized by the government.

No one told Geneva what she being charged with. She was led out into the predawn darkness, loaded into a sheriff's car, driven to a holding cell seventy miles away in Cleveland, booked, photographed, fingerprinted, and shuffled off to arraignment court. "I was more shocked than frightened," she says. "I remember thinking, *This will all be over soon. They made some kind of mistake. They gonna have to let me go.*"

France had no way of knowing, but her long nightmare had only begun.

She had become a small fish caught in a big net. Her arrest on federal narcotics charges was part of a massive drug sweep in Mansfield, Ohio, an economically depressed industrial town of 50,000 inhabitants in the Northern District of Ohio. On the same morning France was arrested, nearly thirty drug busts took place in the area, the culmination of a six-month investigation known as Operation Turnaround.

The case was spearheaded by veteran DEA agent Lee Lucas. In Mansfield, Lucas was dependent on local informant Jerrell Bray, a thug, convicted criminal, and diagnosed schizophrenic. Together Lucas and Bray made street-level crack deals around town for two months, with Lucas often posing as a friend of Bray's. Bray would make the overture by phone and in person, allegedly with someone interested in buying or selling crack or powder cocaine. A location would be set, and sometimes a surveillance team recorded the transaction. Then, one morning in November 2005, the arrests went down in dramatic fashion—doors busted open, drug-sniffing dogs let loose in people's homes, occupants commanded to "get on the fuckin' floor!"

The investigation netted few actual drugs. No narcotics were found at the home of France or most others arrested, but it didn't matter. Informants Bray and Agent Lucas were prepared to identify each and every defendant in court if necessary.

The busts made headlines in Cleveland and the surrounding area; Operation Turnaround was touted as a major success. The star of the show was Special Agent Lucas, local boy made good. In his career, Lucas had handled major drug cases in Miami and South America; now he was back home serving as a white knight in the war on drugs.

Unfortunately, this scenario was seriously flawed and built on a tissue of lies. It will take years to calculate the collateral damage—the mess challenges not only a star DEA agent and those who supervised and prosecuted his cases but the entire criminal justice system in which he operated and the nature of the war in which he served.

Law enforcement personnel in the Northern District of Ohio will tell you it's not difficult to make dope cases in the town of Mansfield. In 2008, Oprah Winfrey devoted an entire hour to Richland County's drug problem, using a panel of local addicts, former dealers, and cops to illustrate her point. As one attorney remarked, "Making dope busts in Mansfield is like shooting fish in a barrel."

The fruits of the Mansfield arrests were numbingly familiar—poor blacks (twenty-five of the twenty-six people arrested were African American), marginally educated, some with previous legal troubles, swept up in a collective show of force. Most quickly copped a plea. Some defendants had been out on parole and were now facing life sentences. Pleading guilty in exchange for a lesser sentence was par for the course, part of the give-and-take that keeps our judicial system from collapsing under the weight of more drug cases than a city, district or state can handle.

There was one small glitch: A startling number of the people charged—including Geneva France—claimed they weren't present during the drug transactions. They had been misidentified, and they could prove it.

Their protests were met with a collective *ho hum* by the authorities. Don't criminals often plead innocence? Assistant U.S. Attorney Blas Serrano, lead prosecutor for Operation Turnaround, was surprised some defendants opted to go to trial. That was unusual, but if they wanted to go through the time and hardship of adjudication, facing ten years to life in prison, the government was ready to take them on.

One parolee defendant was wearing an ankle monitor when his drug transaction supposedly took place, and he could prove he wasn't there. Another was on a plane to Chicago and had a boarding pass and flight records to back that up. The U.S. attorney's response was "So what?" They had Bray and Lucas, who would swear the defendants engaged in drug transactions.

France said she was home braiding a friend's hair at the time Bray and Lucas alleged she climbed into their 1997 Chevy Suburban and sold them more than fifty grams of crack. Who was going to believe a single mother and her friend in the face of a star DEA agent?

In February 2006, after a four-day trial, France was found guilty. Even though she was a first-time offender, mandatory sentencing dictated that she serve ten years behind bars. When she still maintained her innocence at the sentencing, U.S. District Judge Patricia Ann Gaughan berated her and called her a pathological liar.

All these plea bargains, claims of innocence, and guilty verdicts stemming from Operation Turnaround would normally have gone unnoticed. It is a truism of the drug war that arrests and indictments make headlines, but what follows unfolds in obscurity deep within the bowels of the criminal justice system. Unless it's a celebrity or a wealthy white defendant, who gives a damn? No one beyond France's lawyer and family would have lost a moment's sleep over her conviction were it not for an unexpected bombshell delivered by Bray.

In May 2007, the rat who pointed his finger at so many fellow African-American citizens turned against his white overseer, Lucas. "Everything I tell you may spin your head but it's true," Bray told Carlos Warner, a criminal defense attorney with the federal defenders office in Ohio. Bray claimed he and Lucas had railroaded nearly thirty people on fraudulent drug charges.

Bray's confession sent shockwaves that reverberated throughout the country—particularly in jurisdictions where Lucas had made cases and put people behind bars during his nineteen-year career.

In December 2007, then-U.S. Attorney Greg White announced that in light of Bray's confession and after review of the evidence, many convictions could not stand. To date twenty-three people have had their convictions overturned and been released, including France, who served sixteen months in prison for a crime she didn't commit.

In May 2009, Lucas was charged in an eighteen-count federal indictment with knowingly making false statements in DEA reports, obstruction of justice, perjury, and multiple civil rights violations.

The events playing out in Ohio are similar to those in Tulia, Texas, where many of the town's African Americans had been rounded up and convicted on drug charges based on the uncorroborated testimony of Tom Coleman, a highly decorated undercover agent and son of a Texas Ranger. It took years to prove that Coleman was a liar. Eventually, in August 2003, thirty-five of the thirty-eight people convicted were pardoned by Governor Rick Perry, but only after an NAACP call for an inquiry exposed Coleman's malfeasance.

In Mansfield, as in the Tulia scandal, there were early signs that many cases were rotten. Yet prosecutors still sought convictions based on weak evidence supplied by Lucas. They put the agent on the stand and let him use the full authority of his position to frame innocent people.

Working as a DEA agent must have felt perfect to Lee Michael Lucas. At Saint Edward High School the star wrestler often talked about becoming a cop. After graduating in 1986, he enrolled at Baldwin-Wallace College and worked part-time as a bouncer. While in college, Lucas interned with the DEA, the preeminent federal agency in the government's war on drugs. Unlike the buttoned-down types at the FBI, DEA agents tend toward improvisation and daring undercover operations—men of action versus intellectuals or crime analysts.

Lucas graduated from college in 1990 with a degree in criminal justice; within months, he was accepted into the DEA and was trained at its academy in Quantico, Virginia. In early 1992, Lucas received his first assignment, to the hottest spot in the drug war: Miami, Florida.

With his stocky wrestler physique Lucas looked more like a biker than a federal agent. He exhibited an enthusiasm for undercover work—he wore his hair long, sometimes in a ponytail, and dressed

like a man of the streets. Occasionally, he grew a goatee or Fu Man-
chu mustache. If he wanted, Lucas could look like one tough *hombre*.
In the Miami DEA office, agents considered him to be a valuable
asset.

"He was an excellent agent," said Frank Tarallo, Lucas's supervisor in Miami. "He worked really well undercover and did everything.
Today no one wants to do undercover work, but he did. He did surveillance, handled seizures, and worked well with informants."

Tarallo became a mentor to Lucas. A former Los Angeles police
officer, Tarallo had been a member of the Federal Bureau of Narcotics, a precursor to the DEA. He was old school. Says Gary McDaniel,
a Florida-based private investigator, "To understand Lucas, you have
to start with Frank Tarallo. He comes from a law enforcement culture
that believes the end justifies the means. Tarallo is partly responsible
for having created Lucas."

With Tarallo as second in command in Miami, Lucas received
plum assignments. In his early twenties, Lucas became supervising
agent in a major cocaine case right out of *Miami Vice*.

The coke deal in the case involved many moving parts. Two Cuban
drug dealers were sprung from prison so they could circulate as CIs
(confidential informants) in Miami's cocaine underworld. The two
were paid $20,000 each to relocate their families, then assigned to a
joint task force that included Miami police officers; agents from Alcohol, Tobacco, and Firearms; and young Lucas of the DEA.

Setting up a coke deal in Miami in the early 1990s was not difficult. The task force soon organized a major transaction: About 440
kilograms of Colombian coke, with a street value of more than $10
million, would be shipped via speedboat from the Bahamas to a place
called Manny's Marina. (Manny's owner, a convicted dope dealer, was
to receive $500,000 for cooperating.)

That many of the major players were convicted felons working for
the government wasn't unusual. But it was unusual to have a rookie
agent, who spoke no Spanish at the time and was barely one year
out of Quantico, acting as case supervisor. Clearly, Lucas was being
groomed to be a frontline soldier in the war on drugs.

The cocaine arrived in U.S. waters on the night of September 4,

1992. After the bales were transferred to a boat manned by informants and undercover agents, the dope was then taken to a government warehouse.

The shipment was supposed to be delivered to a local smuggler named Gilberto Morales, but Morales was having trouble finding $600,000 to close the deal. The Colombians and the Bahamians grew concerned; they suspected Morales and his partners were planning to rip them off. Two contract killers from Colombia were dispatched to get to the bottom of things. Morales became terrified. And that's when Peter Hidalgo got involved.

Hidalgo had sold Morales boat equipment. "I dealt with many shady characters," says Hidalgo. "Sure, I knew people used power-boats to smuggle cocaine. I don't get to choose my customers, but I was careful. There was a sign on the wall of my store that said IN GOD WE TRUST. EVERYBODY ELSE PAYS CASH. I was not in the cocaine business and made sure I could not be implicated in any way—or at least that's what I thought."

Morales knew that Hidalgo sold boat parts and equipment to the Bahamians who were now threatening to have him killed. The Bahamians trusted Hidalgo. Morales asked Hidalgo to call them and reassure them that he was not seeking to cheat them, that he was a man of his word. Says Hidalgo, "I knew the Bahamians from the boat business. If I didn't do this for Morales, he might wind up dead with his body floating in the Miami River. I defused the entire situation."

Today, speaking by phone from the Federal Correctional Institution in Coleman, Florida, Hidalgo realized that making the call was the biggest mistake of his life. It made it possible for various informants and Special Agent Lucas to set him up as a major player.

On the night of September 8, 1992, Hidalgo was arrested and charged with being the kingpin of the entire operation. Hidalgo was stunned: "I had heard of things like this from movies and TV shows; now I was living it."

Hidalgo was offered a plea deal. If he pleaded guilty, he would receive an eleven-year sentence and likely be released in nine. He was also asked to become a paid informant for the DEA. Remembers Hidalgo, "I turned them down. I was innocent. And it would go against everything I believe to become an informant for any government, even the United States, a country I love."

Though prosecutors had no evidence other than his phone call and the testimony of Lucas and a fellow agent, Hidalgo was found guilty and given four life sentences.

From the stand and in affidavits Lucas testified falsely about the criminal histories of his CIs. Hidalgo and other convicted defendants in the case tried unsuccessfully to use Lucas's misrepresentation to get their convictions overturned. In 2001, commenting on another case in which Lucas was accused of the same misrepresentations about the same CIs, the Eleventh Circuit U.S. Court of Appeals noted, "It is unclear how Agent Lucas could have made such statements of an affirmative character for which there is no basis without having acted either deliberately or recklessly. Accordingly, we will assume that this was a deliberate or reckless misrepresentation."

For more than fifteen years Hidalgo has been confined to various prisons in the United States fighting to get his conviction vacated. Recent developments in Ohio have raised his hopes. Says Joseph Rosenbaum, Hidalgo's attorney, "If you look at the actions of Lucas in our case—allegations of evidence tampering, perjury, withholding evidence in relation to criminal informants—you will see all the patterns that are coming out in Ohio. There's a time line in Lucas's career of misrepresenting the truth, an uninterrupted trail of deceit. And he's been able to get away with it for a long time."

The use of criminal informants—rats, snitches, and stool pigeons—has been part of the prosecution of the drug war since its inauguration in the late 1960s. Its defenders contend it's necessary to use unsavory characters to catch other criminals. But in many cases, the CIs are professional con artists whose experiences in the criminal underworld far outstrip those of the agents and prosecutors who are their overseers. The instances of case agents and government lawyers being played by crooks are far more prevalent than the Department of Justice (DOJ) cares to admit.

One person who has been a vocal critic of the DOJ's dependence on CIs is Michael Levine, former DEA agent and author of the best-selling memoirs *Deep Cover* and *The Big White Lie*. "I can't tell you the number of times," he says, "I've heard fellow agents, cops, training instructors, and prosecutors say, 'Mike, never trust an informant.' But I have never once heard a prosecutor say that to a jury."

He adds, "Over the years, I have seen the DEA and other law enforcement agencies become more and more dependent on rats. The question is: Do you have to put yourself in league with the devil for some higher good? I think the net balance is we lose." Still, Levine does not blame the informants themselves, noting, "A rat cannot take control of an investigation unless the people who are supposed to control him become as immoral and corrupt as he is."

The career of Lee Lucas has been particularly dependent on the use of rats in general and one rat in particular. In the early 1990s, Lucas formed an alliance with Helmut Groebe, a charming German-born con artist who would become his informant benefactor. Lucas and Groebe launched criminal stings around the globe, making Groebe rich and adding international luster to the unpolished former bouncer from Cleveland.

As a young man, Groebe once bilked hundreds of thousands of dollars out of a wealthy German widow and a doctor he'd known for years. After a stint in prison for another fraud, Groebe slipped out of Germany to Rio de Janeiro in the mid-1980s. He promptly ripped off his own twenty-year-old daughter, whom he hadn't seen in eighteen years, for $100,000. During the next decade, Groebe lived the life of an international playboy and predator in Brazil and South Florida.

It is not clear exactly when Groebe signed on as a paid informant for the DEA, but he met Lucas for the first time in the early 1990s. This was a pair made in heaven, or maybe hell: an experienced con man and a young, gung-ho agent.

One Lucas-Groebe sting involved German businessman Wolfgang von Schlieffen. Von Schlieffen had achieved great wealth as an investor in real estate, construction, and the import-export business in the Miami area. He lived the good life, owned a yacht and luxury vehicles, a Rolls-Royce among them.

Von Schlieffen trusted Groebe, who had a polish and mastery of English that he admired, and agreed to meet with Groebe's business associates (Lucas and another undercover agent) interested in condos and cars. At the meeting, much to Von Schlieffen's dismay, the men spoke rapid-fire English and kept steering the conversation to the subject of narcotics. They even flashed a small package he thought was cocaine. A transcript of the conversation shows Von Schlieffen, in fractured English, struggling to explain he was not interested in a cocaine deal. Nonetheless, he accepted a $10,000 down payment from Lucas for what he thought was an automobile transaction. He was arrested on the spot and charged with money-laundering conspiracy charges.

Lucas testified at Von Schlieffen's trial, referring to him as "the Count." He claimed the Count "pacified the thing and put the deal together." Von Schlieffen was found guilty of conspiracy and money laundering. He was sentenced to eight years.

For years, the Count spent hundreds of thousands of dollars on lawyers to clear his name. After serving seven years in prison, he was released when U.S. District Judge Wilkie Ferguson ruled in his favor, dismissing the conviction as fraudulent. The judge was especially critical of the prosecution's lawyers and agents, who he determined had acted in bad faith by using a "treacherous" informant, adding, "The only people who can protect the system against the rogue actions of confidential informants are those who use them: the government."

The Count died in 2003, but his estate was posthumously awarded $356,000 in damages.

Some DEA officials contend that our narcotics problem is less the result of excessive demand or porous law enforcement than it is corruption among foreign public officials. To illustrate this point, in the early 1990s the DEA focused on Faustino Rico Toro, a controversial figure in the Bolivian army. Colonel Rico Toro had been accused of human rights violations and aiding drug smugglers, and after he was named the country's drug czar he was targeted by the DEA.

In 1994, Bolivian police arrested Rico Toro on an extradition request from the U.S. attorney in South Florida. Extradition proceedings dragged on for months until Rico Toro agreed to enter a federal detention center in Miami, where he learned that federal prosecutors had linked him to drug deals, citing five hundred audiotapes and fourteen videotapes. His primary accuser was a man he never met: Helmut Groebe.

The case was weak. Rico Toro had never been caught with drugs, there was no physical evidence, they found no hidden assets typical of a drug kingpin, and he was not on the surveillance tapes. Other than Groebe, who said he met with Rico Toro in Bolivia, there were no witnesses against him. In August 1995, Lucas, now stationed in Bolivia, sought to rectify that. He and other agents paid a visit to Juan Padilla Burela, a co-conspirator in the Rico Toro indictment who was acquitted in 1993.

According to Burela's sworn affidavit, Lucas offered him money for testifying against Rico Toro. Burela had already stated at his own trial that he didn't know the colonel, but Lucas didn't seem to care. Threats were made, and Burela became angry and asked the agent to leave. He later learned that Groebe and additional agents offered cash for testimony to three other co-conspirators.

While detained in Miami, Rico Toro hired private investigator Gary McDaniel of Pretext Services in North Palm Beach to help his defense. McDaniel was the first person to unravel the Lucas-Groebe relationship. He uncovered a mountain of incriminating evidence known to various prosecutors, but never turned over to defense lawyers, in violation of the law. McDaniel was astonished that a case as politically sensitive as the prosecution of a foreign official would be handled by an agent in his mid-twenties, especially one who was "being led around by the nose" by a con artist like Groebe.

Eventually, a financially destitute Rico Toro pleaded guilty to a minor drug charge and was released after serving five years. But the battle had only begun for McDaniel. During the next decade he sought the attention of Lucas supervisors in the DEA and DOJ. Says McDaniel, "I'm an old military man, so I made sure my various letters and inquiries went up the chain of command to supervisors of divisions and ultimately to the DOJ's Department of Professional Responsibility. I made sure everyone signed off on those letters. In some cases, I was told, 'Gary, we are aware of the problem.' But nothing was ever done."

A 1997 German documentary, *King Rat*, detailed the life of Groebe and his relationship with Lucas. McDaniel was interviewed, as was Michael Levine. On camera, Levine refers to Groebe as "a danger to democracy." As to why "reprehensible" CIs are used to make cases, Levine says, "It's done for one reason: to make the agent look good, to make the DEA look good, to make the U.S. drug war look good."

It is not clear why Lucas wound up back in Cleveland. In courtroom testimony, Lucas would claim that nearly five years in Bolivia—known in the DEA as a hardship post—gave him the choice of his next assignment. Others claim Lucas left a paper trail that was potentially embarrassing to the DOJ and was buried in a low-profile regional division. Whatever the reason, Lucas returned home in 2000 as a star agent, a big fish in a small pond.

The DEA's regional office isn't even in Cleveland; it's in Detroit and had a reputation for lethargy. Lucas sought to change that. According to a prosecutor who worked with Lucas, "He was tireless. Some of us wondered if he had any kind of personal life. He fed more drug cases into the system in a year than some agents do in a lifetime."

There were some complaints about Lucas's cases. In a July 2003 confidential memo, FBI agents detailed an interview with Joseph Pinjuh, an assistant U.S. attorney in the Northern District of Ohio. Pinjuh had concerns about the "quality and truthfulness" of Lucas's investigation.

In many cases, a startling number of incriminating conversations that Lucas attested to were mysteriously not recorded due to "equipment malfunction." Many supposedly occurred just before, after, or even between recorded conversations. Pinjuh also found that claims crucial to establishing probable cause for warrants were not backed up by facts or evidence. Also, the FBI memo maintained Lucas and his sometime partner, Detective Jamal Ansari of the Cleveland narcotics squad, had beaten a suspect in custody. Turns out Lucas and Ansari were being investigated by the FBI on charges of official misconduct and excessive use of force. Lucas would eventually be cleared in 2005 but only after his DEA supervisors complained to the DOJ about the FBI's investigation and successfully shut it down.

In June 2003, Pinjuh and another assistant U.S. attorney met with Lucas and Cleveland narcotics cops and criticized the "lack of probable cause in law enforcement stops, lack of control in drug buys, and a continuing theme of pearly handled recorded conversations." The meeting, according to Pinjuh, was "somewhat heated." Lucas bridled at the questioning.

But Pinjuh wasn't the only one. In a pretrial correspondence, U.S. District Judge Peter Economus all but called Lucas a liar. Pinjuh's superiors were worried about the judge's denigration of Lucas's credibility, most likely because he'd created an issue that would be used against Lucas in future cases. So Pinjuh was instructed to approach the judge. According to the FBI memo, "Judge Economus did agree to reword the opinion and dropped a sentence from the opinion regarding Lucas's lack of candor."

Pinjuh told the FBI agents he did not believe the issue of Lucas's problematic testimony was ever forwarded to the DOJ's Office of Professional Responsibility.

The FBI agents filed their memo; one year later, in July 2004, it was forwarded to U.S. Attorney Greg White. The U.S. Attorney's Office decided to restrict the activities of Detective Ansari by having collaborating witnesses available at all his drug buys and interrogations, but the restrictions were not applied to Lucas. No aspersions were cast on an agent who was so prodigiously feeding the beast, making federal prosecutors look busy and effective by handing them a steady stream of dope cases.

In mid-2005, the Richmond County sheriff's department contacted the DEA office in Cleveland. The sheriff's department had picked up local thug Jerrell Bray holding stolen diamond rings. Bray was a career criminal and none too bright. He'd served fourteen years in prison and did not want to go back. He offered his services as a snitch, claiming he could make undercover crack buys all over Mansfield.

Lucas didn't know much about Mansfield, but he agreed to meet. Sheriff's Deputy Charles Metcalf was excited. If Lucas got involved, it would lead to the formation of a task force, which meant federal funding—money allotted for the U.S. government's war on drugs—money to make dope buys, to purchase fancy surveillance equipment, to pay agents working long overtime hours on the company tit.

They met with Bray in the county hoosegow. Thirty-two years old and overweight, Bray was skittish and lacking in self-confidence, a grade-school dropout who had been diagnosed early as a schizophrenic. During his incarceration, Bray was cited for twenty-two violations and served much of his time in isolation. On the street, he was thought of as someone who acted out of fear instead of toughness, the kind of homeboy who shoots first and asks questions later.

Bray's value as an informant was evaluated by a group known as the Metrich Enforcement Unit, an organization that fostered cooperation between various law enforcement agencies in Richmond County. Bray was rejected by Metrich evaluators. City police reached the same conclusion, and told the sheriff's office he shouldn't be deployed and was not to be trusted. The task force proceeded anyway. Lucas had handled Cuban refugees and international playboys; surely he could handle a bottom-feeder like Jerrell Bray.

———

To begin, Lucas, Bray, and the task force made a list of targets. The plaintiff's attorney and many of those falsely accused say task force members gave the list of suspects—and quite possibly the entire investigation—the informal name "Niggers with Rims," as in black males with no discernable income driving around in cars with expensive hubcaps. The theory was they had to be drug dealers—or close enough to be guilty by suspicion. According to Bray, Lucas set the tone by telling him "we get them any way we can" in order to "get the motherfuckers off the street." Lucas accompanied Bray on the first few undercover buys. He knew how to act and talk like a thug; it was part of his repertoire.

The buys went off without a hitch. People knew Bray well; he was an established dealer in town. Later they'd say the reason Bray went into business with the law in the first place was to eliminate his competition.

Operation Turnaround was not designed for random buys; as with any big drug case, the agents needed to establish a conspiracy that connected various suppliers and sellers. They focused on Dwayne Nabors, the thirty-three-year-old businessman and father of three who owned Platinum Status, a custom-made rims and auto accessories store. To the agents, it made sense. If you were going after niggers with rims, why not go after the man who sold them the rims?

Nabors often saw Bray around the shop. "I called him Mister Talk-a-Lot," says Nabors, "because his mouth was always running." Nabors even knew that Platinum Status was under surveillance. He saw what he assumed were narcotics agents' cars parked in a lot across the street. He figured they were tracking Bray. "I used to say, 'Let them watch,' " remembers Nabors. "There was nothing going on here."

A sociable type with an easygoing manner, Nabors had once pleaded guilty to drug possession. He was eighteen at the time, "young and stupid," he says. After serving three and a half years, he married, started a family, and built a successful business, which he first ran out of his home before moving to one of Mansfield's main thoroughfares. By all accounts, Nabors was an exemplary citizen and a shrewd businessman. He rose early, worked six days a week, paid his taxes promptly, and spent much of his free time being a father to his children.

Then in November 2005, the foot soldiers of Operation Turn-around descended on his home at 4:30 a.m. and arrested him on federal narcotics charges. His house was searched. There were no drugs, but cops found two handguns that belonged to Nabors's brother, so illegal possession of a firearm was added to the charges.

While in the county jail, Nabors was astounded to hear that Lucas and Ansari claimed that he had been involved in directing the sale of $10,000 worth of cocaine to Bray. In an affidavit and before a grand jury, Ansari claimed he saw Nabors and a dope dealer named Albert Lee access a secret compartment in a Buick by removing a side panel right before Bray went inside a house to finalize the deal. In addition, the agents identified Nabors as the kingpin of a cocaine conspiracy, with Platinum Status as a front for the sale of dope and laundering of profits.

At trial, he was able to show he was nowhere near the coke transaction, and little evidence was produced to prove him a drug kingpin. The trumped-up charge was likely a ploy to force him to plead guilty in exchange for a reduced sentence. Nabors took a huge risk turning down the plea bargain. He was facing a life sentence. "I was scared," he remembers. "I got kids who were maybe never going to see their father again. I didn't know if I was doing the right thing, but I knew I was innocent."

After a one-week trial Nabors was acquitted of the narcotics charges but found guilty of gun possession. He was sentenced to five years in prison.

Operation Turnaround was like a sick tree, with long branches and plentiful foliage but rotten roots. Investigators knew early on there was reason to believe Nabors was not a coke dealer. Three days before the trial, Ansari and Blas Serrano interviewed the third man in the alleged coke transaction, Albert Lee. After pleading guilty and being sentenced to ten years, Lee told investigators that Nabors hadn't given them cocaine and gave them the name of the person who had. By law, Ansari and Serrano were required to record Lee's statement and put it in a memo, which they did. They were also required to turn such evidence over to the defense. Instead, they buried it.

"That's the kind of conduct that could cost you your ticket to practice law," said Sam Shamansky, Nabors's attorney. "That's the kind of conduct that costs a person his freedom."

Of all the criminal tactics used in Operation Turnaround, the most egregious was the use of stand-ins, willing or unwitting substitutes for the marks Bray, Lucas, and other cops later fingered for crimes. Among the first stand-in cases to be exposed involved Roosevelt Williams, who was on a flight to Chicago—and had documents to prove it—at the time Bray testified that he participated in two separate drug transactions.

Lucas and Bray swore under oath that Williams was their man, though, again, they had been warned they had the wrong person. On the night one transaction took place, a Mansfield police undercover squad just happened to have the same location under surveillance for another investigation. Perry Wheeler, a veteran Mansfield police detective with a long history of investigating dope and gun cases in north-central Ohio, saw the deal go down. Wheeler was familiar with Williams, and he knew the man Lucas and Bray identified as Williams was somebody else. Wheeler met with Lucas, cop to cop, and told him so. He sent Lucas a photo of Williams, all to no avail. Lucas said he was positive he purchased crack from Williams.

When Wheeler attempted to investigate further, Metcalf called a police sergeant and left a message: Word on the street was that if Wheeler kept prying he would be shot at by a Mansfield hood who went by the name of Uncle Wee Wee. Wheeler knew Uncle Wee Wee as an associate of Bray's.

The stand-in used to get Williams indicted was actually a thug named Robert Harris. Bray was slick—he staged the event so that Harris sold $2,000 worth of crack to him and Lucas. Bray identified the dealer as Williams, then Harris gave the money back to Bray.

Another innocent Mansfield man, Lowestco Ballard, was almost framed this way. A crack transaction was videotaped by a backup unit, though it was done so the participants' faces were impossible to identify. At trial, Lucas testified that he was face-to-face with the dealer, who he swore was Lowestco Ballard. Fortunately for Ballard, the man they used was five foot nine, while Ballard is a lanky six foot four. Ballard was able to show he wasn't on the tape. He was found not guilty, but only after he spent nearly a year in pretrial detention.

Geneva France was not so lucky. She was framed by Shaynessa "Shay Shay" Moxley, a female friend of Bray's girlfriend. France knew Shay Shay, and she had also met Bray a few times. Bray once tried to get France to go on a date. When she turned him down, he told her he could put her in the trunk of his car. "I'll take you to Cleveland," he said, "and nobody will ever find you." When France heard Bray had said she'd sold him crack, it sent a chill up her spine. At trial, she was fingered by another man, a person she had never seen before in her life: Lee Lucas.

In order to verify France had sold them crack, Lucas and the task force claimed to have used a photo of France for positive identification.

The photo they used was not entered into evidence at trial, so ruled by presiding Judge Gaughan. Only after France had been convicted was it revealed that the photo they had was a school photo from the sixth grade, when France was eleven years old—a picture that bore little resemblance to the woman they framed on drug charges.

"When I finally saw the photo they used to frame Geneva," says France's attorney, Edward Mullin, an ex-Cleveland cop, "it made me sick to my stomach."

By mid-2007 Operation Turnaround had seemingly run its course. As with most federal narcotics busts, the fear of severe mandatory minimum sentences led to plea bargains in the majority of cases (the Drug Policy Alliance estimates that 95 percent of all federal narcotics cases are plea-bargained). The Nabors and Ballard cases resulted in acquittals, as did two others, but twenty-three people, a good number, had been incarcerated, which justified the federal expenditures and manhours. Niggers with Rims was a success.

It all began to unravel in May, when Carlos Warner of the public defender's office came to handle the case of Jashawa Webb, the only white defendant. Webb had been convicted on minor narcotics charges twice before. In fact, he told Warner, "I'm a drug dealer. I've sold marijuana and powder cocaine to my friends, but I've never sold crack. I didn't do what they said I did."

"Of course I was skeptical," says Warner. "But Josh is the kind of person who, in the past, when guilty of something, would cop a plea and seek the best deal for himself. Here he was saying no to a plea deal even though he was facing a possible life sentence. He insisted he was innocent and Bray and Lucas were lying."

The task force had submitted audiotapes as evidence in the Webb case. Warner listened to them and became convinced the voice identified as Webb was not his client's. Furthermore, the tape had strange gaps and elisions. The lawyer had the tapes analyzed by two separate experts; each concluded they had been altered.

Warner had questions, and only one person could give him answers: Bray.

Since Operation Turnaround concluded, Bray had reverted to form. He had been paid at least $8,450 for the Mansfield drug busts and was back on the street. Emboldened by his Justice Department training, he set up a $700 marijuana purchase. Midway through the deal, a participant pointed at Bray and shouted, "Hey, that's the guy who set up my bro."

Bray pulled out a .38-caliber handgun and opened fire, hitting one of the dealers in the back and stomach. He was caught and charged with attempted murder.

According to Bray, he immediately placed a call to his benefactor, Lucas. Bray told him, "You gotta help me out. After all I did for you, you gotta take care of me." Lucas reassured Bray, telling him, "You're like a brother to me." He said he'd see what he could do.

The next day, Lucas contacted Bray's brother and told him the wounded man was the stepson of a police officer. There was nothing he could do for Bray.

By the time attorney Carlos Warner arrived at Cleveland City Jail, the former star CI had stewed in lockup for a week. In a visiting room, Warner told Bray, "I believe this audiotape has been tampered with."

Responded Bray, "You're only scraping the surface with that tape stuff."

In two meetings, Bray poured his heart out to Warner and another investigator. Bray claimed that at least thirty people were put in jail for crimes they hadn't committed. Even some of the people who had pleaded guilty were innocent. He had been encouraged to make cases by Lucas, Serrano, and the task force.

Bray's confession bordered on hysterical. He cried, pounded the table, and told Warner that by telling the truth his life was in danger. Lucas and Ansari, he said, were bigger than the government, and he was afraid of them. He said, "I'm letting you know, man to man, everything I tell you may spin your head, but it's true. Go look up Dwayne Nabors's case, go look up Geneva France's case, go look up—what's the other?—there are just so many of them."

"There's no investigator that can protect me and my family. . . . I am a no-good, lying scum that slept with this shit."

Bray claimed that when he was on the stand at the France trial, he looked at her face and realized for the first time that what he was doing was wrong: "It was just my thirst for money, and I couldn't get a job." He said prosecutors and agents had told him they could help him out, and Serrano prepared him for trial by telling him if he ever felt like he was lying to say, "I don't understand."

Warner mentioned how federal prosecutors would come down hard on Bray. "They want to shut you up. They don't want you to talk."

"Let me tell you something," said Bray. "From me to you, this might be the universe punishing me for the shit that has happened to other people's lives, not being able to see their kids, their mothers, their sisters, their brothers. Understand what I'm saying: This might be it right here."

After Bray's confession became public, naysayers went on the offensive: Bray was seeking to save his own skin. He had turned on Lucas because Lucas would not help him beat an attempted murder rap. He was a stone-cold liar. But on a tape recording of Bray's second interview with Warner, the anguish and regret in his voice are palpable and real.

Bray was now the proverbial hot potato. Federal authorities placed him in protective custody and assigned as his counsel John McCaffrey, a former FBI agent turned criminal defense attorney. McCaffrey tried to verify many of Bray's claims. It was at first a bumpy ride. Bray failed two polygraph tests. "It was his nature to withhold information," says McCaffrey. "He kept wanting to keep things to himself that he could use for bartering purposes down the road." Eventually, McCaffrey and other investigators obtained signed confessions from many of the people Bray used as stand-ins. Concurrently, the FBI reopened an investigation into the career of Lucas.

Throughout 2008 and into 2009, the dominoes began to fall. First eight people convicted via Operation Turnaround were released from prison, then fifteen more. Bray pleaded guilty to lying on the witness stand and committing civil rights violations; he was sentenced to fifteen years in prison. In May 2009, Sheriff's Deputy Charles Metcalf pleaded guilty to one count of civil rights violation for his role in the Dwayne Nabors case. Later, Ansari agreed to cooperate with federal investigators in exchange for immunity.

In June, three men convicted by Lucas in a separate case involving the sale of PCP demanded and received a hearing regarding circumstances surrounding the trial. Under questing from Special Prosecutor Greg White, Joseph Pinjuh and others in the U.S. Attorney's Office took the stand. They acknowledged that Lucas made cases too quickly and was sometimes sloppy. "He was running at a hundred and fifty miles per hour," said one assistant U.S. attorney. Pinjuh described Lucas as "a loose canon." However, none of them said they doubted his truthfulness or veracity.

One assistant U.S. attorney who tried to sound alarm bells about Lucas was Thomas Gruscinski, a man who felt the consequences of challenging the golden goose. Gruscinski met with Lucas for a 2003 investigation of Akron grocers who were suspected of laundering black market proceeds. Lucas bragged to Gruscinski that "he could make trees talk" and told the assistant U.S. attorney that he planned to pull over a grocer on a routine traffic stop. He would take a drug-sniffing dog so he could claim probable cause to search the grocer and seize his assets. Gruscinski felt the scheme was illegal and wanted no part of it. He later was told that Lucas went over his head to a supervisor for approval to make the stop. When Gruscinski wrote an inter-office memo complaining about Lucas, he was taken off the case.

At the hearing for the three PCP dealers, Gruscinski took the stand and testified that he believed his criticism of Lucas was the reason for his dismissal.

Lucas's trial is scheduled to begin in January 2010. It will be one of the most significant criminal prosecutions ever in the Northern District of Ohio. Testifying against Lucas will be his former CI Bray and his former partner Ansari, not to mention untold agents, deputy sheriffs, cops, prosecutors, dope dealers, and others involved in cases overseen or facilitated by Lucas.

The man has his defenders. At his indictment in May, the courtroom was filled with fellow DEA agents, police officers, prosecutors, and friends, people who contend Lucas is a crackerjack agent who is being used as a scapegoat. A prosecutor who worked with Lucas on numerous drug cases says, "He is the hardest-working law enforcement official I've ever known. The people criticizing [Lucas] don't know the kind of work he put into his cases. He made solid cases and put a lot of bad people behind bars. He did what a law enforcement official is supposed to do."

The defense of Lucas as a good cop is a slippery slope. Even if Lucas were to be found not guilty, Bray has already pleaded guilty to fabrication of evidence, which calls into question a lifetime's worth of criminal cases. Many people currently incarcerated are likely to be set free—not just innocent people but actual criminals and dope dealers Lucas knowingly or unknowingly convicted using bogus evidence. Whether Lucas was corrupt or merely ignorant, his actions will lead to the release of hardened criminals. What kind of law enforcement is that?

His wayward trajectory was charted long ago. Back in 1995 at the trial of Peter Hidalgo, Lucas testified that he was, if anything, overly cautious when dealing with informants. "With everyone I deal with in my job, besides my partners, I am careful," he said. When it came to informants, "You watch them from the nature of what they do. They're informants . . . they're involved with other drug dealers. That is their whole function."

The defense attorney interjected, "You want to corroborate as much as you can, correct?"

"Exactly," answered the agent. "The whole reason you do surveillance is corroboration. It's a large part of our work."

In the Mansfield drug cases, there was little corroboration. The reason a sixth-grade photo of Geneva France was used was because there were no surveillance photos. That may have been intended. If you're attempting to frame innocent people, surveillance can be a problem.

James Owen—a renowned criminal defense lawyer representing France, Nabors (who was released after two and a half years), Ballard, and others in a civil lawsuit against Lucas, the DEA, and Richmond County sheriff's deputies—sees the trial as a possible cover-up. Says Owen, "How was an agent with a checkered career like Lucas—a man whose work had been called into question numerous times in the past—set loose in Mansfield to make wrongful conviction cases, and who knew about it?" To Owen, Lucas was aided and abetted by a criminal justice system that allowed him to operate and encouraged his behavior. With Lucas exposed, the same system seeks to protect itself by cutting off a rogue agent. "Why wasn't Blas Serrano indicted? Why was Deputy Sheriff Metcalf allowed to plead guilty to a minor charge and return to his job, free of any punishment? Why is Greg White allowed to retire into a cushy job as a federal magistrate without having to explain what he knew and when he knew it?"

In August, Owen's clients delivered a letter to Special Prosecutor Bruce Teitlebaum, who is handling the Lucas investigation. The victims demanded to see documents currently under seal by a federal order. They wrote, "We view any refusal to allow us access to this information to be a cover-up that simply continues the crime committed against us."

Owen argues that a federal judge needs to appoint an independent commission to investigate Lucas's career, why he was allowed to make cases and how those cases were facilitated by others.

Nabors remembers when he took the stand and prosecutor Serrano demanded, "Why? Why on earth would a federal agent like Lee Lucas frame you on drug charges? What could possibly be his motive?" Nabors did not have a good answer, and he is still baffled by the question.

What did Lucas have to gain by framing a bunch of innocent African Americans in the small industrial town of Mansfield? The answer is to be found in the inverted morality of the war on drugs.

In the Northern District of Ohio, Lucas had an exalted reputation as an agent who delivered a high volume of cases; he made the world go around. With narcotics charges, you don't need much of a case. Lucas was good at securing an indictment (his word and the word of a CI was usually enough), and severe mandatory sentencing ensured a wealth of plea bargains. Lucas wasn't so good at producing evidence for trial—surveillance videos, corroboration, even believable photos to verify identities. There is a temptation to be sloppy with dope cases because one can be. Lucas and his team could easily have made a dozen legitimate arrests in Mansfield, but that wasn't enough to justify the allocation of federal money and the formation of a federal task force.

The day after the announcement that Lucas had been indicted, the new U.S. drug czar, Gil Kerlikowski, made the startling declaration that the DOJ would no longer use the phrase war on drugs. In the *Wall Street Journal*, Kerlikowski is quoted saying, "Regardless of how you try to explain to people that it's a 'war on drugs' or a 'war on product,' people see a war as a war on them. We're not at war with people in this country."

Kerlikowski's statement seemed to suggest a shift in how the DOJ views narcotics prosecutions. But in the following months, he appeared to backtrack by announcing, "We will continue to vigorously prosecute any violations of the drug statutes in this country." When contacted to comment on drug police in general and, more specifically, the Lucas case, a spokesperson for the U.S. Office of National Drug Policy responded that Director Kerlikowski could not "fit it into his schedule." Official spokespersons for the DOJ, DEA, and U.S. Attorney's Office also declined to comment. Whether or not the drug war is over, or even in remission, remains to be seen. But if anyone wants a clear assessment of how narcotics prosecutions have skewed criminal justice and subverted the notion of due process, they don't need to look far. Innumerable federal agents, cops, U.S. attorneys, prosecutors, and judges facilitated and benefited from the efforts of Lucas. Every case he supervised over the years is now tainted.

In a courtroom in downtown Cleveland, it is DEA agent Lucas who will stand accused, but his co-conspirators are legion.

POSTSCRIPT: On February 5, 2010, Lee Lucas was acquitted on eighteen criminal counts, including perjury and obstruction of justice. Many in Cleveland were shocked, with one local attorney familiar with the case referring to it as "our O. J. Simpson case." However, the verdict had seemed inevitable once the judge in the case ruled that no evidence would be admissible that did not relate exclusively to the Mansfield drug cases. There was no mention of Lucas's previous controversial cases in Miami and Bolivia, no evidence pertaining to his previous uses of confidential informants. Consequently, the entire case rested on the testimony of Jerrell Bray. After the verdict, a juror was quoted as saying that the jury simply did not believe that Bray was a credible witness.

Jerrell Bray died in prison from natural causes on September 9, 2012. He was forty years old.

2.

NARCO AMERICANO

Playboy, February 2011

Juárez, the bloody ground zero for the Mexican drug war:
Two American citizens—a U.S. embassy employee and her husband—
are brutally assassinated in the middle of the day. The message
from the cartels? More violence is coming, and no one is safe.

The killings take place in a crowded area in Ciudad Juárez, Mexico, mid-afternoon.

A white Toyota RAV4 with Texas plates is chased by two vehicles one block from the U.S. border, near the Rio Grande. The driver of the Toyota is a man, age thirty-four. His wife, next to him in the passenger seat, is thirty-five; she is four months pregnant. In the back, a seven-month-old baby is strapped into a car seat.

A black SUV and another vehicle occupied by armed gunmen pull alongside the Toyota. The man driving the Toyota tries to escape; he maneuvers desperately through traffic toward the Paso del Norte Bridge, the border crossing to El Paso, Texas. From the black SUV, gunmen open fire, strafing the side of the Toyota. The driver is hit; the car veers widely out of control, collides with other automobiles, and comes to a halt alongside the curb.

The woman passenger screams in terror. Professional assassins step out of their car. Dressed commando-style in all black, they open fire on the woman and her husband, finishing the job.

After the fusillade subsides, the assassins approach the vehicle.

Some members of the hit team cordon off the area. Although they are less than a block from the border, where dozens of Mexican customs officials and armed military personnel are stationed, no cops approach the murder scene.

The gunmen check to make sure the man and woman are dead. Ignoring the crying baby in the backseat, they gather up spent shell casings and other evidence, then leave the scene. No one chases after them.

Once the killers are gone, military police descend. The couple in the front seat is history. In the backseat, the baby screams amid shattered glass and splattered blood but is miraculously okay. A policewoman reaches in and grabs the baby and clutches her to her chest.

The killings should be shocking. Even in Juárez, called the deadliest city in the world, where the war against narco traffickers has given rise to a staggering body count, this terrible murder—which takes place in the middle of the day in front of dozens of onlookers—is outrageous.

Even so, the flagrant brutality of the hit might have been absorbed into the body politic of Juárez, a city under siege, were it not for a simple fact: The victims are not only American citizens, but also government employees. The female victim, Lesley Enriquez, worked at the U.S. consulate in Juárez. Her husband, Arthur Redelfs, was a corrections officer at the El Paso County Sheriff's Office, across the border in El Paso.

The killings take place on March 13, 2010. At roughly the same time as the Enriquez-Redelfs hit, elsewhere in Juárez another assassination takes place. Jorge Alberto Salcido Ceniceros, the husband of a U.S. consulate worker, leaving the same children's birthday party attended by Enriquez and Redelfs, in a similar white SUV, is also gunned down by a professional hit squad.

The killings have all the earmarks of drug cartels, which have been slaughtering people in Juárez, and all of Mexico, at an ungodly rate. The presidents of Mexico and the United States condemn the killings, with a spokesman for the National Security Council referring to them as "brutal murders." Secretary of State Hillary Clinton expresses regret and denounces the cartels, saying, "There is no question that they are fighting against both our governments."

If there was doubt before, there is no longer. The killings represent a tipping point. What was viewed by some U.S. citizens and public officials as mostly a Mexican problem is now an American problem, with American victims. No one is immune. And no one is safe.

"In all my years in law enforcement, I never imagined it would get this bad," says Phil Jordan, a thirty-one-year veteran of the DEA who, in the mid-1990s, was promoted to director of the El Paso Intelligence Center, or EPIC, the agency's eyes and ears on the borderland and the international drug trade. Although he is now retired, Jordan maintains a network of law enforcement contacts, and he is frequently quoted on narco-related subjects in the press. His interests are professional but also personal. In 1995, his younger brother, Lionel Bruno, was shot dead in a Kmart parking lot in El Paso. A thirteen-year-old hood from Juárez was eventually arrested and prosecuted for the homicide; the official story was that it was a carjacking gone wrong. But Jordan remains convinced the cartels targeted his brother because of his career in the DEA. A version of Jordan's story is chronicled in the 2002 book *Down by the River* by Charles Bowden.

"What you are seeing in Mexico now," says Jordan, "is a new low. The cartels have become like Al Qaeda. They have learned from Al Qaeda."

Jordan is referring specifically to the cartels' use of beheadings to deliver a message. Cartel rivals and other enemies are kidnapped and, on occasion, videotaped being beheaded or dismembered, with the savagery broadcast on YouTube and popular Internet sites such as El Blog del Narco.

Then there are the remote-control car bombings that, throughout the summer of 2010, became increasingly commonplace. The entire country has morphed into a perverse version of the traditional Mexican celebration el Día de los Muertos (the Day of the Dead).

The numbers are shocking. Since December 2006, there have been nearly 30,000 narco-related murders in Mexico. The violence has taken place all around the country, from large municipalities such as Mexico City and Guadalajara to tourist enclaves such as Acapulco and

the Yucatán Peninsula. Mass graves, severed heads and limbs, mutilated bodies left on display in the town plaza with threatening notes
have become a near-daily occurrence.

"These are the techniques of terrorists," says Jordan.

His observations are echoed by Secretary Clinton, who compared
what is happening in Mexico to an "insurgency," with the cartels
attempting to take over sectors of government and whole regions of
the country.

Much of the mayhem is facilitated by corruption, with *federales*,
municipal police and elected officials on the take. The temptations
of narco dollars is seductive, and the threat of violence is persuasive.
Public officials and average citizens are often coerced into the narco
trade by the drug organizations, which make them an offer: *plato o
plomo*, silver or lead. Either you take the cartels money and cooperate,
or you will be shot dead.

Corruption is sometimes a two-way street. Although the United
States does not have the deeply entrenched institutional corruption
that permeates Mexican society, the drug trade is sometimes facilitated by dirty U.S. border patrol agents, law enforcement personnel,
and other government officials on the take.

The killings of the consulate worker and her husband are a case in
point. In July, Mexican authorities arrested a local Mexican member
of the infamous Barrio Azteca Gang, which operates on both sides
of the border (in Mexico it is known as Los Aztecas). According to
the Mexican federal police, this gangster—Jesús Ernesto Chávez Castillo—claims that the target of the hit was Lesley Enriquez, the U.S.
consulate employee. Chávez says he was the organizer of the assassination, which was ordered by the Juárez drug cartel because Enriquez
was corrupt. She was helping to supply a rival gang with visas and had
to die. The other victim, in the other white SUV, was murdered simply
because the hit men weren't sure which car belonged to their target, so
they decided, just in case, to ambush both vehicles.

The FBI office in El Paso publicly expresses doubt about the explanation for the killings, stating it has no evidence that Enriquez was
corrupt. Over the following months, many theories about the killings
appear in the press. This speculation takes place against a backdrop

of further killings, bombings, kidnappings, and extortion that have turned the narco war into a killing field unlike anything else taking place on the planet.

The narcosphere is a battlefield without borders. Politicians, businessmen, lawmen, bankers, drug lords, gangsters, and poor Mexicans and American citizens all have a role to play in an illicit business that generates, according to some estimates, up to $23 million annually from the United States alone. It is difficult to pinpoint the narcosphere's central nervous system, but in terms of violence, the central war zone is Mexico's northern borderland—encompassing the state of Chihuahua and its largest city, Juárez—which produces more victims of narco-terrorism than anywhere else in the country.

Howard Campbell, professor of sociology and anthropology at the University of Texas at El Paso, refers to the phenomenon as "partly an accident of geography." Campbell is author of the 2009 book *Drug War Zone*, a fascinating oral history that explores the Juárez–El Paso narco-economy from myriad perspectives.

For nearly a century, going back to the days of Prohibition and before, America's southwestern borderland has existed as a storied smuggling route. Some of this history, particularly as it relates to the narco trade, is glorified in *narcocorridos*—melodramatic musical ballads that celebrate drug smuggling, usually sung in the *norteño* style in a wavering falsetto accompanied by accordions and heavy brass. The *narcocorridos* have become the soundtrack to the current war. In 2008, when a drug lord from a rival cartel began a violent offensive to take over drug operations in Juárez, police radio frequencies were hacked to broadcast a *narcocorrido* that glorified his organization. To police in Juárez, it was a warning: We are everywhere. Join our cartel, or you will die.

Says Campbell, "Juárez has become a drug war zone primarily because of its proximity to the world's largest marketplace for narcotics—the United States." The professor's comments are an alternative phrasing of the famous observation of Porfirio Díaz, Mexican president in the late nineteenth century. Said Díaz, "Poor Mexico. So far from God and so close to the United States."

Diaz was talking about the entire country, but his words resonate with the force of a shotgun blast in Juárez. Since 2008, when the U.S. government signed the Mérida Initiative—an agreement by which the U.S. Congress earmarked $1.3 billion in training, equipment, and intelligence to facilitate the Mexican narco war—there have been close to 7,000 murders in Juárez, a city of 1.3 million people. (By comparison, New York City, a city of more than 8 million, had fewer than 500 murders in 2009.) President Felipe Calderón and others in the Mexican government have claimed that these murders are mostly a consequence of cartel gangsters killing other gangsters. In fact, the victims comprise a broad swath of Mexican society—women, children, policemen, businessmen, public officials, and journalists—leading some observers to note that what is happening in Juárez as a result of a drug war is the full-scale disintegration of civil society.

I arrive at the border crossing on the El Paso side on a hot August morning at 6:00 a.m. My guide is an *hombre* we shall call Christopher. Although Christopher is a gringo, he knows Juárez like the back of his hand. For seven years, from 1997 to 2004, Christopher lived as a heroin addict in one of Juárez's toughest *colonias*, or slums, situated on the hillside overlooking downtown and across the Rio Grande into El Paso.

My intention is to get a visual sense of the *colonia* known as Felipe Angeles, believed to be a home base of the Azteca Gang, which has been identified as the culprit behind the murders of Enriquez, Redelfs, and Salcido at the border. My guide tells me, "We must go early before most people are awake, like the Comanche used to do it."

We cross through the checkpoint on foot, passing over the brackish, bone-dry Rio Grande, then grab a bus in downtown Juárez. The bus rambles through the mostly deserted streets of downtown, along Avenida 16 de Septiembre toward Felipe Angeles. After ten minutes, we exit the bus and walk the rest of the way, up a steep hill into *el barrio*.

We pass a police station, where half a dozen municipal cops are arriving for work. They look at us, two gringos walking alone through el barrio before the sun has risen, as if we must be escapees from a mental institution. Curiosity becomes hostility; we are outside the norm and therefore suspicious. A few minutes later, I notice a police jeep following us at a distance.

"We are being clocked," I tell Chris.

"No big deal," he says. "The way we're going, they won't be able to follow."

Chris leads me off the streets to narrow gravel pathways, up rocky cliffs, and down hills that no car or jeep could traverse, on our way to find an old friend of his by the name of Chavito. At this hour, the only inhabitants are goats, mangy dogs, and runaway chickens.

We find Chavito, whose home is more like a garage than a house. In the yard is the shell of an abandoned ambulance. We rustle Chavito out of bed. He and Chris embrace.

Chavito is around fifty years old, grizzled, with many missing teeth and a sweet disposition. His stomach is alarmingly distended, he says, from a recent surgery gone wrong. He occasionally winces in pain.

Chris and Chavito talk about old times. Excitedly, Chavito tells a story that is both shocking and familiar.

When Chavito and Chris were at the rehab clinic down the street, they became friendly with two recovering addicts named Carlos and Juan Pablo. Eventually, Carlos and Juan Pablo left and organized their own rehab clinic, a converted house in downtown Juárez that they named El Aliviane. Eventually, Carlos relapsed and again started using heroin; he also became a member of the Aztecas.

The Aztecas have a rule about dope. You can sell it, but if you become a user yourself, oftentimes you are killed. Carlos was targeted for execution. According to Chavito, Juan Pablo met with leaders of the gang and said, "Please don't kill Carlos. In fact, your policy of killing the addicts among you is wrong. It is inhumane. Please let me take in the Azteca dope addicts, and I will show you that they can be cured. They can be saved."

The Azteca leadership agreed. A number of gang members, including Carlos, were allowed to stay at El Aliviane, which supplied a mattress, a place to sleep, and a roof overhead.

The problem was that a rival drug organization caught wind of the fact that a number of Aztecas were now residing at El Aliviane. One night in early September 2009, the Sinaloa drug cartel, which is engaged in a turf war with the Juárez cartel for control of drug distribution routes, sent a team of *sicarios*, or assassins, to the clinic. Wearing hoods and carrying submachine guns, they busted down doors and stormed the house. Although only five or six of the twenty people present were Azteca Gang members, the assassins did not discriminate. They rounded up the rehab patients—including Carlos—and made them line up against a wall, then slaughtered them with staccato blasts of machine-gun fire.

Chavito fights back tears as he says, "Most of the victims were innocent. They were not *vatos locos* [gang brothers]. They were addicts trying to get better. They did not deserve to die."

As we ride the bus out of Felipe Angeles back toward the border crossing to the United States, Christopher tells me he is saddened but not entirely surprised by Carlos's death. "I always had the feeling he needed to be part of a group, to belong to something," he says. "He was big on group identity and group loyalty."

The Barrio Azteca gang, like most street-level criminal organizations, was founded on the concept of group loyalty and identity. Its origins are on the U.S. side of the border, in the Texas state prison system, where, in the mid-1980s, the Aztecas formed from an amalgam of various street gangs. As *vatos* were paroled or completed their sentences and returned to the street, they became prominent in neighborhoods in El Paso and other cities in Texas and parts of New Mexico. Some of the gang members were Mexican nationals who, upon release from prison in the United States were deported to Mexico, where they formed Azteca chapters in Felipe Angeles and other barrios, as well as in the prison systems in Juárez and elsewhere in the state of Chihuahua.

"The gang spread like a virus," says David Cuthbertson, special agent in charge of the FBI's El Paso Division. "In a short time, they became the dominant street organization that sold narcotics in El Paso and conducted other criminal activity such as collecting *cuota* ['tax'] from nonaffiliated drug dealers."

Given the gang's cross-border affiliations, it was natural that the Barrio Azteca would be absorbed into the preeminent cartel in Juárez, led at the time by the ambitious drug lord Amado Carrillo Fuentes. Carrillo died on the operating table in 1997 while undergoing plastic surgery to alter his appearance. While he was alive, Carrillo put the gang to work as street enforcers and contract killers. If anything, the role of the Aztecas under the cartel's current overlord, Amado's brother Vicente Carrillo Fuentes, has grown. The gang organizes and carries out most of the cartel's major hits and also plays a key role in narcotics distribution and sales.

"If you think of the cartel as a corporation," says Cuthbertson, "with a CEO and directors overseeing different aspects like logistics, production, transportation, and so forth, then the Barrio Azteca represents the security wing. Structurally, they are more in the nature of a paramilitary organization, with capos, sergeants, and foot soldiers. They serve as contractors for the corporation, but they also do things on their own; they are not obligated to do crimes only on behalf of the corporation."

Many Barrio Azteca Gang members on the U.S. side of the border have a distinguishing tattoo: Stenciled somewhere on their bodies are the numerals 2 and 1, representing the second and first letters of the alphabet, B and A, which stand for Barrio Azteca. Others may bear Aztec symbols on their skin.

As with most street gangs of any ethnicity, the quickest way to rise within the Azteca structure is through acts of criminal daring and violence.

One person whose pathway into the gang and ascension within the ranks followed the usual pattern is Jesús Ernesto Chávez Castillo, whose nickname is El Camello, "the Camel." Chávez was born in 1969 in Juárez but moved to El Paso with his family when he was seventeen. An early brush with the law came in 1995 when he was arrested attempting to sell marijuana to undercover officers from the El Paso Police Department. He pleaded guilty to a reduced charge and was given probation. Later, in 2001, Chávez was charged with "intoxicated assault"; he was driving drunk when he crashed into another vehicle, seriously injuring four people. Again, he pleaded guilty, but this time he was deported from the United States to Mexico.

Chávez seems to have moved back and forth between Juárez and El Paso on a semi-regular basis. He had two marriages in the United States and fathered three children. In February 2003, he was detained on the U.S. side of the border. When he lied to border patrol agents about his status—a federal offense—he was charged with illegal reentry.

Chávez's lawyer at the time was Carlos Spector, a renowned El Paso immigration attorney who recently represented several Mexican journalists seeking asylum in the United States on the grounds that their lives had been threatened not only by gangsters, but also by members of the Mexican military. Spector remembers Chávez as "a tough *hombre*, obviously a guy from the streets" but not a high-ranking or connected member of any cartel or gang. The manner by which Chávez, a lowly street thug, became the notorious El Camello is a tale that Spector says could be called "the making of a *sicario*."

After being found guilty of illegal reentry, Chávez received a mandatory sentence of twenty years. He was sent to the notorious Las Tunas Federal Correctional Facility, ruled from within by the Barrio Azteca. By the time Chávez was released after serving five years, he was a hardened gangster with the criminal contacts on both sides of the border.

A spokesman for the Mexican federal police in Juárez says that Chávez confessed not only to his role in the killing of Enriquez, Redelfs, and Salcido in March, but also to the January slaughter of fifteen people, including eleven teenagers, at a birthday party in the Villas del Salvárcar barrio of Juárez. That killing, authorities say, was a case of mistaken identity; Chávez participated in the slaughter believing the students were members of a rival gang known as Artistas Asesinos ("Artist Assassins").

Since his arrest, Chávez has been paraded on Mexican television, and his confession is cited as a major victory for the forces of the law. But for some who follow the narco scene in Mexico, the confession has a bad smell. It is not uncommon, they say, for a member of the Barrio Azteca to step up and take the fall for a crime he may or may not have committed, simply to satisfy the demands of the system. It is an arrangement designed to benefit both law enforcement and the gang: Government authorities get to parade the "perpetrator" before the public, and in return the investigation goes no further.

The gang member who is put forth to "take one for the team" goes off to prison, which is, in fact, the central base of operations of the Barrio Azteca. He enters prison revered by his fellow gang members for having sacrificed his freedom, and he leaves prison an even higher-ranking member of the gang than he was before he went in.

FBI Special Agent Samantha Mikeska, who heads a special unit devoted solely to investigating the Barrio Azteca Gang, is aware of the quandary. Like many cops and agents working the borderland, Mikeska has a personal as well as a professional imperative. In 2002, while participating in a sting against thieves who targeted cargo trains at the border, Mikeska and another agent were brutally assaulted with sticks, rocks, and a baseball bat until a fellow agent arrived and opened fire, chasing the gangsters away. Mikeska suffered a fractured cheekbone, a fractured orbital bone of the left eye, retinal hemorrhaging, fractured vertebrae, a ruptured cervical disk, and external wounds to her face and body. When she returned to work six weeks later, it was with seven plates and two pins in her left eye area and a plate of four screws in her neck.

"I got my butt kicked," she says. "Afterward there were psychological issues, physical issues, but you have to learn to separate what happened from the responsibilities of your job. This is what I do; I'm sworn to try and make the world a better place. You adapt and overcome."

In 2008, Mikeska was part of a task force that arrested and successfully prosecuted six Barrio Azteca leaders and associates on RICO charges. "To be honest," she says, "I sometimes think we made them stronger. We basically put them in the same area, where they are not one hundred percent monitored. At least when they are out on the street, we could monitor them; we knew what they were up to. Prison commingles them into one big unit, and they have access to smuggled telephones, letters, phone privileges; they have a line of communications within the prison system that is strong."

Since the 2008 convictions, Mikeska and her unit have been on the hunt for one Azteca in particular: Eduardo "Tablas" Ravelo, believed to be the gang's boss on the Juárez side of the border. Ravelo is currently on the FBI's Ten Most Wanted list. There is a warrant out for his arrest in both the United States and Mexico. "He is a thug and a ruthless killer," says Mikeska. "His power is based partly on the fact that he has a lot of law enforcement in his pocket. As we all know, there are some corrupt law enforcement personnel over there. Things are not investigated to the fullest."

Given the nature of corruption in Mexico, I ask Mikeska if she is able to share information with her counterparts across the border. She looks at her supervisor, who has been sitting in on our interview, and asks, "How do I answer that?"

"Carefully," says the supervisor.

Mikeska smiles ruefully and says, "I don't share anything with the Mexican government. I really don't. I have not been successful in gathering information from that side. A lot of the investigation I do is strictly in the United States. Ravelo's name comes up; we know he is in Juárez. The names come up, but to actually go over and pursue investigative techniques in Mexico is pretty much impossible. Does that answer your question?"

In the narcosphere, things are not always what they appear to be. Four months after the killing of the U.S. consulate worker and her husband, an incident occurs in Juárez that, at the time, represents a new downward demarcation in the narco war. On Avenida 16 de Septiembre, a car bomb is detonated, killing four people and injuring eleven others. It is the first use of a car bomb in Mexico's drug war, evoking the tactics of Iraqi insurgents and the narco-terrorism that wracked Colombia in the 1990s.

The bombing is the result of a diabolical deception. Earlier that day, gangsters affiliated with the Juárez cartel kidnap the owner of an auto repair shop, dress him in a police uniform, and then shoot him—not to kill him but to fill him with bullet holes so he bleeds profusely. They then leave him incapacitated near Avenida 16 de Septiembre and Bolivia Street. A doctor in a nearby office hears the man screaming for help and responds to the scene. A policeman also responds, arriving to aid what appears to be a fellow officer in distress. What they do not know is that the gangsters placed a call to emergency services to bring officials into the trap, or that they have planted twenty-two kilos of C-4 explosives in a nearby car, which they detonate via cell phone. The doctor, policeman, rescue worker, and a bystander are blown to smithereens.

Almost immediately, Mexico's federal police issue a statement that the ambush was perpetrated by La Línea, a wing of the Juárez cartel, in retaliation for the arrest days earlier of a prominent cartel leader. Soon after, a statement—understood to be from La Línea—appears pinned to the fence of a local primary school. It claims responsibility for the incident but states it was in response to corrupt Chihuahua police intelligence officials acting in consort with La Línea's main rival, the Sinaloa cartel. The statement reads, "FBI and DEA, start investigating officials who give support to the Sinaloa cartel, because if not, we will use more car bombs [against] those federal agents."

For those who closely follow the narco war, La Línea's accusation of corruption has a familiar ring. Ever since President Calderón unleashed the Mexican military to become more directly involved in the conflict, La Línea and the Juárez cartel have been taking a beating at the hands of the Sinaloa cartel. Led by Joaquín "El Chapo" Guzmán— a ruthless drug lord who, according to *Forbes* magazine, is one of the wealthiest men in the world—the Sinaloa cartel has emerged as the most powerful criminal organization in all of Mexico. Compared with the Juárez cartel, its crackdowns at the hands of Mexican military police have been remarkably low. The Sinaloa cartel appears to be operating with near impunity.

Some in the press—including National Public Radio, which broadcast an investigative report in May—have suggested that the Calderón administration has formed an alliance with the Sinaloa cartel. A benign interpretation of the theory is that by establishing hegemony in the narco trade, officials feel one cartel in charge will cause less mayhem and murder across the land. Calderón's administration has denied the accusation.

The car bombing in Juárez is followed by events that seem to be aimed at U.S. interests in Mexico. A series of threats forces the closing of the U.S. consulate in the city for periods of three and four days throughout the summer. After La Línea's demands that the U.S. government investigate connections between corrupt Mexican government officials and the Sinaloa cartel or by a specified date there will be a massive bombing, the U.S. consulate closes. When the date passes without incident, the consulate reopens.

The question arises: Why is the Juárez cartel and its security arm, La Línea, focusing their wrath on the U.S. government?

One organization that is very interested in this question is Stratfor, an Austin-based company whose team of intelligence professionals analyzes world events for business leaders, investors, law enforcement officials, and government agencies. In August, in an internal report entitled "Mexico's Juárez Cartel Gets Desperate," Stratfor notes that the actions of the Juárez cartel appear designed to prevent the Sinaloa cartel from taking over "the Plaza."

In Mexican narco-speak, the Plaza refers to a cartel stronghold, secured by the complex set of relationships among traffickers, law enforcement agencies, and local governments that makes it possible for an organization to control the narco trade in a given region. Whoever controls the Plaza by paying off police and public officials—and through extortion, intimidation, and murder of the civilian population—reigns as the supreme overlord of crime in that area.

"As we noted some months back," states the Stratfor report, "there have been persistent rumors that the Mexican government has favored the Sinaloa cartel. . . . Whether or not such charges are true, it is quite evident that the Juárez cartel believes them to be so, and has reacted accordingly." In a reference to Jesús Ernesto Chávez Castillo, alleged mastermind of the Enriquez-Redelfs hit, the report adds, "According to *El Diario* [a daily newspaper published in Juárez], the arrested Azteca member said that a decision was made by leaders in the Barrio Azteca Gang and Juárez cartel to attack U.S. citizens in the Juárez area in an effort to force the U.S. government to intervene in the Mexican government's war against the cartels and act as a 'neutral referee,' thereby helping to counter the Mexican government's favoritism toward El Chapo and the Sinaloa Federation."

The Stratfor conclusions resonate throughout U.S. law enforcement; many agents I interview tell me it is a "solid theory." It is also an advanced state-of-war strategy in which lives are cruelly sacrificed for a larger objective and events are presented in the public domain in a way that is often a deliberate obfuscation of the manipulations and maneuverings for control that lie below the surface.

It is a sweltering afternoon, and I am back in Juárez. This time my guide is José Mario Sánchez Soledad, a former assistant to the mayor of Juárez and former head of the city planning commission who is now a proud member of the Juárez city council. Sánchez is erudite and passionate. Along with his career in politics, he is an opera singer and the owner of a modest-sized furniture-manufacturing business.

Like many people born in Juárez, Sánchez grew up on both sides of the border. "I used to tell people I was very lucky. I grew up in two cultures: the strong family life of Mexican culture and, on the other side, the economic and educational opportunities of the United States." In the borderland, it is common for families and family businesses to exist in a binational universe, but with the narco terror have come drastic changes. According to Alfredo Corchado, who covers the border beat for the *Dallas Morning News*, Ciudad Juárez has lost more than 10,000 private businesses in recent years. Many have closed or moved across the border to El Paso due to extortion and kidnappings by gangsters. The climate of violence has brought about a mass exodus; the civilian population has decreased by about 200,000 since late 2006.

"It is heartbreaking," says Sánchez. "We can feel our city slipping through our fingers, and there is nothing we can do about it."

The devotion that Sánchez feels for Juárez is infectious; he begins his tour downtown, near the Mission de Guadalupe, with a treatise on the historical forces that shaped what has traditionally been Mexico's most unique and thriving border culture. It is the middle of a workday afternoon. Traffic on the streets, which used to crawl with migrant *comerciantes* ("merchants") from all over Mexico, as well as with U.S. tourists and soldiers from Fort Bliss across the border in El Paso, has slowed to a trickle. Fort Bliss now forbids its soldiers from crossing the border. The reasons for this were made clear in October when a soldier from the Texas National Guard, Private First Class José Gil Hernandez, twenty-two, was shot dead on a street in south Juárez. The reasons for this killing are being investigated but remain unknown.

Unsolved murders contribute to a mood of fear, which descends over Juárez as the day wears on, with people hustling to take care of business and cross to the U.S. side before nightfall. After dark, the sound of gunfire is not uncommon; the bodies of murder victims are dumped in the streets, in parks or on the dusty banks of the Rio Grande.

Pointing out the sites of narco murders, body disposals, and other criminal atrocities is a familiar parlor game in Juárez. In Sánchez's car, as we drive along Avenida 16 de Septiembre, my guide casually points out the location where, three weeks earlier, La Línea detonated its car bomb. The sidewalk has been blown away, and the wall of a nearby building is pockmarked with shrapnel from the explosion. It looks like exactly what it is: an urban street corner that has been hit by a bomb.

We head out of the city into the desert. Sánchez wants to show me the *maquiladoras*, the massive factories that expanded exponentially in the wake of the North American Free Trade Agreement. Sánchez is not entirely critical of the factories; he acknowledges that right now they are the only form of steady employment in the area. But he notes that they have sucked the economic life out of the city center. The working population has been lured into the desert by multinational corporations to work the assembly lines and manufacturing plants for wages as low as $4.21 a day. The multinationals pay low taxes and are provided cheap labor. Business is good. Last year, the industrial parks on the outskirts of town added more company permits and jobs than in the previous two years combined.

Meanwhile, back in Juárez, the manufacturing base of the city has been gutted. Into the breach have stepped drug lords and gangsters who shoot it out with one another, as well as with municipal police, *federales*, and the military, on a nightly basis.

"The city has been left to die," says Sánchez. "There is no movement toward urban planning or commercial development. Is there any wonder that those who are left behind in the city turn to illegal activities? The illegal activities in Juárez are thriving, while legal commercial employment is going nowhere."

Even more depressing than the hulking factories in the desert is the tract housing that has been constructed for the *maquiladora* employees. Squat, confining, monotonous by design, the desert projects are a crass form of human warehousing. In the city, *colonias* like Felipe Angeles are poverty-ridden and perilously unsanitary, but at least they feel like communities compared with the *maquiladora* industrial parks, where company buses pick workers up for their shift and take them to the factory and back in a soul-destroying cycle of cheap labor and subsistence.

Of the desert housing complexes, Sánchez says, "Many of these projects have become prime locations for recruitment by gangs like the Aztecas and Artistas Asesinos."

We continue farther into the desert. It is Sánchez's intention to show me the flimsy, near-comical border fence, which runs for a few miles and then abruptly ends in the middle of the desert. He points out surveillance posts and border patrol checkpoints, where vehicles are routinely stopped and searched for illegal contraband. As we drive along through fields of brown desert soil and sagebrush, I ask Sánchez about living with the fear and threat of violence that is so prevalent in the area.

He tells me a story: One night, his two teenage sons attended a birthday party outside the city, not far from where we are now driving. The party was held at a friend's house. There were close to two dozen guests, all of them teenagers. Two of the attendees, friends of Sánchez's sons, left the party early—around 9:00 p.m.—to return home. As they were driving back through the desert, they were forced off the road by another car. Gunmen got out of the car, pulled the two teenagers from their car, and executed them along the side of the road. Like many killings in Juárez, it made no sense: It is believed that the murders were a case of mistaken identity.

"It was horrifying," says Sánchez. "My sons were in shock."

As he remembers these events and relates them to me, Sánchez begins to cry. He is a grown man, driving through the desert with a recent acquaintance, and he is weeping uncontrollably. The sense of tragedy is overwhelming.

Sánchez gathers himself, wipes the wetness from his eyes and says, "I want you to know, I am not crying for myself or even for my children. I am crying for my city. I am crying for Mexico."

———

After two weeks of investigations in Juárez, I am not satisfied. The Mexican authorities' acceptance of Chávez's explanation that Lesley Enriquez was murdered because she was corrupt is typical, part of a dubious pattern. In Mexico, when a prominent person is murdered, authorities often present to the public that the victim was in cahoots with the cartels and therefore his or her death was perhaps inevitable. I speak with Redelfs's former partner, a corrections officer in El Paso named Mike Hernandez, who worked alongside Redelfs for five years. "He was a total professional," Hernandez says of his murdered partner. "He was a good family man and great all around guy. What [authorities in Mexico] have said about him is bullshit."

A memorial service for Redelfs and his wife is held at a Mormon church. Redelfs was active in the church (Enriquez was not a member) and the couple appeared squeaky clean according to those who knew them.

I am prepared to believe they are innocent victims who have been slandered in death, but then I hear from a source in the DEA who has agreed to pass along the results of an internal investigation. He is an active special agent currently on the job; I am not able to use his name because he is not authorized to communicate with me.

Of Enriquez and Redelfs, in three simple words the DEA source says, "They were dirty." I ask for more details, which he declines to divulge, saying only that a federal law enforcement investigation in the United States confirms what the Mexican authorities have alleged: that Lesley Enriquez and her husband were on the take.

I speak with Phil Jordan, the retired DEA director who spent more than thirty years investigating drug trafficking. I tell him I am still having a hard time accepting Enriquez and Redelfs as having been in bed with *narcotraficantes* when, by all outward appearances, they were, as one source told me, "goody two-shoes" and churchgoers.

"Well," Jordan says, "don't you think that if you were involved in corrupt activities with narcos, to present yourself as upstanding citizens and religious people might be the best possible cover?"

By fall 2010, their murders are no longer a major news item. A story that had initially riled the righteous indignation of U.S. officials, including the president, a story of innocent U.S. citizens and federal employees gunned down for no good reason, has evolved into something far more complex and disillusioning. As is often the case in the war on drugs, it turns out that corruption was at the heart of the matter after all.

The shocking level of violence has accelerated. In late July, eight severed heads of murder victims are found neatly lined up along a highway in the state of Durango. No one knows how they got there. In that same month, it is reported that the warden of a prison in the state of Sinaloa allowed inmates to leave the prison, carry out murders for the local cartel and then return safely to their cells. This story is presented as a positive development, seeing as the warden was arrested for the crime. In late August, the bodies of seventy-two people who were attempting to enter the United States are found in a mass grave, one of numerous such sites discovered in the desert in the past year. This particular massacre is attributed to Los Zetas, a fearsome cartel composed of former members of the Mexican military who were originally trained by the U.S. military.

In late November, Mexican authorities arrest a man they claim is the leader of the Azteca Gang in Juárez. The suspect allegedly tells federal police that he is responsible for 80 percent of the city's killings since August 2009. This is given major play in the press, including the *New York Times*, even though U.S. agents say this man's name does not appear anywhere in their records of known Azteca leaders.

A victory for the forces of the law or a cheap PR stunt? It is hard to know. Meanwhile, the cycle of violence continues to escalate, partly because the governments of Mexico and the United States have committed themselves to a strategy of all-out war from which they say they will never back down. In the public domain, the fog of war hov-

ers along with the pollution and dust that sometimes engulfs Ciudad Juárez. When atrocities occur, key details are omitted from news
reports, public officials put forth version of events that are incomplete
or outright lies, people are terrified and afraid to tell anyone what they
have seen or what they know. There appears to be no end in sight.

Welcome to the narcosphere.

IV.

THE BULGER CHRONICLES

*B*y the summer of 2011, I had good reason to believe that I would never again be writing about the Irish-American gangster. I had more or less exhausted the topic, having written two books on the subject and contributed to numerous cable television documentaries that profiled various Irish mobsters of the nineteenth and twentieth centuries. I had chronicled the phasing out of the Irish Mob in New York and Boston, which, along with the decline of the Mafia, represented the end of what people in law enforcement refer to as "traditional organized crime," meaning old-style racketeering with roots going back to the days of Prohibition. It seemed as though there was nothing left to say on the subject of the Irish Mob.

And then they captured Whitey Bulger.

I had written about Bulger before, in the book Paddy Whacked (2005), which was an attempt to lay bare the entire unholy universe of the Irish-American gangster, from the time of the Irish potato famine to the present day. I opened and closed that book with a meditation on Whitey, who had served as the Mob boss of Boston for more than twenty years, and who was still on the lam at the time.

[Bulger] was the last of the last, inheritor of a tradition that had once pretended to represent the rising of a people and inevitably degenerated over the generations into a bloody netherworld of treachery, deception, betrayal, wholesale murder, and dismemberment. To some, the story of the Irish-American gangster is the stuff of legend, a tribute to the rebellious, defiant, tough-as-nails side of the Irish temperament. To others, the saga is shameful, a best-forgotten example of antisocial behavior at its most homicidal and a desperate survival mentality personified in the diabolical, sociopathic tendencies of Whitey Bulger and his ilk.

Either way, the lives were lived, the bodies buried, and the history remains the same. Out there somewhere, Whitey exists as a living relic, or a ghostly reminder, that no criminal underworld in the history of the Unites States started as early or lasted as long as the Irish Mob.

By 2010, I'd come to the conclusion that Bulger was most likely deceased. There hadn't been any recent sightings of the aging gangster, who first disappeared in 1995 along with his girlfriend, Catherine Greig. My guess was that after the terrorist attacks in the United States on September 11, 2001, with the increased security around the globe, he'd gotten stranded somewhere. Eastern Europe, perhaps, where there had allegedly been a Bulger sighting in the late-1990s. He might have died there under an assumed name, a vaguely anonymous U.S. citizen with no known family contacts. There would have been no reason for foreign authorities to make any kind of announcement regarding such an undistinguished passing. As for Catherine Greig, I would not have been surprised if Bulger had resolved that problem. If she had showed signs of weakness, or had begun to crack under the pressure of life on the run, it was not inconceivable that Bulger might have strangled her to death and gotten rid of the body.

It did not cross my mind that America's most wanted fugitive was living basically out in the open, in a popular section of Santa Monica, California, not far from the town's famous bluff overlooking the beach and Pacific Ocean. Under the assumed names of Charles and Carol Gasko, Bulger and Greig strolled the beach and the Third Street Promenade in Santa Monica like any number of mature couples who had left the urban hustle of their native cities behind to retire to the gentle climes of Southern California. Neighbors at their apartment building, the Princess Eugenia, were reportedly shocked that the sweet, slightly eccentric couple living on the third floor was, in fact, among the most wanted fugitives in the United States.

Vanity is what finally tripped up Bulger and Greig. After sixteen fruitless years of searching for Whitey, having exposed and detailed his criminal career on TV shows like America's Most Wanted and Unsolved Mysteries, the FBI and U.S. marshals shifted their strategy to focus on Greig, who was a creature of habit. She liked to go to beauty salons on a regular basis. A media campaign with photos of Greig and information about her personal habits led to a tip from a woman who had seen Greig regularly at a Santa Monica salon. Based on that tip, the feds staked out the apartment of "Carol Gasko," leading to the arrest of Greig and her notorious gangster paramour.

John Connolly, the former FBI agent who was Bulger's benefactor back in Boston, later convicted on second-degree murder charges stemming from his relationship with Whitey, would later tell me from prison, "If it had been just Bulger on his own without Catherine, they never would have caught him."

A few days after Bulger was returned to Boston and indicted on charges that included nineteen counts of murder, I received a communication from an editor at Newsweek magazine. Would I be interested in writing about the Bulger case in a series of articles leading up to and including his trial on charges of murder and racketeering?

I was hesitant. In the sixteen years that Bulger had been on the lam, close to twenty books had been written about Whitey from every conceivable angle. Bulger's gangster history in South Boston; his relationship with brother William "Billy" Bulger, the powerful state senator; his role as an FBI informant and how he'd used that to further his criminal oper-

ations—all of these subjects had been investigated and presented in print. It seemed as though the Bulger story had been thoroughly worked over, sent to the morgue and further penetrated, probed, and dissected until the corpse no longer served any earthly purpose. And then it occurred to me: no, not exactly. There was one final chapter to the Bulger saga yet to be told: his prosecution.

Could Bulger be brought to justice, fairly and judiciously, even though his criminal activities were partly underwritten by the same criminal justice system that would now be putting him on trial? And what new or unanswered questions about Whitey might be raised or resolved by a full regurgitation of the Bulger saga in court? The possibilities were enticing. And so I packed a bag and hopped on an express train from New York City to Boston.

Beginning in early 2011, I became a semi-regular commuter, staying in Boston, usually at the Seaport Hotel on the harbor, not far from Bulger's old stomping ground of Southie, and also walking distance from the federal courthouse.

For anyone entering the orbit of the Bulger story, a mood of creepiness and depression are the likely consequence. Bulger's grip on Boston was unlike anything seen since the days of Al Capone in Chicago. Unlike Capone, whose reign was characterized by outrageous drive-by shootings and gang warfare in the streets, Bulger's reign of power was more insidious, a subterranean culture of corruption that enveloped much of the city's political and law enforcement structure and ate away at the fabric of justice from deep within the system.

While I was covering this story, some in Boston would tell me that they didn't care about the Bulger story, that it didn't really affect them or the city. They were in denial. The story of Bulger's reign and his prosecution, as much as any other public event—for better or for worse—had come to define the city of Boston over the last quarter century.

Boston can sometimes seem like a small town, and covering the Bulger story meant getting to know a circumscribed cast of former gangsters, family members of murder victims, local crime journalists, former cops, and criminal defense lawyers who seemed trapped in an ongoing horror that never ended. There were Bulger's years as Mob boss, his years on the lam, and now his prosecution, which promised to drag everyone back out into the limelight to regurgitate stories and events they thought had been put to bed decades earlier. As Pat Nee, a former criminal rival and then reluctant partner of Bulger's put it to me, "It's like being trapped in a nightmare. We just want it to all be over."

How insular was the cast of characters in the Bulger story? One time, in the lobby of the Seaport Hotel, I was interviewing the relative of a man that Bulger and an accomplice were alleged to have murdered. My next interview, also scheduled to take place in the hotel's lobby on the heels of this one, was with the person who was thought to have been Bulger's accomplice during that murder. Though it was common knowledge to many—including the victim's relative—that this man may have been an accomplice to the murder, the man had never been charged with the crime. It was nerve-wracking trying to quickly finish up the interview with the victim's relative so that the two men, victim and killer, did not stumble upon each other. Covering the Bulger story offered many potentially explosive juxtapositions.

The various articles in this section represent a mishmash of assignments and styles. Three of the articles are full-fledged investigative pieces, one a book review, another a spot reporting assignment, and another a personalized obituary written for my Internet blog page. Most of the articles were written months apart from one another and were never intended to be read back to back. If read successively, the reader will find numerous informational repetitions in these articles, a consequence of having to remind the reader of salient details and factual matters relating to the Bulger story. Also, you may notice a repeat of certain adjectives or phrases that I use as shorthand over the course of these articles to describe Bulger and his criminals activities. I was tempted to go back and reedit these pieces to make them appear more seamless for this anthology but, ultimately, felt it was a more accurate representation of my work—extremis and on deadline—to let them appear exactly as originally intended in print and on the Web.

1.

WHITEY'S PAYBACK

Newsweek, September 19, 2011

Mob boss Whitey Bulger might be behind bars, but as his trial
approaches, former associates, FBI agents, and victims' families speak
about why he might get away and how Boston has never recovered.

O f all the murders James "Whitey" Bulger is alleged to have committed in his twenty-year run as the Mob boss of Boston, the killing
of Debra Davis stands alone. Whitey is alleged to have strangled the
woman with his bare hands.

Davis, age twenty-six, was the girlfriend of Bulger's gangster partner, Steve Flemmi. Bulger and Flemmi were concerned that Davis,
a blond-haired beauty, had learned that they were both informants
for the FBI. One night in September 1981, Flemmi, forty-six at the
time, brought Davis to a house on Third Street in South Boston, or
"Southie," a tight-knit neighborhood that served as the base of Bulger
and Flemmi's criminal operations. Flemmi and Davis had been arguing. After nearly nine years together, Davis wanted out of the relationship. Flemmi wanted her out also, but not in the way Davis planned.
Waiting in the house on Third Street was Whitey Bulger, fifty-two
years old. Bulger suddenly emerged from the shadows and wrapped
his hands around Davis's throat. She struggled to break free. Squeez-
ing tightly, never letting go of her neck, Bulger dragged Davis down to
the basement, where he finished the job. Afterward, using a pair of pli-
ers, Flemmi pulled the teeth from Davis's head so that the body could

not be identified by dental records. They later trussed and wrapped up the body and dumped it in a shallow grave near the Neponset River in Quincy, Massachusetts.

Steve Davis never got the chance to say good-bye to his sister. She had disappeared seemingly without a trace. Two or three times Flemmi came to Steve's mother's house in tears, professing not to know where Debra was or why she had disappeared, but then they didn't hear from him anymore.

Looking back now, thirty years later, Steve, at age fifty-three, has some regrets. He had his own run-ins with the law, and, from neighborhood scuttlebutt and street knowledge, knew all about Bulger and Flemmi. "I tried to warn her," he remembers. "I said, 'Your boyfriend is not a nice guy. He's dangerous. People fear him.' She would say, 'Yeah. But what's he gonna do to me?' "

The Davis family suspected Bulger and Flemmi of having killed Debra, but they didn't know for sure. Debra's mother had conversations with FBI agents who claimed they were investigating the disappearance, but they seemed more interested in what she knew about Flemmi than the whereabouts of Debra. Steve wanted to talk to the FBI, to go with his mother, who was meeting with agents at strange locations and odd hours, but she said, "No." Says Steve, "When an agent told her, 'You have nine other kids to worry about now,' she took that as a threat and stopped meeting with them."

It took nearly twenty years for the Davis family to learn that Debra had been the victim of a homicide, and that Bulger and Flemmi were the culprits. The details of the killing, and Bulger and Flemmi's role as Top Echelon informants for the FBI, was revealed by Flemmi in the late-1990s, when he was arrested and later found his calling as the biggest snitch in the history of the Boston underworld. In court, Flemmi described the murder, the removal of teeth, and how they wrapped up the body of Debra Davis and buried it near the river. While Flemmi sang his treacherous song from the witness stand, Bulger was on the run, where he remained for sixteen years, living, as we've now learned, for most of that time near the beach in Santa Monica, California. When he was spectacularly apprehended last June, Bulger had $822,198 cash hidden in the wall of his condo and an arsenal of thirty guns, including semi-automatics, a machine gun, and a sawed-off shotgun.

Steve Davis remembers the day he received word they had captured Whitey. A cousin called: "They got him!" Davis watched the early reports of Bulger being transferred from Santa Monica, where he had been cohabitating with his female companion, Catherine Greig, while on the lam. He heard of the multitude of charges that Bulger would now be facing. Davis thought then and still thinks: *It's not a done deal. With the power Bulger has had in politics and with the FBI, he could find a way to manipulate the situation to his advantage.* Now Davis is less fixated on what will happen to Bulger in court than he is on what he'd do to Bulger if he got his hands on him.

"I'm an eye for eye kind of guy," says Davis. "I'd do to him what he did to my sister. . . . They talk about closure. Fuck closure. Give me fifteen minutes with Bulger and I'll give him closure. I'll shoot him in the fuckin' head."

In Boston these days, revenge is a dish best served cold. Since last June, when news of the capture of Bulger and Greig first settled over the city like a bad weather pattern, the city has been stewing in its own juices. Family members of Bulger's many victims (he is charged with nineteen murders) have been vocal in their demands that the full weight of the criminal justice system be brought to bear on Whitey. Federal prosecutors have begun strategizing: In July, all of the racketeering counts in the indictment against Bulger were dropped, so that the U.S. attorney's prosecution team can zero in on the multiple murder charges. The thinking is, this way, the road to justice will be accelerated and less encumbered by Bulger's staggering multitude of criminal acts stretching back to the mid-1960s and across the country with outstanding murder indictments in Florida and Oklahoma.

Justice in court is one thing and outside the courtroom something else entirely. Forty years ago, when Jim Bulger first rose to power in the city's organized crime structure, he did so as the result of a gangland revenge war that lasted almost a decade. From the mid-1960s to the mid-1970s, mobsters and innocent bystanders were shot, knifed, strangled, and mangled. Sixty-six murders were attributed to this internecine gang war, a tit-for-tat series of killings that were more about underworld retribution than anything else.

When it was all over, in 1975, Bulger emerged as a key powerbroker. It was also around this time that he secretly began to work as an informant for the FBI, under the supervision of Special Agent John Connolly. Bulger fed Connolly information about the local Mafia, with whom Bulger did business. In return, Connolly tipped off Whitey about local law enforcement investigations in which he was a target, which gave Bulger a tremendous edge throughout his long criminal career.

And then there was the brother, State Senator William "Billy" Bulger, who for close to twenty years was the most powerful politician in state government. Billy sometimes ran interference for Whitey by inquiring about law enforcement investigations involving his brother and making implied threats.

Over the decades, untold people, both criminals and average citizens, were drawn into and/or burned by what the *Boston Globe* christened "the Bulger Mystique." Many are now looking for justice. But to those who know Whitey best, their concern is how Bulger might try to use his current predicament to exact revenge on his enemies.

"Since at least the early 1990s, he's had a strategy for when he got pinched," says Kevin Weeks, who stood alongside Bulger as his right-hand man when the gangster was at the height of his power. "It's his nature to be manipulative. Machiavellian. He'll be looking to hurt people who hurt him. To even scores. He will want to rewrite history."

At one point in his life, Weeks looked up to Bulger as if he were a big brother, or an uncle. At the age of nineteen, he was handpicked by Whitey to serve as his "muscle." When Bulger wanted someone physically threatened or assaulted, Weeks was his man. Brawny and physically capable, Weeks broke bones, once beating a man who owed Bulger money so brutally that he shattered the bones in his own hand.

Weeks was also frequently called upon to help Bulger and Flemmi dispose of the bodies of their many murder victims.

In 1999, after Bulger went on the run and Flemmi began to spill his guts to the Feds, Weeks cut his own deal with the government. He literally told investigators where the bodies were buried, including the body of Debra Davis, who Weeks had helped bury. Weeks testified in court and served five years in prison. He was paroled in 2004 and lives once again in Southie.

Of his time with Bulger, Weeks says, "I ain't gonna lie to you, I had some exciting times with the guy. We had fun out on the street. But then we all found out he was a rat for the FBI. I felt betrayed. And for a while I was angry. But I've had time to think about things. Mostly, I blame myself."

What Weeks remembers best about Bulger is this: "He was a hard guy, tough as nails. A stone-cold killer. I know he's eighty-two now, but still, he's in great shape, mentally strong. I hear they've got him in protective custody to protect him from other inmates. But don't put it past him: He might try to kill somebody himself. Put a shank in his hand, and he'd know what to do with it."

Richard Marinick is another former South Boston criminal who had dealings with Bulger. Marinick is unique. In the early 1980s, he was a Massachusetts state trooper. He then crossed over to the other side of the law and became a criminal, a robber of armored cars. Eventually, Marinick got busted on an armed robbery charge and served ten years at the Massachusetts Correctional Institution in Norfolk, but before that he had numerous encounters with Bulger.

It was a rule of the Boston underworld that any criminal activity that took place in Whitey's jurisdiction, he was supposed to get a cut. Bulger heard that Marinick's crew was making scores locally, and he wanted a piece of the action. Remembers Marinick, "I'm walking along the street in Southie one day, and Bulger's car pulls up. He says, 'Get in.' I'm sitting in the backseat, face-to-face with Jimmy. He says, 'You're a health nut, right, a healthy guy?' Bulger was into good health, eating right, taking vitamin supplements; we'd talked about it before. 'Well,' he says, 'what you're doing now is not very healthy.' He explained to me, 'Our primary line of business is racketeering. Our secondary line of business is killing people. You do not want to be part of our secondary line of business. . . . I will kill you and run your body through the meat-grinding plant. I will grind up your body, put it in a plastic bag and leave it on your mother's doorstep.' "

The whole time Marinick was receiving this threat from the city's preeminent Mob boss, he noticed that he was wearing a chain around his neck—on the outside of his T-shirt—that had on it a silver Christ's head with two red rubies on either side. "As he's yelling at me, I see that Christ head looking at me and, I swear, it looked like those two red rubies were glowing."

As a negotiator, Bulger's tactics were simple. "He absolutely terrified people, made them literally piss and shit in their pants," says Marinick. "His high was making people afraid of him; that's how he got pleasure from what he did."

Marinick, like Weeks, sees Bulger as an obsessive manipulator and schemer, proclivities he is now likely to apply to his current predicament as an incarcerated criminal and potential defendant.

Among criminals in Boston who interacted with Bulger both as a rival and a partner, few were in as privileged a position as Patrick Nee. Like Bulger, Nee grew up in South Boston at a time when it was very much an insular Irish enclave. A former Marine who served in Vietnam in the early-1960s, Nee returned home in 1965 just as the Boston gang wars were heating up. He was a prominent member of the Mullen Gang, who clashed with Bulger's crew, led by the Killeen brothers, Donald, Eddie, and Kenneth. On multiple occasions, Nee and Bulger tried to kill one another, with Whitey shooting at Nee and Nee stalking Bulger with a rifle. Today, whenever he is asked if he has any regrets in life, Nee responds, "I wish I'd killed Whitey Bulger when I had the opportunity."

By the 1980s, Nee was in business with Bulger. They took part in an arms-smuggling operation in an attempt to send weapons to the Irish Republican Army. Nee was arrested and served eight years in prison. Afterward, Nee began to have suspicions about Bulger. "I knew something wasn't right," he says. "Others were getting arrested and sent to jail, but Bulger and Flemmi never seemed to get touched. We knew they had a relationship with Connolly; our understanding was that they were paying Connolly, he was on the take. But we didn't know Whitey and Stevie were rats, supplying Connolly and the feds with information about us."

Whitey's power, says Nee, was based on his ability to play the game. "He was a master at keeping everyone in the dark. He had his relationship with Howie Winter in Somerville, with the Italians in the North End, with us in Southie. And he made sure we didn't know what he was doing with those other groups."

When asked what Bulger will do now that he's been caught and faces seemingly insurmountable charges, Nee says, "All I know is that Bulger probably planned for this. He was always five or six steps ahead of everybody else."

Bulger may want to exact revenge and manipulate his current predicament, but the question remains: Does he have any cards to play? His court-appointed attorney is J. W. Carney, a respected Boston lawyer known as the Patron Saint of Hopeless Cases. Carney's last big case involved John Salvi, who shot up two abortion clinics in suburban Boston, killing two and injuring others. Salvi was found guilty at trial and sentenced to life without parole. Currently, Carney's law firm is pouring over more than 17,000 pages of discovery material related to the Bulger case delivered to them by the U.S. Attorney's Office. At a press conference in front of the Moakley courthouse in Boston, Carney told reporters, "I am always at the direction of my client, and I will do whatever Mr. Bulger instructs me to do."

Bulger's choices are limited. He could possibly plead guilty to the murder charges in exchange for a better deal for Greig, his companion, who is facing five years in prison for aiding and abetting a fugitive. He might also cop a plea to avoid the death penalty, like Flemmi did. Or he could throw a Hail Mary pass and go to trial.

Paul Griffin is an attorney who represented the family of Debra Davis in a civil lawsuit against the FBI and U.S. government. The suit alleged that the Davis family and other families of Bulger and Flemmi's victims were entitled to damages, since the U.S. Justice Department had virtually underwritten the criminal careers of two notorious mobsters. Griffin is a former Boston cop. He believes that Whitey currently faces insurmountable odds. "Any plea that he agrees to, he gets a telephone pole shoved up the ass. If he goes to trial, he gets a telephone pole shoved up the ass."

Bulger's maneuverability is hindered by the fact that all of his criminal co-conspirators have already cut deals with the feds. Flemmi pleaded guilty to ten murders in October 2003 and was spared a lethal injection in exchange for his testimony. He is currently serving a life term in prison. Johnny Martorano, another prolific hit man who did murders with Bulger, confessed to twenty killings in 1999. In exchange for his testimony, he received a light fourteen-year prison sentence and was released in 2007. Kevin Weeks also cut an immunity deal with the feds, and will likely be called to testify against his former mentor in the Boston underworld.

"I hope Bulger enjoyed his years on the run," says Anthony Cardinale, a criminal defense attorney who was among the first to uncover the Bulger-Connolly informant relationship. "Because now he's late to the game. All of the others have made their deals, told their version of events. Bulger is facing a solid wall of discovery evidence going back decades, and there's no one left for him to take down."

For many, the deep stain of the Bulger years will never be expunged until his alliance with the government is exposed and supervising agents in the FBI are prosecuted or at least publicly excoriated. Bulger's case agent, John Connolly, is in prison on obstruction of justice and second-degree murder charges stemming from his relationship with Bulger. Connolly's supervisor, John Morris, pleaded guilty to taking $7,000 in bribes and gifts from Bulger; he was granted immunity in exchange for his testimony. But others in the FBI and the political arena who facilitated Bulger's "unholy alliance," from Boston to Washington, D.C., have never been held accountable.

Retired FBI agent Robert Fitzpatrick, a lonely voice during the Bulger years who tried to call attention to corruption in the bureau's Boston office, has always maintained that the culpability should be spread far and wide. "I don't believe in the rogue agent theory," he says. "Connelly didn't do it alone. His dealings with Bulger were facilitated by the entire system."

For nearly a decade, Fitzpatrick tried to right the ship. A veteran special agent who served at the Academy as an instructor on how to develop informants, Fitzpatrick was sent to Boston by his supervisors to evaluate Bugler's "suitability" as an informant. Specifically, there had been complaints by the Massachusetts State Police that an investigation they had initiated into Bulger's gambling operations was being undermined by the Boston FBI, who were leaking confidential details to Bulger.

Fitzpatrick was brought by John Morris, who supervised the FBI's organized crime squad in Boston, to see Bulger at his condo in Quincy. "On the way there, in the car, Morris can't stop telling me what a great guy Bulger is. He was overselling the guy, which made me suspicious."

When Fitzpatrick met Bulger, the Mob boss was wearing a Red Sox's baseball cap and sunglasses, even though they were indoors, standing in Bulger's kitchen. Fitzpatrick extended his hand for Bulger to shake, but Whitey would not shake his hand. "He proceeds to tell me what a tough guy he is, starts bragging about his prison experiences in Leavenworth and Alcatraz." Bulger bristled when Fitzpatrick referred to him as an informant; he made it clear that although he would supply the agents with underworld scuttlebutt, he would not testify in court.

"I got the impression that he was withholding," says Fitzpatrick. "The meeting was a half hour to forty-five minutes. I cut it short. It was clear to me that Bulger could not be trusted, and that he likely had a propensity for violence. He was dangerous."

The FBI agent filed a two-page report recommending that Bulger be "closed" as a confidential informant. Not only was the report overruled, but thus began a long period in which Bulger-related cases initiated by Fitzpatrick were mysteriously derailed. "We had four Bulger-related informants murdered, as we now know, by Bulger and Flemmi. Information about CIs was leaked to Bulger by our own people in law enforcement." After five years of trying to close Bulger, Fitzpatrick became frustrated. "I was becoming a pain in the ass to people. I was bucking the tide. I started to feel as though I wasn't part of the team. I lost my trust in the system."

In the years since the Bulger House of Horrors began to unravel, Fitzpatrick has emerged as a rare good guy in the story, and his concerns have been proven correct. Now, Fitzpatrick worries that Bulger will resume his Svengali-like gaming of the system. "This guy controlled the entire criminal justice system in the state of Massachusetts. And he's still got that attitude. He's going to be cute. He's going to try to manipulate people, just as he's always done."

Like many people who had encounters with Jim Bulger over the years, Fitzpatrick is clear about how he would like to see things play out for the most infamous mobster in Boston history. "I hope they fry the bastard," he says.

The prospect of a trial has many in Boston licking their chops. Howie Carr, a popular radio personality and author of a bestselling book on the Bulger brothers, thinks that a long criminal proceeding with many witnesses would be good for the city. "There are still a lot of loose ends," he says.

Of all the loose ends relating to the Bulger story, some of the most intriguing involve Billy Bulger. "I would like to see Billy indicted," says Carr. The feeling among many is that Whitey would do almost anything to protect his brother.

With subpoenas being rendered and grand jury hearings underway, the U.S. Attorney's Office appears to be focusing on who may have aided Bulger while he was a fugitive. Fresh criminal charges stemming from Bulger's years on the run could be used to implicate others, perhaps, say, Billy Bulger, which would aid prosecutors in their efforts to demythologize the Bulger Mystique once and for all.

Meanwhile, Bulger is locked away at Plymouth County Correctional Facility. He has a lot to be concerned about, given that his life literally hangs in the balance. But according to those familiar with Bulger from his years as boss of the Boston underworld, he is likely hunkered down, feeling vengeful, while plotting to get even.

2.

THE MAN WHO SAW THROUGH WHITEY

The Daily Beast, January 27, 2012

For more than twenty years, crime boss Whitey Bulger was protected by the FBI. Now former agent Robert Fitzpatrick tells his story of trying to stop the gangster and why the FBI wouldn't listen.

In the two decades that James "Whitey" Bulger served as a secret FBI informant while extorting citizens, peddling cocaine and killing people to protect his Boston-based criminal empire, there is only one federal agent who tried seriously to shut him down: Robert Fitzpatrick.

For his efforts, Fitzpatrick was frustrated at every turn, not by Bulger and his fellow gangsters, but by his own, the FBI.

After being introduced to Bulger in 1981, Fitzpatrick warned his regional supervisor that Whitey was "sociopathic . . . untrustworthy . . . likely to commit violence" and suggested that he be "closed" as an informant. Not only were his memos and recommendations ignored, some in the FBI sought to discredit Fitzpatrick and destroy his reputation.

The aggrieved former G-man finally has the opportunity to tell his side of the story in *Betrayal*, an explosive memoir of his years as assistant special agent in charge of the FBI's Boston office. The book has the feel of an ongoing therapy session, as Fitzpatrick seeks to make sense of a sprawling conspiracy of agents, cops, judges, criminals, and politicians who for decades enabled Bulger and made it possible for his campaign of corruption and terror to infect an entire city. Currently,

Bulger awaits trial on nineteen counts of murder, after having been on the lam for sixteen years.

It is a sickening story, one that Fitzpatrick and his coauthor Jon Land allow to unfold slowly, like a toxic oil spill that envelopes and destroys the surrounding ecosystem—in this case, the entire criminal justice system of the state of Massachusetts.

It is now common knowledge that Special Agent John Connolly, Bulger's primary handler in the Bureau who is presently in prison on murder charges, and former state senator William "Billy" Bulger, Whitey's powerful politician brother, formed a support system that made it possible for the Bulger era to sustain itself. But in *Betrayal*, Fitzpatrick broadens the conspiracy, detailing the culpability of a vast matrix of enablers, including, most notably, the late Jeremiah T. O'Sullivan, who, as lead prosecutor for the state's Organized Crime Strike Force, undermined potential prosecutions of both Whitey and Billy Bulger, and Lawrence Sarhatt and James Greenleaf, successive special agents in charge of the FBI's Boston office, who buried reports, including Fitzpatrick's recommendation that Bulger be "closed" as an informant.

Fitzpatrick does not attempt to portray himself as a hero; the dominant tone of the book is one of frustration and astonishment as the author, who was sent to Boston by FBI headquarters in Washington, D.C., with the expressed task of evaluating Bulger's "suitability" as a Top Echelon informant, encounters malfeasance and corruption at every level.

Early in the book, he describes being a young boy at the infamous Mount Loretto orphanage in Staten Island, New York, where he encountered bullies and institutional abuse. Late at night, he sought solace by laying in the dark and listening to the popular radio program *This Is Your FBI*. Fitzpatrick's belief in the FBI as both an avenue of personal salvation and an institutional force for justice haunts the book, as the reality of corruption and careerism crushes his idealism much the same way Bulger strangled, shot, and mutilated his murder victims.

Fitzpatrick came to Boston well suited to deal with subterfuge and corruption. He had gone undercover in the Deep South in the mid-

1960s in an attempt to penetrate and bring down white supremacist organizations. In the 1970s, he'd been one of the lead agents on the ABSCAM investigation, a sting operation involving corrupt public officials that led to numerous high-profile arrests, including the indictment of a sitting U.S. senator.

In Boston, Fitzpatrick spent nearly a decade trying to unravel what he calls "the Bulger arrangement." As a veteran G-man who had trained budding agents on the proper cultivation of criminal informants at the FBI academy in Quantico, Virginia, he recognized all the telltale signs of a disaster in the making. He saw that Connolly and his supervisor, John Morris, were too close to Bulger. Also, as Fitzpatrick noted to anyone who would listen, the Bulger situation violated one of the most basic tenets of informant cultivation: The proper strategy with informants is to get someone mid-level who can help take down the boss and therefore an entire organization. You cannot have an organized crime kingpin as an informant, because it is inevitable that person will choose to manipulate the information they reveal to their handlers as a way of *staying* in power.

When it became apparent to Fitzpatrick that his warnings about the Bulger relationship were being ignored, he sought to build his own cases against the Mob boss. He developed informants like Brian Halloran, a sad-sack career thug who worked for Bulger, and John McIntyre, a naive Irish Republican Army (IRA) sympathizer who partnered with Bulger on a scheme to send guns to Northern Ireland in exchange for shipments of marijuana and cocaine. Agents in Fitzpatrick's own office leaked information to Bulger about the informants; Halloran and McIntyre were both brutally murdered by Bulger, as were other informants whose identities were compromised and revealed to local gangsters by Connolly and Morris.

In the end, Fitzpatrick's reputation within the Bureau as a potential whistleblower and general "pain in the ass" began to wear him down. It took a personal toll on him and his wife. Fitzpatrick began to get the sense that Bulger and his gangster partner Steve Flemmi, who was also a longtime FBI informant, were more important to the local office than he was. "Apparently, Bulger and Flemmi were the FBI's 'guys' while I, somehow, wasn't," writes Fitzpatrick. "While busting [the Mafia] remained every bit a top priority in Washington, my efforts and accomplishments were being demeaned by a group-think mentality that led to a scenario of 'us versus them,' with me inexplicably linked with 'them.' "

When Fitzpatrick, frustrated and disillusioned, resigned from the Bureau in 1987, the full dimensions of Bulger's partnership with the FBI was not yet known, even to the agent. It wasn't until the late-1990s, when Bulger went on the lam allegedly after being tipped off by his FBI contacts that he was about to be arrested, that the truth started to come out. In a series of hearings and depositions, the Bulger cohorts who were left behind turned "rat" and testified in court. In a groundbreaking hearing presided over by federal judge Mark Wolf, Fitzpatrick testified, and for the first time the story of his efforts to rectify the Bureau's sinister alliance with Bulger began to take shape.

In January 2000, after Whitey's right-hand man provided details on a series of murders, including where the bodies were buried, Fitzpatrick stood in the rain alongside Dorchester gully as the remains of John McIntyre, his one-time informant, were dug up. "As I stood on that embankment," writes Fitzpatrick, "steaming over confirmation of what I'd suspected ever since John McIntyre had disappeared in 1984, I never imagined I was looking at the means to achieve my long sought vindication."

Fitzpatrick's vindication would come in court, where he testified as part of a civil lawsuit brought by the McIntyre family—and other families of Bulger's victims—against the FBI and the U.S. government for having underwritten Bulger's murderous criminal career. In 2006, the McIntyre family was awarded $3.1 million in damages. All told, litigation from cases related to the Bulger debacle would result in damages more than $20 million.

Betrayal provides the most complete overview to date of the culture of corruption that made Bulger possible. Fitzpatrick names names and offers an appendix filled with FBI memos, letters, and excerpts from depositions and court proceedings. The cumulative effect is a devastating reaffirmation of the findings of a U.S. congressional committee that declared the Bulger-FBI relationship to represent "one of the greatest failures in the history of federal law enforcement."

The final chapter on Bulger has not yet been written. Whitey is scheduled to stand trial sometime in 2012, and Fitzpatrick will likely be called to testify.

In this sordid saga of homicidal gangsters and dirty federal agents, Fitzpatrick's perspective—and his book—offers a rare beacon of light.

3.

THE UNLIKELY MOLL

The Daily Beast, March 14, 2012

Catherine Greig's guilty plea means she is unlikely to receive more than
thirty-two months in jail for conspiracy and identity fraud—an outcome
that outraged relatives of the victims of boyfriend James "Whitey"
Bulger's many alleged murders.

You can hardly hear the voice of Catherine Greig, sixty, longtime
paramour of notorious gangster James "Whitey" Bulger, as she
stands before a federal judge and says the words, "Guilty, your honor."

Dressed in blue prison fatigues over a long-sleeved white T-shirt,
her gray hair cropped short, Greig is a figment of her former self.
An attractive woman who once lavished money on various surgical
procedures to further enhance her beauty, Greig's vanities have been
punctured—if not decimated—by nine months of maximum-security
incarceration. The permanent tan she acquired after sixteen years on
the lam with Bulger in such sunny climes as the Gulf Coast of Louisi-
ana and Santa Monica, California—where she and the Most Wanted
gangster were apprehended in June—is long gone now, replaced by the
permanent gray pallor of a convict.

As had been leaked to the media earlier in the week, Greig is in
U.S. District Court in Boston to plead guilty to charges of conspiracy
to harbor a fugitive, conspiracy to commit identity fraud, and identity
fraud. By signing a statement that she "engaged in conduct that was
intended to help Bulger avoid detection from law enforcement and

to provide him with support and assistance during his flight from law enforcement," Greig avoids a trial and any further charges U.S. Attorney Carmen Ortiz may have been planning on bringing against her.

Bulger, currently in prison at the Plymouth County Correctional Facility, faces nineteen counts of murder stemming from his twenty-year reign as the Mob boss of Boston. After being indicted on racketeering charges and fleeing with Greig in January 1995, it was revealed that Bulger also had been a confidential FBI informant since 1975.

Last June, when Bulger and Greig were arrested in Santa Monica—after a tip from a woman who had spotted Greig at a local beauty parlor—federal agents found an arsenal of weapons on the premises, along with more than $800,000 in cash hidden in the wall of their apartment.

Known as a bright but subservient woman, Greig is believed to have had little involvement in Bulger's life as a racketeer. She enjoyed the financial largesse of his criminal pursuits without having to partake of his crimes, until they set out together on the lam. For sixteen years, Bulger and Greig lived as con artists, opening bank accounts and making medical appointments and purchases under false identities, using stolen birth certificates and Social Security numbers to create fraudulent identities.

Wednesday, at the Moakley Courthouse in Boston, Greig was brought into court in handcuffs, which were removed once she was seated at the defense table. The hearing lasted just over one hour. Greig showed emotion only once, when Judge Douglas Woodlock asked her a series of routine questions about her health.

"Have you ever sought or been through psychiatric evaluation or therapy?" asked the judge.

"One time," said Greig. She attempted to explain that she sought therapy following the suicide of a family member but was too overcome with emotion to finish her sentence. As Greig wept openly, her attorney, Kevin Reddington, seated beside her at the defense table, patted her on her shoulder.

Greig regained her composure and listened without emotion as prosecutor Jack Pirozzolo outlined details of the charges against her. Later, after it was explained to Greig that she could still be called to testify in a criminal proceeding against Bulger, and that her sentencing would be determined by the judge irrespective of the guilty plea, Judge Woodlock asked, "Do you understand that?"

"I do, Your Honor," responded Greig.

After Greig entered her plea and the hearing ended, she was again handcuffed by a court officer. On the way out of court, she waved to her twin sister, Margaret McCusker, who had observed the proceeding from the front row of the spectators' gallery.

Outside the courtroom, family members of victims of Bulger's many alleged murders vented their frustration. Steve Davis, brother of Debra Davis, who, at the age of twenty-six, was allegedly strangled to death by Bulger, called Greig "a monster." In an exclusive interview with the *Daily Beast*, Davis said, "For thirty years, my family has been waiting for justice to prevail. That woman helped keep a mass murderer at large. She knew exactly what she was doing. She doesn't deserve a break."

U.S. Attorney Ortiz, speaking to the press following the hearing, denied that Greig had received any kind of "sweetheart deal." Said Ortiz, "We believe that bringing this to a swift conviction is in the best interest of justice."

Ortiz noted that Greig faces a maximum charge of five years on each count to which she pleaded guilty. The sentences, however, would run concurrently, meaning that even if she receives the maximum sentence, Greig is unlikely to receive more than thirty-two months, of which she has already served nine.

Says Steve Davis, "For sixteen years, the families been paying for her actions, suffering, not knowing. For what? So Catherine Greig can be back on the street in two years? It ain't fair."

Greig is due back in Judge Woodlock's courtroom to be sentenced on June 12.

4.

WHITEY'S WOMEN

The Daily Beast, June 11, 2012

As Catherine Greig awaits sentencing for helping fugitive Whitey Bulger, she becomes the latest girlfriend of the Mob boss to suffer for her love. T. J. English exclusively speaks to "the other woman" in the Bulger saga, Teresa Stanley, and other mobster ex-girlfriends about the terror and glamour of their lives.

When Catherine Greig, girlfriend and fugitive partner of gangster James "Whitey" Bulger walks into U.S. District Court in Boston this week, she will face her moment of reckoning. After sixteen years on the lam with Bulger, most of those years spent living in an apartment in Santa Monica, California, under assumed names and false identities, Greig, age sixty, pleaded guilty three months ago to charges of identity fraud and harboring a fugitive. She is expected to receive a sentence somewhere between three and five years. Having already served one year in prison, she could walk free in thirty-three months. Not bad, considering that some of the women who entered the realm of Bulger and his gangster partner, Steve Flemmi, were strangled to death and buried in a shallow grave.

When twenty-six-year-old Debra Davis sought to end her relationship with Flemmi, she was lured to an apartment on Third Street in South Boston and strangled in the basement, allegedly by Bulger. Four years later, a similar fate befell Deborah Hussey, also twenty-six, Flemmi's stepdaughter from a relationship with his common-law wife, Marion Hussey. When Deborah Hussey openly accused Flemmi of having sexually molested her as a teenager, she wound up garroted by Bulger, her teeth extracted, and her body dumped in a grave not far from Whitey's condominium in Quincy, Massachusetts.

The killings are disturbing enough, but for the women who circulated in the orbit of Bulger and Flemmi, there were other costs. Appearing in U.S. District Court for her guilty plea, Greig seemed fragile and traumatized. Her voice rarely rose above a whisper. When asked by the judge if she had ever sought psychiatric counseling, Greig wept openly.

At least two other women who had relationships with Bulger and Flemmi can identify with the state of post-traumatic stress that Greig might be experiencing. To them, her story is a cautionary tale. These women also could have wound up dead, or on the run with a murderous gangster and psychotic control freak, or in prison awaiting sentencing. Instead, they are alive and free, though, like Greig, they carry with them a lifetime's worth of psychological baggage from their years of deceit and paranoia as the girlfriends of underworld criminals.

For nearly twenty years, Teresa Stanley has endured a checkered legacy as "the other woman" in the Whitey Bulger saga. Her feelings about this are mixed. On one hand, she regrets that she was ever any kind of woman to Whitey Bulger, a man who romanced, dominated, and then betrayed her. On the other hand, she resents being known as a second-class paramour when, in fact, she lived with Bulger for thirty years. If anything, Stanley believes it was Catherine Greig who was the other woman.

"It's hard to live with," says Stanley. "Not only did I share my life with a man who is now accused of these terrible things. But he deceived and betrayed me by having this other life with Catherine. He humiliated me in the eyes of the town."

In the media, Stanley is often portrayed as Whitey's attractive but dumb common-law wife. At age seventy, her fresh, girl-next-door good looks have faded, but she is certainly not dumb. In two separate interview sessions, Stanley—who rarely talks to the media—was thoughtful and reflective, as she looked back over her thirty-year relationship with a man whose criminal history, and upcoming trial, has riveted the city.

"To me, he was just Jimmy, the man I lived with," she says. "I never thought of him the way other people do."

Bulger and Stanley are both products of Southie, a close-knit, mostly Irish Catholic enclave nestled along the Boston waterfront at Castle Island. When Stanley first met Bulger, in 1966, she was a twenty-six-year-old woman with four children. Bulger had recently returned to Boston from a stint in prison on armed robbery charges. Stanley had no idea that he'd also once been charged with rape, in Montana, during a stint in the air force in the 1950s. Bulger was not rich at the time or the mobster of legend that he would later become. To her, he was a strong male figure offering to play a significant and much-needed role in her life as a protector and father figure to her children.

"There was a strong physical attraction," says Stanley. "He was very handsome. And he was classy, always looked sharp, everything in place. He liked quality. He used to brag about the value of things he owned, a watch or shoes or whatever. And he was smart. He could intimidate people with his intelligence. He used big words, spoke in complete sentences with proper grammar. You couldn't win an argument with Jimmy; he was too smart. When I watched him with other people, he stood out. He was a leader. I thought, *Gosh, maybe some of that will rub off on me.*"

Bulger told Stanley, "With me, you will never have to work a day in your life. I will take care of you. I will be a father to your children. I will provide for your every need." In return, Bulger had Stanley learn to cook, "though I never really liked it." He set her up in a home in Southie and made sure she kept it spotless. He turned her into the woman he wanted her to be.

Stanley knew her boyfriend was some type of criminal. Southie had a long tradition of gangsters and racketeers going back to the Prohibition era, when illegal booze was off-loaded at Carson Beach. She believed he made his money from illegal gambling and maybe loan-sharking. She heard stories that he had killed people during the Boston gang wars of the early-1960s. This did not dissuade her.

"It could be exciting," she admits. "You walk into a restaurant or neighborhood place, and everyone notices you. You get the best tables. People treat you like you are special. It's very easy to be seduced by that."

Given that Bulger was a professional criminal, there was a lot of secrecy in his life. Though he usually checked in with Teresa, he could be gone for days at a time. Stanley had no idea that, along with being a rising star in the city's criminal underworld, Whitey and his partner Flemmi were both confidential informants for the FBI.

By the late-1970s, Bulger and Flemmi used their secret relationship with law enforcement authorities as a way to eliminate underworld rivals and take over the rackets in Boston. They allegedly fed information to the FBI and U.S. Attorney's Office, making it possible for prosecutors to take down the most powerful Mafia family in Boston. Bulger and Flemmi became gods of the underworld. Virtually any criminal operating in Boston or the New England area paid tribute to them.

Stanley knew little about this, mostly by choice. She avoided newspaper articles about Bulger, though sometimes neighborhood rumors were hard to ignore. In the late-1980s, when a cocaine operation in Southie was broken up, leading to many arrests and prosecutions, neighborhood people asked an obvious question: How could this level of criminal activity be taking place without Whitey knowing about it and getting a piece of the action? Whitey told Teresa, "You'll hear rumors, but let me ask you: Have you ever seen me around drugs? Have you ever seen me spending time with the kind of people who use or deal drugs?"

Stanley chose to believe Whitey. Later, it would be revealed that Bulger—who often bragged that he was keeping cocaine, heroin, and other hard drugs out of Southie—was, in fact, receiving a cut of all major dope transactions in the area.

The money rolled in. Stanley remembers being given the opportunity to select diamond rings, necklaces, and other goodies from boxes of jewelry, likely the bounty from robberies. Whitey paid for the house, school for the kids, and all other bills. Every week she was given an envelope filled with $500 cash, her "table money" for personal use.

Stanley and Bulger took trips to Europe and around the United States, always staying at the best hotels.

But there were problems. "He could be a very difficult man," she says of Bulger. He was a control freak with an unpredictable temper. In attempting to be a father to Stanley's four children, he was a harsh disciplinarian. The kids were grounded for minor infractions and sometimes physically threatened. Bulger ran background checks on the families of people Stanley's daughters were dating. He clashed especially hard with Stanley's oldest son, Billy, who both worshipped and despised Bulger.

Then there was Bulger's temper. Stanley remembers one time they were in a hotel elevator and she exchanged pleasantries about the weather with another passenger. When they arrived in the lobby, Bulger grabbed Teresa by the arm and looked at her with eyes that could kill. "Don't you ever make eye contact with another man like that ever again." Another time, when she mentioned she'd helped a friend move some boxes into a car and accepted a twenty-dollar payment, Bulger went ballistic, calling her "low class" and a "whore." Says Stanley, "You never knew what was going to set him off. It was unpredictable. I was afraid to say anything that would get him going. So mostly I said nothing."

Although Bulger never struck Stanley, he was physically menacing. He grabbed and pushed and threatened like a true gangster. Stanley's fear of Bulger was such that whenever she smoked a cigarette—which Bulger, a health nut, was adamantly opposed to—she would have to sneak it when he was wasn't around.

By the early 1990s, Stanley began to crack under the years of control and psychological domination. She and Bulger were arguing constantly, sometimes violently, at home and in public. Once, at a wedding party, Teresa was approached by Bulger's partner, Flemmi, who said, "Teresa, I know you and Jimmy are going through a rough patch, but there's something you need to understand. That man will never let you go."

Stanley felt trapped. She went into a deep depression. She had become financially and emotionally dependent on Bulger; she could see no way out. Then, the "other woman" entered the picture.

Stanley was home alone one night when she got a call. An unfamiliar female voice said, "I think we need to talk."

Teresa agreed to meet the woman. At a designated location, they arrived by car. A window rolled down and Teresa saw Catherine Greig, whom she did not know. When Teresa sat in the passenger seat of Greig's car, she asked, "What is this all about? Who are you?"

Catherine answered, "I'm Jimmy's girlfriend."

Teresa suspected there had been other women, floosies, she assumed, who Bulger used for sex and then discarded. She asked Catherine, "For how long?" thinking the answer would be three or four months.

"Twenty years," said Catherine.

Teresa felt as if she'd been kicked in the stomach. She and Catherine drove back to the condominium in Quincy where Whitey had set up an entirely separate domestic life with Greig. There, Greig told her the entire story of her long relationship with Bulger. Says Stanley, "Here's the man I have a life with, he's been a father to my kids, walked my daughter down the aisle on her wedding day, I've devoted my whole life to him—and he has this entirely other life!"

As Stanley was absorbing this information, in walked Whitey, with his gangster underling Kevin Weeks.

Bulger had no idea that Greig had contacted Stanley and deliberately blown his cover. When he saw the two women together, he exploded. Remembers Stanley, "He grabbed Catherine around the neck and started choking. 'You bitch, what have you done?' She shoved him back. He fell over the arm of the couch and grabbed the Venetian blinds, accidentally tearing them down." Catherine pointed at Teresa and shouted at Jimmy, "I can't believe you put this woman in the same ballpark as me!"

Now Teresa was irate. *The same ballpark!* "I lived with this man for thirty years, and here they are talking about me like I was nothing."

Kevin Weeks, who had been at Bulger's side during murders and the disposal of bodies, vividly remembers the incident. "It was wild. I thought Jimmy was gonna kill Catherine. I grabbed him to stop him from choking her. Teresa didn't want to leave, but I grabbed her, too, and got her out of there."

In the wake of this incident, Bulger supposedly ended the relationship with Greig. He said to Stanley, "I see I've been hard on you. Let's go on a trip. Anywhere you want to go."

In December 1994, Bulger and Stanley set out on a drive across the country. It was supposed to be a one-month trip all the way to California. As they drove through the Midwest, Stanley stared out the window at the passing scenery. She had fallen deeper into depression, feeling that she was hopelessly trapped in an abusive relationship.

When they pulled off the road and into a lodge for an overnight stay, Bulger could see that Teresa was upset. "Why the sour puss?" She seethed and said, "Maybe it's because I belong in some other ballpark." Then she did something she'd never done in the thirty years her and Bulger were together. She pulled out a cigarette, lit it, and puffed away, right in front of Whitey. It was her way of saying, "This charade is over. I want to go home."

On the drive back to Massachusetts, Stanley and Bulger heard over the car radio that Steve Flemmi had been arrested and Bulger was being sought by a federal task force. They detoured to New York City. From there, Bulger communicated with underlings back in Boston, determining he would have to go on the lam. He asked Teresa to accompany him. "I knew it was a mistake. My mother told me not to do it. But where I come from loyalty is an important value. I'd spent thirty years with this man. He needed me."

Stanley said she would do it, but then the depression set in again. She had four children and a whole lifetime of relationships she would be leaving behind. She couldn't do it. She told Whitey she wanted to go home.

Under cover of darkness, they drove back toward Boston. Late one night, Stanley was dropped off at her daughter's house in Hingham. She never saw Bulger again. He drove immediately to Malibu Beach, in Dorchester, where he'd made arrangements to pick up Catherine Greig.

Teresa Stanley's thirty-year personal relationship with Whitey Bulger was over, but the repercussions of that relationship continued. With Bulger on the FBI's Ten Most Wanted list right behind Osama Bin Laden, Stanley was hounded by the FBI. She and her family were under constant surveillance. As details about her former boyfriend's criminal life exploded into the public domain through sensational revelations in court, her feelings of betrayal deepened. Eventually, she cooperated with investigators by giving them information about one of Bulger's aliases, Thomas Baxter, which led them to seize a bank account in Tampa, Florida, one of many Bulger had opened around the country to facilitate his life on the run.

Stanley is still in a state of shock from the legacy of deception and depravity left by Whitey Bulger. Learning that Bulger and Flemmi are alleged to have murdered women with their own hands, she says, "It's horrible. You ask yourself, *What kind of people are these? And why didn't I see it or recognize it?*"

Mostly, Stanley tries to stay out of the media glare. She works as a waitress at the Boston Convention Center and rarely talks to reporters. Recently she was offered $10,000 to do an on-camera interview for the cable television program *I Married a Mobster*. She turned it down. She was relieved to learn that her name is not on the list of potential witnesses to be called by the government to testify at Bulger's trial, scheduled for November 5. Even so, there is no escaping the consequences of her years with Whitey. "It never ends," she says.

Back in the mid-1970s, Marilyn Di Silva, sixty-four, also found herself slipping deeper and deeper into the seductive parallel universe of the Winter Hill Mob, as Bulger and Flemmi's criminal crew was known to law enforcement. At the age of twenty-six, a divorced mother with three young daughters, she landed a much-needed waitressing job at Chandler's, a bar in Boston's South End that was, unbeknownst to Di Silva, partly owned by Mob boss Howie Winter. The bar was a gathering place for gamblers, mobsters, Mafiosi, and, occasionally, corrupt cops and agents.

At Chandler's, Di Silva met Stevie Flemmi, who was fifteen years her senior. He was handsome, flirty, and always had a wad of cash from which he dispensed ten- and twenty-dollar bills. Di Silva knew that Flemmi had an estranged wife and a live-in girlfriend named Marion Hussey, but that was okay with her. "I had three daughters who I went home to every night," says Marilyn. "I wasn't really looking for anything permanent. I was a better prospect as a mistress than as a wife."

The relationship with Flemmi was based mostly on sex and good times. Unlike Teresa Stanley, who was sweet and pliable with her gangster boyfriend, Di Silva was spunky and had a sharp tongue, which Flemmi found amusing. She learned early on that her new sugar daddy was a criminal of some type. Flemmi had recently returned to Boston after several years on the lam; he'd been ducking a murder charge that was eventually thrown out, likely with the help of the FBI. He didn't hide his lifestyle. Within the first month they were together, Flemmi bought Di Silva a two-toned Cadillac and showered her with jewelry. "He was extravagant, very generous," she remembers.

Flemmi set up Di Silva in an apartment next door to Marshall Motors, an auto garage in Somerville that served as the clubhouse of the Winter Hill Mob. "Because I was Italian, I was designated to cook lunch for them. In the apartment, I'd make sandwiches, with cold cuts, or pasta. If I had my mother there, we'd make extra sauce, then walk it over to the garage." Di Silva became the unofficial mascot for what would become the most notorious criminal gang in the city's history.

As the daughter of a cop who grew up over a meat market in East Cambridge, Di Silva knew better than to ask a lot of questions. Clearly, the men who passed through Marshall Motors were not doctors and university professors. "I figured they were loan sharks, leg breakers, bookies. Yeah, bookies. Money. That seemed to come up a lot."

The garage is where Marilyn first met Whitey Bulger. "He was there almost every day," she remembers. "Along with Stevie, Johnny Martorano, and sometimes Johnny's brother, Jimmy. Whitey was always impeccable, with his jeans starched, the tight leather jacket. He was kind of a know-it-all, talked with a lot of authority on different subjects. Eventually, I could see that he was sort of taking over as the leader. He'd sit behind a big desk, his foot up, cleaning his nails with a knife he kept tucked in his boot."

On numerous occasions, Di Silva hung out socially with Flemmi and Bulger together. "They took me to buy my first gun," she remembers. Di Silva's father had taught her how to shoot. "We went to this little shop, the three of us standing over the gun case. 'That's a nice one, I like that. The snub nose.' "

Occasionally, they all went on double dates. Di Silva would set Whitey up with one of her friends. "One time, we were at Café Budapest. It was late. Whitey and his date, a friend of mine, were in another area. Suddenly, Stevie and I hear this blood-curdling scream. We run over there. Whitey had pulled this big knife out of his boot, was flashing it around. It scared the hell out of my friend."

Sometimes, Di Silva clashed with Bulger, who could be "uptight." At the garage, after she cursed one time, Whitey said to Flemmi, "Listen to the mouth on that broad. She talks like a truck driver. Why you want a truck driver in your life?" Di Silva got right in Whitey's face. "Fuck you," she said. "This is the way I talk. You don't like it, you can leave the room." The others laughed. Bulger let it slide. At the time, Di Silva found the encounter comical, but looking back now, with what she knows about Bulger and Flemmi, she feels lucky to be alive.

It started to turn sour in 1978, after she and Stevie had been together four years. Flemmi had encouraged her to get a criminal justice degree at a local community college. He wanted her to be a cop and even helped get her name on a five-year waiting list. Only the name on the list was not Marilyn Di Silva. Flemmi had created an entirely false identity for Di Silva, with a fake name, driver's license, and birth certificate. Di Silva now believes that Flemmi and Bulger were angling to get her on the police force so she could serve as a mole for the Winter Hill Mob.

Di Silva now found herself being followed home by police cars and sometimes other unidentified vehicles. When her phone records were seized, she became worried. "God forbid if something happened to me, who would take care of my girls? I asked Stevie, 'What's going on here?' But he had a way of not answering questions. He told me not to worry."

The last straw came on a night in 1978. Flemmi had gotten Di Silva a job as a barmaid at Blackfriars, a bar in the city's financial district that was "mobbed up." Di Silva was scheduled to work that night, but Flemmi called her and said, "Don't go. Not tonight." Di Silva stayed home. At Blackfriars that night, there was a slaughter. The owner of the bar and two others were shot dead. Flemmi has denied any involvement in the Blackfriars shooting; it remains one of Boston's most notorious unsolved crimes.

Di Silva's dual life as a mother and a gangster's girlfriend had lost its charm. She drove over to Marshall Motors one night and handed the keys to the Cadillac to Flemmi. "I can't do this anymore," she said. "I got my kids to worry about. It's over for us."

"Oh, boy, if looks could kill, I think he could have killed me at that moment. He was, like, 'What!? Nobody walks away from me.' I think maybe the only reason I got away with that was because I had kids. I was a little older than his other girlfriends and had a life of my own. For whatever reason, I walked away from it. I was lucky."

Though Di Silva moved out of the area, to Arizona and Costa Rica and Florida, she never stopped worrying about her past connections to Flemmi and Bulger, partly because she was frequently contacted by the FBI and other law enforcement sources seeking details about her time with the gang. In the late 1990s, when Bulger went on the run and Flemmi turned stool pigeon, the lurid details started to come out.

"I was shocked," says Di Silva. "I'm still shocked." The grisly details of Flemmi and Bulger strangling Debbie Davis, who Di Silva knew, and Deborah Hussey were "sickening," but equally disturbing was the revelation that Flemmi began a sexual relationship with the fourteen-year-old daughter of his common-law wife. "I remember him always asking me about my oldest daughter," she says. "Did he have his eyes on her so he could move in when I got older? Was that his plan?"

Like Teresa Stanley, Di Silva is haunted by the knowledge that she could have circulated among men who were psychopathic killers, and what that says about her. "You can't take back the past," she says. "It is what it is. But when I think back about it, it gives me the creeps."

To some, Catherine Greig, like Teresa Stanley and Marilyn Di Silva, is guilty only of having made bad choices. She fell for a professional criminal and likely became enamored by the excitement and, most of all, the financial security it provided. She remained loyal to Bulger for thirty-six years, with sixteen of those years under extreme pressure as co-fugitives from the law. Greig was either in love with Whitey, or living in fear, or under the throes of some manner of Stockholm syndrome.

Others see a more conniving co-conspirator. In the wake of Greig's guilty plea, it was revealed in court that she was attempting to transfer co-ownership of her house and bank accounts into the name of her twin sister, Margaret McCusker. Rather than a woman in a state of trauma, claimed federal prosecutors, she was calculating ways to protect her property and bank accounts. U.S. District Judge Douglas P. Woodlock has ordered that her assets be frozen until after she is sentenced.

One person who could feel vindictive toward Greig but does not is Teresa Stanley. "I have nothing to gain by Catherine doing a long time in prison," she says. Stanley remembers a day last summer, after Bulger and Greig were apprehended, when she was approached by Catherine's sister, who said, "Teresa, I'm sorry about what you're having to go through," adding, "you know, Whitey really loved you."

"I thought about that," says Stanley. "Did he love me? Really? How can you say that about a person who deceived you and lived a double life and shamed you in the eyes of everybody?"

Still, she does not blame the other woman. "All those years cooped up with Jimmy, traveling, living on the run, having to answer to his every command, that couldn't have been easy."

5.

THE SCAPEGOAT

Newsweek, June 25, 2012

FBI Agent John Connolly went to jail for enabling the bloody reign of gangster Whitey Bulger. Now, in his first interview since Bulger was caught, he says the extent of the Feds' cover-up may never be known.

In the twelve months since notorious mobster James "Whitey" Bulger was captured, he has been revealed to have feet of clay. Stripped of his power, with few cards to play, Bulger awaits some form of justice, be it death from old age (he's eighty-two), or adjudication in federal court, where he stands accused of nineteen murders. Either way, Bulger will be made to pay, though, increasingly, it has become apparent that the many people and institutions of government that made Bulger possible will not be held accountable. One of the most violent and pernicious criminal conspiracies in the history of America is over, but for those who hoped that the prosecution of Bulger would be some form of final exposé on the Bulger era, the trial is shaping up to be a whitewash.

Having lived sixteen years on the run, twelve of those in an apartment near the beach in Santa Monica, California, with $822,198 cash and an arsenal of weapons stashed in a wall, Bulger was finally pinched after a tipster contacted the FBI with information about his fugitive girlfriend, Catherine Greig. Bulger and Greig, age sixty-one, were arrested on June 23, 2011 and returned to Boston, where Whitey had for nearly a quarter century maintained a criminal business that included extortion, loan sharking, narcotics, fraud, illegal gambling, and murder.

Last week, Catherine Greig received an eight-year prison sentence and $150,000 fine for aiding and abetting a federal fugitive. With time served and allowable reductions for "good behavior," she is likely to serve seventy-six months. Bulger's trial is scheduled to begin on November 5.

The evidence against Whitey is formidable. Since he went on the run in January 1995, most of his closest associates have cut deals with the government and testified at various hearings and trials, and they are likely to testify against Whitey at his trial. Any attempt to prosecute Bulger, however, is complicated by the fact that at the same time he was committing most of the alleged murders, he and his gangster partner, Steve Flemmi, were also working as top informants for the FBI.

It is Bulger's role as a government informant, and how that role was fostered, facilitated, and kept confidential by a vast array of public servants, that has led many to suspect that the true nature of Bulger's criminal career will never be fully explored in a court of law. Actions taken since Whitey's arrest one year ago underscore these claims.

"The prosecution of Bulger is being carefully orchestrated," says Harvey Silverglate, a renowned Boston criminal defense attorney and author who has written about the case. Silverglate uses the word *cover-up* to describe the prosecution's motives, adding, "If they wanted to convict Bulger swiftly, they could have tried him in California on gun possession charges. Would have been an open-and-shut case. He'd have received a thirty-year sentence. Or in Oklahoma, where one of the murders occurred, they have the death penalty. But the U.S. Attorney's Office in Boston is not about to let this case out from under its control. Because then details might come out that show a pattern of secrecy and cover-up going back generations."

The cover-up kicked into gear last July when the U.S. Attorney's Office announced they had dropped all counts in the indictment except for the murder charges. "It is in the public interest to protect public resources—both executive and judicial—by bringing the defendant to trial on the government's strongest case," said U.S. Attorney

Carmen Ortiz. Dropping the racketeering counts had another benefit: It greatly diminished the possibility that Bulger's trial would explore how his racketeering career was underwritten, in large part, by the U.S. Department of Justice.

One person who concurs with the cover-up theory is John Connolly, the former FBI man who was Bulger's case agent in the years that he was an informant. Since 2002, Connolly has been in prison on numerous charges stemming from his relationship with Bulger and Flemmi, including a second-degree murder conviction. "The Justice Department is going to do everything within its power to try to make sure the full story never comes out," says Connolly, via phone from a correctional facility in Chipley, Florida, where he is currently serving a forty-year sentence. Since Bulger's apprehension, Connolly has not granted any public interviews—until now.

Born and raised in the insular blue-collar neighborhood of South Boston (Southie), Connelly knew Bulger from childhood. He was even closer friends with William "Billy" Bulger, Whitey's younger brother, who would rise through the ranks of state politics to become president of the state senate and, arguably, the most powerful politician in the Massachusetts state legislature.

In 2008, after a two-month trial in Miami, Connolly was convicted of having fed information to Bulger's crew that led to the murder of John Callahan, a crooked business partner of Bulger's who the mobster was concerned might cooperate with a criminal investigation. Callahan was shot in the head by a Bulger associate, his dead body left in the trunk of a Cadillac near Miami International Airport. Before being convicted for his involvement in the Callahan murder, Connolly was sentenced to ten years on a federal conviction in Massachusetts for accepting gratuities, falsifying evidence, and obstruction of justice, including the charge that he tipped off Whitey about his imminent arrest back in late-1994, making it possible for Bulger to run.

Says Connelly, "[The Justice Department] put a hit out on me back in 2000. They decided I would be targeted to take the fall for this whole arrangement. And they've stuck to it ever since."

Connolly hopes that the apprehension of Bulger will lead not only to his murder conviction being overturned, but also to his public exoneration. "My lawyers have information that since Bulger was brought in, he spoke to FBI agents and told them I had nothing to do with tipping him off [about a pending federal indictment]. And he told them I had nothing to do with this murder in Florida, not one damn thing."

From 1975, when Connelly first enlisted Bulger as a Top Echelon informant, until 1990, when Connelly retired from the FBI, Bulger and the agent met often, shared meals, and traded information. Connolly acknowledges that Bulger was involved in criminal activity, but, he says, "I didn't ask about that. My role was to protect Bulger and Flemmi so we could make cases against criminals based on information they gave us. That was my job. Everyone knew that they were top criminals and murderers."

Though he insists there was nothing criminal in his relationship with Bulger, Connolly acknowledges there was a natural affinity between him and the Bulger brothers based on their shared Southie upbringing. In fact, in the early-1990s, following his retirement, Connolly says he'd heard that criminal investigations of "Jimmy" (Bulger's friends never called him Whitey) were under way. He had a friendly conversation with Senator Billy Bulger, saying, "You know, I hear your brother is involved in things that could get him into big trouble. You should tell him maybe it's time to change his lifestyle and retire to Florida." Says Connolly, "Billy sighed, looked at me, and asked, 'John, you ever try to tell an older brother what to do?' I knew what he meant."

The crucial question about Bulger's trial is whether or not the evidence might reveal that Connolly was merely a foot soldier in a much larger campaign of secrecy and corruption that spanned generations. The forces that sustained Bulger involved not only the entire Boston office and regional supervisors of the FBI, but stretched into the U.S. Attorney's Office and possibly involved federal judges.

Federal prosecutors are on a track to make sure this version of the Bulger narrative does not surface at his upcoming trial. "The DOJ has no appetite for any kind of self-examination," says Thomas Foley, a former colonel with the Massachusetts State Police who spent the better part of his career in law enforcement trying to take Bulger down.

"To air all this out now would give a lot of people a black eye. They just want it all to go away."

The roots of Bulger's "special relationship" with law enforcement goes back before Bulger was a big player in the city's underworld. In the early hours of March 12, 1965, in a dark back alley in Boston, a low-level hood named Teddy Deegan was filled with lead and left for dead. Deegan had fallen afoul of a psychotic Mafia-connected hit man named Joe "the Animal" Barboza. It was Barboza who murdered Deegan after asking for permission from Raymond Patriarca, boss of the Patriarca crime family, which then controlled New England. Barboza was assisted in murdering Deegan by another gangster named Vincent "Jimmy the Bear" Flemmi, brother of Steve Flemmi, who would one day be Bulger's partner in crime. The murder of a small timer like Deegan would normally have been a minor event. But the government had a problem. The killers, Barboza and Flemmi, were both Top Echelon informants for the FBI.

The feds knew that these two men murdered Deegan. In fact, the FBI had bugged Raymond Patriarca's home in Providence, Rhode Island, and captured on tape the conversation where Barboza asked for and received permission to whack Deegan. But the FBI did not want to lose their highly prized Top Echelon informants. What they did next would alter the trajectory of criminal justice in the region for a generation. The FBI and prosecutors had Barboza take the stand and tell a fabricated version of the murder that would lead to the conviction of two innocent men, Peter Limone and Joe Salvati. After being declared guilty, Limone and Salvati were sentenced to death row.

The framing of innocent citizens in a capital murder case by withholding evidence and suborning perjury—all to protect notorious criminals who were government informants—became the dirty secret of federal law enforcement in New England. In the years that followed, the convictions of Limone and Salvati would be challenged in various local jurisdictions but the government always fought back. It is difficult to know how many agents, assistant U.S. attorneys, district attorneys, and cops were in on the conspiracy. Prosecutors understood that they were to do everything within their power to preserve the convictions and ensure that no further examinations of the evidence would ever take place in court. Virtually the entire system became part of an effort to safeguard the false conviction so that criminals, protected by the government, could remain free.

By the time John Connolly recruited and signed up Whitey Bulger as a FBI informant in the mid-1970s, the Boston underworld had descended into a murky, murderous pit of rats with cops and federal agents as active players. Connolly's predecessor and mentor in the Boston FBI office, Special Agent H. Paul Rico, would eventually be indicted on charges of obstruction of justice and murder. Rico was believed to have supplied key information for gangland murders, and may have even taken part in actual Mob hits himself. He died in prison in January 2004 while facing prosecution.

The Boston FBI office has been publicly excoriated for its handling of Bulger and Flemmi, and rightfully so. Connolly and many others in law enforcement defend the concept of using criminals to catch other criminals. "Nobody wants to see how the sausage is made, but in the real world that's how cases get made," says Connolly. At the very least, the Bulger case reveals a shocking lack of oversight. Federal agents fed information to two mobsters that led to murders and the thwarting of potential criminal investigations spearheaded by other law enforcement agencies. They helped turn Bulger and Flemmi into the most powerful gangsters in the history of Boston.

Connolly's supervisor, Special Agent John Morris, head of the Organized Crime Squad, pleaded guilty to charges of accepting bribes and gratuities from Bulger, and obstructing justice. He served no jail time, in exchange for his testifying at 1998 hearings into the Bulger affair. In his testimony, Morris put forth a scenario—since expounded upon by prosecutors and the media—that John Connolly was a "rogue agent" who promoted and protected Bulger's informant status within the Bureau solely for personal profit and aggrandizement.

John Connolly is not without culpability, but he did not devise the Top Echelon Informant Program, and whatever he did to maintain Bulger's viability as an informant was authorized and, in many cases, rewarded via promotions and special citations from six different FBI directors.

"There were enablers throughout the system, from top to bottom," says retired FBI agent Robert Fitzpatrick. An assistant special agent in charge of the Boston office, Fitzpatrick was Connolly's nemesis. After meeting Bulger and Connolly together, Fitzpatrick recommended that Bulger be "closed down" as an informant. His recommendations were ignored and his two-page report about Bulger was buried by two successive special agents in charge of the Boston office. Over time, Fitzpatrick began to sense that the conspiracy to protect Bulger went all the way to headquarters in Washington, D.C. His suspicions were later verified in U.S. congressional hearings that concluded, "What happened in New England over a forty-year period is, without doubt, one of the greatest failures in federal law enforcement history."

That conspiracy went beyond the FBI. Among the friends of Whitey Bulger who ran interference for the mobster was Jeremiah O'Sullivan, head of the U.S. Attorney's Organized Crime Strike Force, who would, thanks to his successes during the Bulger years, rise to become U.S. attorney in Boston.

As early as 1977, agent Connolly informed O'Sullivan that he had "turned" someone who could help them make major cases against the Mafia. When O'Sullivan heard it was Bulger, he wanted to meet him. Remembers Connolly, "I asked him, 'Are you sure? You don't have to.'" It was highly unusual for an assistant U.S. attorney to meet face-to-face with a top informant while an investigation was still ongoing. O'Sullivan insisted.

Connolly set up a meeting between the city's top mobster and its top organized crime prosecutor in a hotel room on a rainy afternoon around Christmas. "I was there," says Connolly. "Jimmy met Jerry. As I remember it, they were both quite impressed with one another."

Jeremiah O'Sullivan was one of the best things that ever happened to Bulger. In 1979, when an investigation targeted an array of mobsters on charges of fixing races at horse tracks, O'Sullivan dropped Bulger and Flemmi from the indictment. As Flemmi would later put it, "We believed we were authorized to commit crimes as long as we didn't kill anybody. That's what we were told."

O'Sullivan's desire to protect his prize informants didn't end with Whitey and Stevie. In 1989, information was brought to O'Sullivan that Billy Bulger, Whitey's senator brother, had received a legally questionable payment of $240,000 as part of a real estate deal at 75 State Street in downtown Boston. According to Bob Fitzpatrick, who investigated the deal, "It was a clear violation of the Hobbs Act. We had Billy Bulger dead in his tracks." But O'Sullivan made the decision to not go forward with charges against Senator Bulger. After the deal was exposed in the media, Bulger gave the money back.

In 2003, long after Whitey went on the run and his associates began cutting deals with the government, pieces of the puzzle began to fall into place. Hearings were held by the U.S. House Committee on Government Reform that proved to be an unprecedented foray into the criminal history of the Bulger era. The hearings most famously exposed Billy Bulger, who was forced to resign from his job as president of the University of Massachusetts after it was revealed he had been in contact with his fugitive brother.

Far more revealing was the testimony of O'Sullivan, also retired, who, in the years since Bulger's disappearance, had publicly denied that he'd known that Bulger was an informant until he read about it in the press. This bold-faced lie was exposed when internal Justice Department memos were produced that showed O'Sullivan had known about Bulger since the late-1970s. "You got me," said the former U.S. attorney to the congressional committee.

Even more damaging were FBI and DOJ memos and correspondence subpoenaed by the committee, after a fierce legal battle with the Bush administration. Records showed that O'Sullivan's mentor and predecessor as U.S. attorney, Edward Harrington (later a federal judge), had been complicit in the framing of Limone and Salvati for the Deegan murder. At the hearings, a picture began to emerge of a generation of agents and prosecutors who were the metaphorical offspring of those who had conspired to make sure that the truth about the Deegan murder would never be revealed. Thus, protecting Bulger and Flemmi became a way of repressing this potentially explosive history—Whitey and Stevie became the keepers of the Justice Department's dirty little secret.

A final report on the findings of the House Committee was issued in 2004. Entitled *Everything Secret Degenerates: The FBI's Use of Murderers as Informants*, it remains the single most detailed exposé on the Bulger era. The findings helped expedite a financial settlement for Peter Limone and Joe Salvati, who had their convictions overturned in 2000. In 2007, they were awarded $101.7 million in damages—paid by U.S. taxpayers—for having unjustly served thirty-four years in prison. The U.S. government has also been forced to pay, collectively, $20 million in damages to family members of some of Bulger's victims, who filed suits against the FBI and DOJ, claiming that the man who killed their loved ones did so while being sponsored and protected by the government.

Those who advocate for the U.S. attorney's current streamlined prosecution of Bulger make the argument that the Bulger conspiracy has been fully aired at various hearings and trials in the sixteen years that Bulger was basking in the California sun. In 1999, the justice department claimed they were going to get the bottom of the Bulger fiasco, and that no one would be spared. John Durham, a Connecticut prosecutor, was appointed by Attorney General Janet Reno to spearhead an investigation, but the Durham report was never completed or delivered, and the government has never explained why. The sole significant result of Durham's efforts was the prosecution of John Connolly.

Despite decades of corruption, obstruction of justice, and suppression of evidence, no government official in a supervisory position has ever been held accountable. Many who benefited most from Bulger's tenure as an informant have since passed away.

Some doubt that a trial will ever come to pass. Bulger may choose to stall and run out the clock and eventually die in prison, though his lawyer denies that is the case. The prosecution—though they claim to be eager to proceed—also has reason not to be overly enthusiastic about a trial, given the potential for unanticipated revelations.

Amidst the uncertainty, one thing is clear: As the U.S. Justice Department prepares to put on trial one of the most murderous gangsters in the last half century, it is in no position to claim the moral high ground.

6.

R.I.P. TERESA STANLEY

TJ-English.com, August 26, 2012

Her life was defined and perhaps ruined by thirty years as the common-law wife of Mob boss James "Whitey" Bulger. Now, maybe, Teresa Stanley has finally found peace.

I was saddened to hear of the death of Teresa Stanley, seventy-one, long-time companion of James "Whitey" Bulger who passed away last August 16 of lung cancer.

I interviewed Teresa on two separate occasions earlier this year, before she knew anything about the cancer. I found her to be haunted by the legacy of personal deception and violent crime left by her ex-common-law husband, James Bulger. Teresa was a twenty-six-year old divorcée with four kids when she first met Bulger in 1966. He was not the legendary crime figure he would later become. By her own account, she became comfortable in her life with Bulger, who she knew was in "the illegal gambling business" and possibly a loan shark. She says she did not know of Bulger's many murders.

I first met and interviewed Teresa at Marisola's restaurant in South Boston, a neighborhood bistro well known to the locals. I was introduced to Teresa by Pat Nee, a friend and former criminal rival of Bulger's who, among other things, once did eight years in prison for smuggling guns to the Irish Republican Army back in the 1980s. Teresa used to chuckle whenever I mentioned Pat's name, because she knew Pat didn't care for Bulger, and, in fact, tried to kill him once or twice before they finally formed an uneasy partnership. Teresa later conceded that Nee was probably right in his negative assessment of Whitey.

The second time I interviewed Teresa was over breakfast at the Seaport Hotel on the harbor in Boston. Both interview sessions were lengthy—two hours or more. And Teresa was very forthcoming and frank about her feelings and emotions. I liked her instantly. My feeling was that she was a good person, very sensitive and sweet, who had made a horrible choice in her life by settling down with a master deceiver like Bulger. She would later pay a heavy price for her associations with Bulger, as she became the subject of FBI and other investigations, was called to testify numerous times at hearings and trials, and was ultimately painted with a "scarlet letter" for having been Bulger's paramour for thirty years.

I spoke with Teresa one last time, earlier this year, when I called her on behalf of *Newsweek* magazine, which was looking to take her photo to accompany my article. Though she had not told anyone outside her closest family members of her cancer, she told me. I was shocked. Not only had she just learned of her condition, she was told that the cancer was far advanced. I told her I was sorry and that she deserved better; she was a good person.

There are those who vilify Teresa and hold her partly responsible for Bulger's crimes. I do not. She made a bad choice in love, was perhaps naive, maybe even chose to stick her head in the sand during Whitey's reign of power. When it came out that her lover was alleged to have killed so many people, including young women, she was stunned. When I met her, she still seemed to be partly in a state of shock about the whole thing.

Teresa has now arrived at her place of peace. Let the haters spew their venom. They never had to walk in her shoes.

EPILOGUE

January 2013: It is a gloomy drive through the frozen tundra of upstate New York to Sullivan County, for another visit with Mad Dog Sullivan. As we greet one another in the prison visiting room, as usual, I joke with the aging gangster about the fact that he is named Sullivan, incarcerated at the Sullivan Correctional Facility, in Sullivan County. "They were so worried you were gonna try to escape," I say, "they wanted you to feel as welcome as possible."

Sully looks amazingly fit considering the cancer surgeries and his most recent prognosis: There is a cancerous field in his one remaining good lung. It is only a matter of time before the cancer becomes active. Sully's days are numbered. You wouldn't know it by looking at him, though, thanks to his daily visits to the prison gym and a rueful acceptance of his mortality. "Nobody lives forever," says the former hit man.

We settle into our regular spot in the prison visiting room. As usual, Sully reminisces, and I take it all in. These days, he doesn't have much to hide. There is a Wikipedia entry about Mad Dog Sullivan on the Internet that details a criminal life that is almost impossible to believe. Son of a New York police detective who died when Joe was thirteen; institutionalized and later criminalized by a hardscrabble life on the streets; many hired killings carried out under contract with the Genovese crime family and other organized crime groups; more time spent in prisons than on the street.

It's all true, Sully admits, except for one fact on the page that gets his goat. Wikipedia and other Internet sources claim that Sully was given the moniker "mad dog" in prison, so named by other inmates due to a salivary gland problem. "Total bunk," says Sullivan. He tells me the true story about the origins of the nickname.

It was 1981, and Sullivan had been contracted to murder a mobbed-up Teamster official named John Fiorino. Sullivan killed Fiorino with a shotgun blast in a restaurant parking lot in Rochester, New York. He and his getaway driver were pursued. After their car crashed into a large snowbank, the driver was captured, but Sullivan got away by hiding in that freezing snowbank for nearly eight hours. A team of state police and FBI agents descended on the scene in pursuit of Sullivan. The lead lawman told the others, "Be careful. This man is armed and dangerous. He is a mad dog killer."

That night, Sullivan got away, but the nickname stuck when the *New York Post* and other newspapers, upon his eventual arrest weeks later, plastered it in headlines such as MAD DOG HIT MAN NABBED! and HOW COPS PUT LEASH ON MAD DOG.

In most accounts of Sully's life, his many murders stand out like a horrible gash, an open wound so gruesome that anyone pondering the life of this man is unable to see anything beyond his penchant for destruction. I have never asked Sullivan exactly how many people he murdered. It is a long list. He knows now that these killings were the product of a deep-seated sickness, though he notes that the people he killed were almost always people in the criminal life—gangsters, or even killers themselves. Sullivan did not have a psychological compulsion to kill people. He did it for the money. He did it because it was his job.

Sully is not proud of his role as an angel of death, but there is one aspect of his long criminal career that does warm his heart, and that has to do with his many escapes from jails and prisons. His early life was driven by a deep-seated fear of entrapment, which, subconsciously, led him to embrace a philosophy based on Newton's third law of motion, that for every action there is an equal and opposite reaction. Up until his most recent extended incarceration, Sully's life was a cycle of entrapment and escape, escape and entrapment.

At the age of fourteen, not long after his father died, he ran away from home. He was apprehended by police and sent to the New York State Training School for Boys in Warwick, and later the New York State Vocational Institution in Coxsackie, both notorious reformatories in upstate New York. When Sullivan was released at the age of nineteen, he went on a petty burglary spree out west with a boyhood friend. They were apprehended by police in Cheyenne, Wyoming. There, Sully pulled off his first escape by diving through a plate-glass window at a police station. Bloodied and on the run, he walked into an Army recruitment station and joined up, mostly as a means to escape the law.

In the Army, he went AWOL on numerous occasions and fled back to New York City, where he was captured and thrown in a military stockade on Governor's Island, in New York harbor. Sullivan escaped from that facility by covering his body with Vaseline, throwing himself into the frigid waters of the harbor, and swimming all the way to Brooklyn.

Sully's course in life was set: His hatred of institutional authority meant that he would never hold a legitimate job. In his early twenties, he undertook a more serious life of crime, with a series of robberies and stick-ups, until he was caught and thrown in prison in New Jersey. In Trenton State Prison and later in Rahway, Sully witnessed prison rapes and killings, and was in the middle of a horrific prison riot. He was released in 1965. Not long after that, he killed a man at the Willow Bar and Grill, near his home neighborhood in Queens, and was sentenced to prison for manslaughter. This led to his most daring escape, in 1971, from Attica, a maximum-security facility.

The Attica escape is perhaps the most noteworthy item on Sully's résumé. Using a pole constructed from pieces of pipe, he shimmied over a prison wall, dropped to the ground, and sweet-talked an unwitting visitor in the parking lot to drive him to the nearest town. From there, he hopped a Greyhound bus to parts unknown. He was captured a couple of months later in Manhattan's Greenwich Village, with a sawed-off shotgun stuffed in the leg of his pants.

Sullivan smiles when I tell him that I live two blocks from where he was pinched, at East 10th Street and University Place. "Nice area," he says. "Some nice diners, a few good bars. I used to go down there to visit my wife. That's how I got caught. They staked out the office building where Gail worked and nailed me when I tried to see her."

Talk of Gail, Sullivan's wife of thirty-seven years, is a subject that often brings a tear to the eyes of this unreconstructed tough guy. They were married in 1976, after Sully—having served ten years for manslaughter—was paroled, thanks in part to the help of former U.S. Attorney General Ramsey Clark, who had befriended Sullivan and served as his attorney before the parole board. Gail was an account executive at a small advertising firm who met Joe through a friend. They soon had a child who they named Ramsey, in honor of the man who got Joe out of jail. Three years later, they had another boy named Kelly.

Gail did not know that her husband was a hired killer for the Mob. It was her understanding that he worked at various construction jobs that he had secured through union connections.

After my first prison visit with Sullivan, I met Gail at a diner in Manhattan, and she told me, "Joe could be difficult. He had a problem with drugs and alcohol, and I suspected he was having affairs, but he was a good provider. He cared about his family and his kids. Most of the time, he was a good man."

Gail is no dummy. She is not naive. Through arrests, trials, and incarceration, she has stuck by Sullivan because she believes, "inside of him, along with everything else, there is a good person. That's the part of him I fell in love with." Gail made sure their two boys grew up knowing their father, with regular visits to prison. They have become fine young men, never in trouble with the law, with kids and families of their own.

The idea that Sullivan has somehow managed to maintain a marriage and healthy nuclear family while being a hit man and longtime prison inmate does not fit the profile of a psychotic mad dog. Sully gives Gail most of the credit. "I told her if she wanted to leave me and get on with her life, I would understand," says Sullivan. "I told her, 'You have a choice.' She stayed. I owe everything I have to her, no doubt about that."

The dedication that Gail has shown to the man she married, and the relationship Sullivan has been able to salvage with his two sons, is—in the savage narrative of Joe Sullivan's life—as miraculous as the Immaculate Conception. Improbably ennobled by family relationships that have survived and grown stronger over a forty-year period, Sullivan, the inveterate gangster and cold-blooded killer, can't talk about any of this without choking up: "Gail, my sons, the grandkids—it's more than I deserve. I don't know why or how I got to be this lucky. It's all I have to live for."

It's getting late in our visit, and Sully wants to hear more about Whitey Bulger. He has followed my writing about Bulger in *Newsweek* magazine, and he is fascinated by how Whitey maintained his power by gaming the system for all those years.

The Bulger story, of course, is right up Sully's alley. He never met Bulger, but he knows the type. "He reminds me of Joey Gallo," says Sully. "Machiavellian. Always playing one side against the other." Gallo was one of numerous Mafia bosses who, in the late-1970s, hired Sully to whack out their enemies in the underworld.

Sully admires Bulger's mastery of the criminal universe in which he operated, but he is not pleased to hear that Whitey's attorney has announced that Bulger will take the stand at his trial and reveal all about his criminal career, particularly as it relates to his relationship with the U.S. Department of Justice. Sully sees my excitement as I detail how Bulger, realizing he has nothing left to lose, will finally tell all and name names of people in the government who, he says, promised him immunity from prosecution as long as he supplied them with information about the Mafia. Says Sully, "See, you're all for it because you're a writer and it makes for a good story, but from where I'm sitting, it's the lowest thing a guy can do."

Sully, of course, is referring to "the code," the principle that under no circumstances does a person rat out anyone, not even his enemies. Sully is in prison because his accomplice in the Fiorino hit cooperated with the government and testified against him at trial. Sully would rather be dead than be a rat, and he has paid a heavy price for adhering to the code. It is likely that he would be out on the street right now, his sentence reduced by many years, had he offered up testimony against the many Mob bosses with whom he did business.

Sticking to this principle of never being a rat under any circumstances has caused Sully distress within his own family.

"Him and his code," says Kelly Sullivan, Sully's son, whom I met and interviewed after my first meeting with Sully. Kelly told me that he and his father have often had arguments over the issue. "I've said to him, 'Dad, what good has your code done for you? Many of your enemies are out on the street because they cut deals with the government. You're in here . . . in prison for life. What you're saying is that your code means more to you than your own family.' "

Sully knows that it is hard for anyone to understand, especially law-abiding citizens—civilians—who have never been in his shoes.

I attempt to explain the nuances of the Bulger situation, how this is slightly different, Bulger naming names of people in the government who he feels have sold him out, but Sully is not interested. He's spent an entire lifetime living by his code; it is the only thing he has, other than his family. Though, like his son, I may have issues with it, I respect Sully for sticking to what he believes is the highest principle of the streets—even if, in this day and age, it makes him seem like the last of the Mohicans.

As our visiting time nears an end, Sully and I have our picture taken. It's part of the visiting ritual: Girlfriends, wives, brothers, and other visitors stand in front of a fake background—a wide-open sky and trees, or some other nature scene that will never exist in reality within the prison walls. Sullivan and I lean in close together as a prison guard, for the price of two dollars per photo, snaps our picture with a Polaroid camera.

As we are waiting for the photo to develop, I mention to Sully that I'm currently working on a magazine article about some armed robbers who used state-of-the-art synthetic masks to disguise themselves while robbing a check-cashing store in Queens. I tell him, "Two black guys pulled off a couple of robberies disguised as white cops. That's how good these masks are. You can completely alter your identity."

I see Sully's eyes lighting up. He's like a cocaine addict who hasn't done blow in thirty years when someone just placed a bowl of coke in front of him.

"Hey," he says, "do you think they could make one of those masks according to specifications? Like, if I gave them a photo of someone, say, a guard in here, could they make a mask that looked like that?"

I smile, because I know where this is headed. "I don't know, Sully. Maybe they could."

We're both smiling now. Riffing. It is a lark—a fantasy—that Sullivan, age seventy-four, down to one cancer-infested lung, could pull off one last glorious escape.

"How would I get it in here?" I ask.

"You fold it up and stuff it down the front of your pants, in your crotch area. You could get by security with that."

I nod. Yeah, maybe I could.

"You pass it to me here in the visiting room. I'll take it into the bathroom. I can get a guard's uniform. I'd put on that mask and walk right out of here. They'd think I was a guard."

Sully says all this with a twinkle in his eye. We both know that, although I write about criminals in books and magazine articles, and attempt to do so with knowledge and even a certain degree of intimacy, I am, after all, a civilian. I am not going to help Mad Dog Sullivan break out of prison.

I chuckle and say, "Okay, Sully, I'll check and see if they can make that mask."

"Yeah," he says, "would you do that?"

Visiting time is over. There is a common practice for both visitor and inmate as a visit comes to an end: The inmate is escorted by a guard to a door on one side of the room, and the visitor is also escorted by a another guard to different door on the other side of the room. Visitor and inmate, knowing they will not see each other for months or years or maybe ever again, watch each other being led from the room, wanting to get one last look at their friend or loved one.

I shout across the room, "Take care, Sully. And stay out of trouble."

Sully gives me a pumped-fist salute. He knows what I mean. Nearly on his death bed with lung cancer, bowed but unbroken, I watch him disappear through the electronic, steel-plated door, a twinkle in his eye, a smile on his face, visions of escape dancing in his head.

ACKNOWLEDGMENTS

This book represents more than two decades' worth of labor, all of it enabled and supported by contacts in "the field"; by editors and their staffs in the magazine, newspaper, and webzine trades; and by fellow journalists and friends who helped usher these articles from the proposal stage to published/posted reality. It is impossible to name them all. Some contributors have been lost to memory. Nonetheless, I have attempted to reassemble a list of those who played a role, either through professional obligation or personal generosity, in these articles having originally appeared in some of the best periodicals in the country.

You will notice that many of the pieces in this collection were first published in *Playboy* magazine. That is no accident. Over half a century, *Playboy* has been a tremendous supporter of quality journalism, especially crime journalism. I am particularly indebted to two former *Playboy* editors, Peter Moore and Chris Napolitano, who helped conceive and line edit some of the most complex and lengthy pieces in this collection. I also owe much respect to Hugh Hefner. Although we have never met, I tip my hat to Hefner for having created such a valuable forum for good work; for commissioning the best writers and paying them accordingly; and for being a tireless advocate for First Amendment rights, civil liberties, and courageous reporting.

The following acknowledgments are organized into sections, according to the particular piece for which an individual made a vital contribution.

Introduction and Part I: Bullet in the Ass

Special thanks to Gail Sullivan and Kelly Sullivan for facilitating my time with Joe Sullivan; to the late Mike McNickle, who worked with me as a research assistant on many of the earliest pieces in this collection; to Laurie Gunst, who graciously led me to many key sources in Jamaica and in Brooklyn; to Flo O'Connor at the Jamaican Council on Human Rights in Kingston; and to Steven Wong, who for many years served as my *dai lo*, or big brother, in New York City's Chinatown, and who also led me to many key sources in Hong Kong, the city of his birth.

Part II: American Dream, American Nightmare

Thanks to the late Bob Callahan, who introduced me to the Mitchell brothers; to Susie Bright, renowned author and "sexpert," who helped me understand the world of adult entertainment; and Tom Caldarola, a longtime friend who remains my "go-to" person in San Francisco. Thanks to the Chinese Staff and Workers' Association in New York's Chinatown for their assistance and for their tireless advocacy on behalf of Asian immigrants in the United States; to legendary civil-rights attorney Myron Beldock, who first helped me track down George Whitmore; to Regina Whitmore, George Whitmore's beloved daughter; to Pulitzer Prize–winning journalist and friend Jim Dwyer; and to Sewell Chan, deputy Op-Ed editor at the *New York Times*.

Part III: Narco Wars, at Home and Abroad

As a magazine writer in pursuit of a story, often I have found myself at the mercy of local reporters. Few were more gracious than John Caniglia of the Cleveland *Plain Dealer*, who shared sources and contact information on the Lee Lucas story. Also helpful in Cleveland were attorneys John McCaffrey and James Owen. Special thanks to Geneva France in Mansfield, who suffered a grave injustice at the hands of the criminal justice system in the Northern District of Ohio, and who remains a friend.

My investigations in Ciudad Juárez, Mexico, were aided by a host of people across the border in El Paso, Texas. Special thanks to Valentin Sandoval, a well-connected filmmaker and poet who led me to contacts in Juárez and El Paso; to the lovely Valerie Anne Garcia, who kept me safe and sound at the Holiday Inn Express in downtown El Paso; to Howard Campbell, a professor at the University of Texas at El Paso and a highly knowledgeable source on the effects of the narco war in the borderland region; and to Carlos Spector, a civil rights attorney who continues to do essential work on behalf of Mexican immigrants and others whose lives have been thrown into chaos by the narco war.

Part IV: The Bulger Chronicles

I have been covering the Whitey Bulger beat for years and am greatly indebted to local reporters in Boston who have been on the front lines of this story, most notably Shelley Murphy and Kevin Cullen of the *Boston Globe*. For leading me to important sources; helping with logistics and the cultivation of contacts in Boston; and helping me to understand important details about the Bulger era, I would like to thank the following people: Pat Nee, Kevin Weeks, Jimmy Martorano, John Martorano, Marilyn Di Silva, Tommy Lyons, Paul Griffin, retired FBI agent Robert Fitzpatrick, Steve Davis, Richard Stratton, Sharon Branco, John Connolly, Jim Connolly, the late Teresa Stanley, and lawyer and author Harvey Silverglate. Special thanks also to Jim Carmody, manager at the Seaport Boston Hotel, and Lucas Whitmann, editor at *Newsweek/Daily Beast*.

Special thanks to Joel Millman, a friend and highly skilled reporter at the *Wall Street Journal*, for serving as a welcome sounding board over the years. And to Sophia Banda, friend, confidant, and sometimes personal assistant, who has been and remains a ray of sunshine in my life. And, as always, to my longtime agent Nat Sobel and his crew at Sobel Weber Associates, Inc., who were instrumental in making sure this book found its proper home.

Finally, *muchas gracias* to legendary publisher Otto Penzler at MysteriousPress.com, who is responsible for getting this book into print and published as an ebook in record time. Having presided over the genre of crime writing—both fiction and nonfiction—as a publisher for nearly forty years, Penzler knows the terrain. And he and his new partners at Open Road Media have established themselves as skillful practitioners at the commingling—and transition—of books from the printed page to electronic formats.

Mostly, I am grateful to the Spirit that put me on this path, and am thankful for the confluence of circumstances that have made it possible for me to make a living doing what gives me the most fulfillment: investigating subjects that engage my head and my heart, and writing stories for the entertainment and edification of those who revere the written word.

EBOOKS BY
T. J. ENGLISH

FROM MYSTERIOUSPRESS.COM
AND OPEN ROAD MEDIA

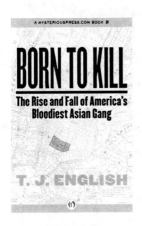  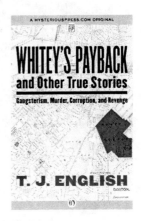

Available wherever ebooks are sold

MYSTERIOUSPRESS.COM

Otto Penzler, owner of the Mysterious Bookshop in Manhattan, founded the Mysterious Press in 1975. Penzler quickly became known for his outstanding selection of mystery, crime, and suspense books, both from his imprint and in his store. The imprint was devoted to printing the best books in these genres, using fine paper and top dust-jacket artists, as well as offering many limited, signed editions.

Now the Mysterious Press has gone digital, publishing ebooks through **MysteriousPress.com**.

MysteriousPress.com offers readers essential noir and suspense fiction, hard-boiled crime novels, and the latest thrillers from both debut authors and mystery masters. Discover classics and new voices, all from one legendary source.

FIND OUT MORE AT

WWW.MYSTERIOUSPRESS.COM

FOLLOW US:

@emysteries and Facebook.com/MysteriousPressCom

MysteriousPress.com is one of a select group of publishing partners of Open Road Integrated Media, Inc.

OPEN ROAD
INTEGRATED MEDIA

Open Road Integrated Media is a digital publisher and multimedia content company. Open Road creates connections between authors and their audiences by marketing its ebooks through a new proprietary online platform, which uses premium video content and social media.

CPSIA information can be obtained at www.ICGtesting.com
Printed in the USA
LVOW102234030513

332280LV00003B/15/P